D1030315

AQUINAS

on the Divine Ideas as
Exemplar Causes

To President Garvey,
with best wishes
Greg Doolan
12/20/2010

GREGORY T. DOOLAN

AQUINAS

on the Divine Ideas as Exemplar Causes

The Catholic University of America Press

Washington, D.C.

The Catholic University of America Press
All rights reserved
Printed in the United States of America

LIBRARY OF CONGRESS CATALOGING-IN-PUBLICATION DATA
Doolan, Gregory T.
Aquinas on the divine ideas as exemplar causes / Gregory T. Doolan.
p. cm.
Includes bibliographical references and index.
ISBN 978-0-8132-1523-5 (cloth : alk. paper)   1. Thomas, Aquinas, Saint,
1225?–1274.   2. God—Attributes.   3. Idea (Philosophy)   I. Title.
B765.T54D588 2008
111'.2—dc22   2007045815

To John F. Wippel

for all that he has taught me

CONTENTS

ACKNOWLEDGMENTS

I would like to offer my thanks to all those who helped me in writing this book: Barry Jones for always offering a ready ear to listen to my ideas; Peter Kwasniewski and Daniel O'Connell for providing me with philosophical insights; Giuseppe Butera, Patrick Harmon, Gerald Russello, and my mother, Elisabeth Doolan, for helping me with the occasional translation; Joseph Tylenda, S.J., Susan Karp, and the entire staff at the Woodstock Theological Library for their assistance with my research; and everyone at the Catholic University of America for their support during my final revisions of this work.

My special thanks go to Eric Perl who first inspired me to write about the divine ideas, John F. Wippel who offered invaluable insights and advice on this topic, Timothy Noone and Brian Shanley who challenged me to consider different perspectives, and my wife, Kelly Doolan, who provided the love and support that helped me to bring this work to completion.

Finally, I would like to express my appreciation for my father, Thomas Doolan, who made my study of philosophy a possibility in the first place.

ABBREVIATIONS

AUGUSTINE

De civ. dei	*De civitate dei*
De div. qq. 83	*De diversis quaestionibus LXXXIII*
De Gen. ad litt.	*De Genesi ad litteram*
De lib. arb.	*De libero arbitrio*
De Trin.	*De Trinitate*
De ver. rel.	*De vera religione*
Tr. in Ioann.	*In Ioannis Evangelium tractatus*

THOMAS AQUINAS

Comp. theol.	*Compendium theologiae*
De ente	*De ente et essentia*
De malo	*Quaestiones disputatae de malo*
De oper. occult.	*De operationibus occultis naturae*
De pot.	*Quaestiones disputatae de potentia*
De prin. nat.	*De principiis naturae*
De spir. creat.	*Quaestio disputata de spiritualibus creaturis*
De sub. sep.	*De substantiis separatis*
De ver.	*Quaestiones disputatae de veritate*
De virt. in comm.	*De virtutibus in communi*
In De an.	*Sentencia libri De anima*
In De caelo	*In libros Aristotelis De caelo*

ABBREVIATIONS

In De div. nom.	*In librum beati Dionysii De divinis nominibus expositio*
In De hebd.	*Expositio libri Boetii De ebdomadibus*
In De Trin.	*Super Boetium De Trinitate*
In Eth.	*Sententia libri Ethicorum*
In Hebr.	*Super Epistolam S. Pauli Apostoli ad Hebraeos*
In Lib. de caus.	*Sancti Thomae de Aquino Super librum de causis*
In Meta.	*In Metaphysicam Aristotelis commentaria*
In Phys.	*In octo libros Phyiscorum Aristotelis*
In Post. an.	*Expositio Libri Posteriorum*
In Sent.	*Scriptum super libros Sententiarum*
Lect. super Ioann.	*Lectura super evangelium Johannis*
Quaes. disp. de an.	*Quaestiones disputatae de anima*
Quod.	*Quaestiones de quolibet*
SCG	*Summa Contra Gentiles*
ST	*Summa theologiae*

INTRODUCTION

🐾

In *Le Thomisme,* Étienne Gilson observes that "exemplarism is one of the essential elements of Thomism."[1] Such a claim might take the reader by surprise: if we consider medieval philosophy, it is not Thomas Aquinas who is commonly associated with the doctrine of exemplarism but Bonaventure. Indeed, for Bonaventure exemplarism is the defining characteristic of any true metaphysics.[2] To make the same statement of Thomas would be to exaggerate the significance of this doctrine for him. Nevertheless, a reading of his corpus reveals that exemplarism is an important element in his philosophy: the word *exemplar* and variations thereof occur more than eight hundred times in his writings, and *ex professo* treatments of the divine ideas occur in each of his major systematic works.[3] In short, the

1. Étienne Gilson, *Le Thomisme,* 6th ed., rev. (Paris: Librairie Philosophique J. Vrin, 1965), 86. "Sans doute, une telle recherche n'aboutirait pas si nous ne faisons intervenir l'idée platonicienne et augustinienne de participation; mais nous verrons que, pris en un sens nouveau, l'exemplarisme est un des éléments essentiels du thomisme." All translations are my own unless otherwise noted.

2. See Bonaventure, *Collationes in hexaemeron,* 1.13 (Quaracchi ed., 331); 1.17 (Quaracchi ed., 332). Regarding Bonaventure's doctrine of exemplarism, see Christopher M. Cullen, *Bonaventure* (New York: Oxford University Press, 2006), esp. 71–77; Étienne Gilson, *The Philosophy of St. Bonaventure,* trans. Dom Illtyd Trethowan (Paterson, N.J.: St. Anthony Guild Press, 1965), 127–46; Luis Diego Cascante-Fallas, "La metafísica de la luz, una categoría de la ontología bonaventuriana," *Revista de Filosofía de la Universidad de Costa Rica* 36 (1998): 341–48; Ewert Cousins, "Truth in St. Bonaventure," *Proceedings and Addresses of the American Philosophical Association* 43 (1969): 204–10.

3. Regarding the number of times that the word *exemplar* and its vari-

doctrine of divine exemplarism is one that is essential to his metaphysical thought.

To have a complete understanding of Thomas's metaphysics, then, one must be familiar with his account of the divine ideas as exemplar causes. Together with other important theories, this one helps to define his metaphysical system. And since Thomas's metaphysics *is* defined by a number of such theories, each has rightly received scholarly attention to some degree. As John Wippel has observed, moreover, various scholars have singled out one of these theories "as offering a key or even *the* key to his metaphysical thought. Thus," Wippel continues,

his theory of a real distinction between essence and existence, his metaphysics of act and potency, his views concerning analogy of being, and his stress on the primacy of the act of existence *(actus essendi)*, all have been emphasized in due course. Much more recently, J. Aertsen has stressed the importance of the transcendentals in his thought. And each plays an important role within Thomas's metaphysics.[4]

In the present work, my hope is to add to this list precisely by emphasizing the causal role of the divine ideas in Thomas's metaphysics. In doing this, my intention is not to present this doctrine as if it were *the* key to understanding his metaphysical thought; for, simply put, it is not. Rather, my intention is more modest: it is to show how his doctrine of divine ideas is *a* key to such an understanding, that is, it is to show how exemplarism, as Gilson notes, is *one* of the essential elements of Thomistic philosophy.

The topic of the divine ideas is addressed by Thomas from the time of his earliest writings. He argues that just as in the mind of the human artisan there are ideas that act as exemplars or patterns for the things that he makes, so too in the mind of the *divine* arti-

ants occur throughout Thomas's works, see *Thomae Aquinatis Opera omnia: cum hypertextibus in CD-ROM,* 2nd ed. Robert Busa, S.J. (Milan: Editoria Elettronica Editel, 1996). A search using the term *exemplar* reveals 810 occurrences.

4. John F. Wippel, *The Metaphysical Thought of Thomas Aquinas* (Washington, D.C.: The Catholic University of America Press, 2000), 94. Following these observations, Wippel proceeds to consider the role of participation within Thomas's metaphysics.

san there must analogously be such exemplar ideas. Thomas presents these divine ideas as serving three principal roles: (1) They are epistemological principles, for in knowing them God knows creatures; (2) they are ontological or causal principles, for it is in their likeness that God creates all things; and (3) inasmuch as they fulfill the first two roles, they are veridical principles for human knowledge, since the truth of our judgments must ultimately be in accordance with them.[5] In the present work, I will focus principally on the role of the divine ideas as causal principles. Hence, I will not address the veridical role that they play in human knowing.[6] Regarding their epistemological role in divine knowing, I will address that only as it sheds light on the status of the ideas as exemplars, that is, as causal principles.[7]

The topic of the divine ideas is one that has been written on before but never with a detailed analysis of their causality. Authors have tended instead to focus on the question of their multiplicity

5. See Mark D. Jordan, "The Intelligibility of the World and the Divine Ideas in Aquinas," *Review of Metaphysics* 38 (1984): 17.

6. On this role of the divine ideas, see *De ver.*, q. 1, a. 4, ad 5 (Leonine ed., [Rome], vol. 22.1.14–15:239–50): "Veritas secundum quam anima de omnibus iudicat, est veritas prima: sicut enim a veritate intellectus divini effluunt in intellectum angelicum species rerum innatae, secundum quas omnia cognoscunt, ita a veritate intellectus divini procedit exemplariter in intellectum nostrum veritas primorum principiorum, secundum quam de omnibus iudicamus; et quia per eam iudicare non possemus nisi secundum quod est similitudo primae veritatis, ideo secundum primam veritatem dicimur de omnibus iudicare." See also *Quod.* 8, q. 1, a. 1 (Leonine ed., vol. 25.1.52:113–17): "intellectus divinus est ratio naturae absolute consideratae vel in singularibus, et ipsa natura absolute considerata vel in singularibus est ratio intellectus humani et quodam modo mensura ipsius." See Joseph Owens, "Deo Intus Pandente," *Modern Schoolman* 69 (1992): 369–78; Vivian Boland, *Ideas in God According to Saint Thomas Aquinas* (New York: E. J. Brill, 1996), 279–84; Bernard B. Lonergan, *Verbum: Word and Idea in Aquinas,* ed. David B. Burrell (Notre Dame: University of Notre Dame Press, 1967), 87–88. Regarding the role of the agent intellect in human cognition, see John Haldane, "Aquinas on the Active Intellect," *Philosophy* 67 (1992): 199–210; Patrick Lee, "Saint Thomas and Avicenna on the Agent Intellect," *Thomist* 45 (1981): 41–61; Francis A. Cunningham, "A Theory on Abstraction in St. Thomas," *Modern Schoolman* 35 (1958): 249–70; Louis B. Geiger, "Abstraction et séparation d'après s. Thomas *In de Trinitate*, q. 5, a. 3," *Revue des sciences philosophiques et théologiques* 31 (1947): 3–40; Lonergan, *Word and Idea*, 151–68; Boland, *Ideas in God*, 279–81.

7. See chaps. 3 and 4.

and the status of divine ideas for pure possibles.[8] Vivian Boland provides a more complete consideration of the divine ideas in his recent book *Ideas in God According to Saint Thomas Aquinas.* This work offers both a helpful overview of the history of the theory of ideas as well as an analysis of Thomas's own doctrine. Nevertheless, it does not offer a consideration either of how Aquinas views the causality of the divine ideas in relation to that of natural agents or of how their causality fits within the framework of his theory of participation. This is in part because Boland's goal in examining the divine ideas differs from my own. As he notes, his desire is "to examine the meaning and function of the notion of divine ideas in the theology of Saint Thomas."[9] By contrast, my desire is to exam-

8. See Vincent P. Branick, "The Unity of the Divine Ideas," *The New Scholasticism* 42 (1968): 171–201; Norris Clarke, "The Problem of the Reality and Multiplicity of Divine Ideas in Christian Neoplatonism," in *Neoplatonism and Christian Thought,* ed. Dominic J. O'Meara (Albany: State University of New York Press, 1982), 109–27; Lawrence Dewan, "St. Thomas and the Possibles," *The New Scholasticism* 53 (1979): 76–85; id., "St. Thomas, James Ross, and Exemplarism: A Reply," *American Catholic Philosophical Quarterly* 65 (1991): 221–34; John Lee Farthing, "The Problem of Divine Exemplarity in St. Thomas," *The Thomist* 49 (1985): 183–222; Louis B. Geiger, "Les idées divines dans l'oeuvre de s. Thomas," in *St. Thomas Aquinas: Commemorative Studies,* vol. 1 (Toronto: Pontifical Institute of Mediaeval Studies, 1974), 175–209; Roger Miller Jones, "The Ideas as the Thoughts of God," *Classical Philology* 21 (1926): 317–26; Jordan, "Intelligibility of the World"; Armand A. Maurer, "James Ross on the Divine Ideas: A Reply," *American Catholic Philosophical Quarterly* 65 (1991): 213–20; James F. Ross, "Aquinas' Exemplarism; Aquinas' Voluntarism," *American Catholic Philosophical Quarterly* 64 (1990): 171–98; id., "Response to Maurer and Dewan," *American Catholic Philosophical Quarterly* 65 (1991): 213–20; John F. Wippel, "The Reality of Nonexisting Possibles According to Thomas Aquinas, Henry of Ghent, and Godfrey of Fontaines," *Review of Metaphysics* 34 (1981): 729–58; id., *Thomas Aquinas on the Divine Ideas,* in The Etienne Gilson Series, no. 16 (Toronto: Pontifical Institute of Mediaeval Studies, 1993); Beatrice Hope Zedler, "Why Are the Possibles Possible?" *New Scholasticism* 55 (1981): 113–30.

In his dissertation, *Exemplary Causality in the Philosophy of St. Thomas Aquinas* (Ph.D. diss., The Catholic University of America, 1967), Theodore Kondoleon does go beyond these questions to examine both the mode of causality exercised by the divine ideas as well as their nature as measures. However, he does not offer a consideration either of how this causality is related to that of natural agents or of how it fits within the framework of Thomas's theory of participation (*Exemplary Causality in the Philosophy of St. Thomas Aquinas* [Ann Arbor, Mich.: UMI (1967)], microfilm, ProQuest document ID: 758691971).

9. Boland, *Ideas in God,* 13.

ine the causality of the divine ideas within Thomas's *philosophical* thought. Moreover, while granting the theological significance of Thomas's theory of ideas, I shall argue that his doctrine is fundamentally a philosophical one.

Although the point of focus in my work differs from Boland's in these respects, there is a basic concurrence between us regarding the historical influences on Thomas's doctrine. The theory of divine ideas is not new with Thomas. Indeed, he himself acknowledges the influence that prior thinkers had on his theory, most notably Augustine and Dionysius. As Boland observes, the list of such influences is long, for: "Besides the texts of Augustine and Dionysius, the entire range of authors used by Saint Thomas dealt with the question of divine intelligence and divine ideas."[10] This list of names grows longer still when we consider that Thomas's doctrine is influenced not only by those authors whom he himself had read, but even by those whom he had never read: authors such as Iamblichus and Plotinus whose writings exercised a profound influence on the historical development of the doctrine of divine ideas. To recount this development, therefore, would be an enormous undertaking and one, furthermore, that Boland himself has already done. For this reason, in the pages that follow I will focus instead on Thomas's own doctrine of divine ideas, addressing historical influences only when necessary to provide the reader with relevant background information.[11]

The current work thus begins in chapter 1 by examining Thomas's understanding of the nature of exemplarism in general as well as how an idea can act as an exemplar cause, and it will do so by looking at human art, since we are more familiar with our own ideas than we are with God's. Having identified what constitutes

10. Ibid., 192.

11. For the reader who wishes to learn more about these influences, I would recommend reading Boland's work. See part 1 for the history of sources that shaped Thomas's doctrine of divine ideas (*Ideas in God*, 1–192). What still remains for future scholarship is an investigation of the influences that Thomas's thirteenth century contemporaries may have had on his doctrine.

an exemplar idea for Thomas, I shall consider in chapter 2 whether such ideas exist in the divine mind. Assuming the existence of God, I shall examine Thomas's arguments for the existence of divine ideas. Chapter 3 will then address how he reconciles the multiplicity of these ideas with the divine simplicity. Chapter 4 will examine this multiplicity further, considering the kinds of things for which God has ideas and identifying which ideas Thomas considers properly to be exemplars. In chapter 5, I shall consider how these exemplar ideas act as causes without compromising the causality of natural agents. The work will culminate in chapter 6 with a consideration of the role the divine ideas play within the structure of Thomas's theory of participation.

Throughout these chapters, my methodology will be to provide a close textual analysis of Thomas's theory of the divine ideas, following the chronology of his writings. The advantage of this approach is that it will reveal any developments in his doctrine. Such analyses, I believe, are valuable to the reader who wishes to have a thorough understanding of Thomas's thought on this topic. Nevertheless, I recognize that some readers may desire a more general overview. For this reason, I have also provided summaries of my findings, both at the end of the aforementioned analyses as well as at the conclusion of each chapter. Thus, the reader who so desires can turn straightaway to these précis.

The philosophical issues that I have outlined above I believe to be the most fundamental ones regarding Thomas's doctrine of the divine ideas. Examining them will reveal why the otherwise Aristotelian Aquinas would adopt this Neoplatonic doctrine. My hope is that, in considering these issues, the reader will come to have a better understanding of the role of the divine ideas as causes in Thomas's metaphysics and, moreover, that he will come to appreciate why it is that exemplarism is one of the essential elements of Thomistic philosophy.

ONE

IDEAS AS EXEMPLAR
CAUSES

⌇

"[I]n the divine mind," Thomas Aquinas tells us, "there
are exemplar forms of all creatures, which are called ideas,
as there are forms of artifacts in the mind of an artisan."[1]
Time and again throughout his career, Thomas affirms
the existence of such forms in the mind of God, and time
and again he presents these ideas as the exemplars of created things.[2] The type of causality that the divine ideas exercise can thus be described as exemplar causality, or exemplarism. Exemplarism, however, is not limited to the
divine ideas. As the above quotation suggests, the ideas of
a human artisan can also be considered exemplars. In fact,
Thomas holds that exemplars need not even be ideas at
all. In order to begin to understand the causality of the
divine ideas, therefore, we must first consider what exemplar causality is in general and in what way an idea, whether human or divine, can be said to be an exemplar.

1. *Quod.* 8, a. 2 (Leonine ed., vol. 25.1.54:23–26): "In mente diuina sint
omnium creaturarum forme exemplares,quae ideae dicuntur, sicut in mente artificis formae artificiatorum."
2. See, e.g., *In I Sent.,* d. 36, q. 2, a. 1 (Mandonnet ed. [Paris: Lethielleux,
1929], vol. 1.839–40); *De ver.,* q. 3, a. 3 (Leonine ed., vol. 22.1.107–8:85–174);
In V De div. nom., lect. 3, n. 665 (C. Pera, ed. [Turin and Rome: Marietti,
1950], 249); *ST,* I, q. 15, a. 1 (Leonine ed., vol. 4.199).

WHAT IS AN EXEMPLAR?

Central to exemplarism is the characteristic of similitude or likeness *(similitudo)*. Likeness, however, is not a trait that is unique to exemplars—indeed, likeness implies that there is another that shares in the similitude. As Thomas explains, a likeness can exist in something in one of two ways: either as in a principle or as in something that shares a likeness *to* a principle. Only the former such likeness, however, has the character *(ratio)* of an exemplar; the latter has, instead, the character of an image *(imago)*. Thomas notes that an image is called such because it is produced in imitation of something else, that is, in imitation of an exemplar.[3] Hence, he commonly describes an exemplar as "that in the likeness of which something is made."[4]

Consequently, Thomas sees a dependence of an image upon its exemplar for the likeness that is present in it. The notion of "image" adds something to that of "likeness," namely, that the image is the expression of another *(ex alio expressum)*. Thus, for example, no matter how much one egg is similar and equal to another, Thomas explains that we would not call the first egg the image of the second because the likeness of that second egg is not expressed by the first.[5] Conversely, we might add that neither, therefore, is that second egg the first one's exemplar. Here we begin to get a better sense of the philosophical notion of exemplarism. It is true that in common parlance we often refer to the finest example of something as an exemplar. In this sense, a perfect egg might well be described as an exemplar for other eggs, or a perfect student as an exemplar

3. *SCG* IV, c. 49 (Leonine ed., vol. 15.34.51–56); *ST* I, q. 35, a. 1, ad 1 (Leonine ed., vol. 4.372); q. 93, a. 1 (Leonine ed., vol. 5.401).

4. *In Lib. de caus.*, prop. 14 (Saffrey ed. [Fribourg and Louvain: Société philosophique de Fribourg, 1954], 85.12–13): "exemplar est id ad cuius similitudinem fit aliud." Cf. *De ver.*, q. 3, a. 1 (Leonine ed., vol. 22.1.99:177–82); *Quod.* 8, q. 1, a. 2 (Leonine ed., vol. 25.1.54:42–3); *In V De div. nom.*, lect. 3, n. 665 (Marietti ed., 249); *ST* I, q. 35, a. 1, ad 1 (Leonine ed., vol. 4.372).

5. *ST* I, q. 93, a. 1 (Leonine ed., vol. 5.401).

for other students. But as Marie-Charles Perret observes, "when they [philosophers] speak of a thing's exemplar, it is not for them a given member of a series; it is not simply the first member, the 'first edition,' the prototype of which all of the other members in the series are repetitions. Rather, for them it is about the original, the model itself and not the reproduction."[6] For the same reason, Thomas describes exemplars as being superior to *(praestantius)* and exceeding *(potius)* that which they exemplify.[7]

This relationship between exemplar and image is clearest as regards human art. Real things are in a sense the exemplar forms of pictures.[8] When, for example, an artist paints the portrait of a man, there is a likeness of that man in the painted picture. The man is the model for this image. Thus, we may consider the man himself to be the exemplar of that picture. Still, while Thomas does describe this sort of likeness as a manner of exemplarism, he more frequently reserves the term "exemplar" for the form that is in the *mind* of the artisan. That form is more truly the exemplar of the work of art because it—and not the external object—is the principle of the artisan's operation.[9] Hence, the work of art is more properly said to be made in likeness to the form or *idea* that is in the mind of the artisan.

As we have seen, it is from this artistic model of exemplarism that Thomas draws an analogy to explain God's creative knowledge, for he notes that "the divine knowledge that God has of things is comparable to the knowledge of an artisan in this respect: that it is the cause of all things as art [is the cause] of works of art."[10] In or-

6. Marie-Charles Perret, "La Notion d'Exemplarité," *Revue Thomiste* 41 (1936): 450: "«Exemplaire» revêt un autre sens dans la bouche des philosophes: quand eux parlent d'exemplaire d'une chose, il ne s'agit plus de tel ou tel numéro d'une série, il ne s'agit pas seulement du numéro *un*, de l'édition «princeps», du prototype dont tous les autres numéros sont la répétition, il s'agit pour eux de l'original, du modèle même et non plus de la reproduction."

7. *In III Sent.*, d. 20, q. 1, a. 3 (Moos ed. [Paris: Lethielleux, 1933],vol. 3.621.56); *ST* II-II, q. 26, a. 4, *sed contra* (Leonine ed., vol. 8.213).

8. *In III Sent.*, d. 27, q. 2, a. 4, *solutio* 3, ad 1 (Moos ed., vol. 3.889.176).

9. *SCG* IV, c. 11 (Leonine ed., vol. 15.34).

10. *De ver.*, q. 2, a. 5 (Leonine ed., vol. 22.1.62:245–53): "Et ideo simpliciter conce-

der to understand Thomas's doctrine of divine exemplarism better, therefore, we must first consider the exemplarism of human art in more detail; doing so will allow us to discern both what exemplar causality entails and how an idea can act as an exemplar cause.

Thomas's most systematic treatments of the exemplarism of human art are found, interestingly enough, in his texts on the divine ideas. Looking at these passages, the reader discovers that Thomas's doctrine of exemplarism does not change dramatically from text to text. There is, however, a development in his *terminology*. By the period of Thomas's later works, he is using a refined sense of the term "exemplar," lending greater precision to his account of the causality of ideas. In order to see the significance of this development, we turn now to a chronological consideration of the principal passages in which Aquinas discusses the exemplarism of human art.

TEXTUAL ANALYSIS

In I Sententias (1252–1256)

The earliest work in which Thomas discusses exemplarism is his commentary on Peter Lombard's *Sentences* (*Scriptum super libros Sententiarum*,1252–56).[11] Thomas directly addresses the divine ideas in *In I Sent.*, d. 36, q. 2, a. 1. There, he examines what is meant by the term "idea." He begins by observing that artificial forms have a twofold act of existence. In one way, they exist in act inasmuch as they are in matter; in another way, such forms exist in po-

---

dendum est quod Deus omnia singularia cognoscit, non solum in universalibus causis sed etiam unumquodque secundum propriam et singularem suam naturam. Ad cuius evidentiam sciendum est quod scientia divina quam de rebus habet comparatur scientiae artificis eo quod est causa omnium rerum sicut ars artificiatorum." Even though Thomas makes this comparison between God and the human artisan, he is careful to acknowledge the limits of the analogy and to avoid any anthropomorphism, as we shall see.

11. Unless otherwise noted, dating of Thomas's texts follows Jean-Pierre Torrell's *Saint Thomas Aquinas*, vol. 1, *The Person and His Work*, trans. Robert Royal (Washington, D.C.: The Catholic University of America Press, 1996).

tency inasmuch as they are in the mind of an artisan—a potency that Thomas describes as active rather than passive. He explains, furthermore, that the term "idea" comes from the Greek word *eidos,* which means "form." Since the principle of both practical and speculative knowledge is the form of a thing that exists in the intellect, Thomas concludes that the proper meaning of the term "idea" belongs equally to each type of knowledge. He grants that according to common usage, the term is taken for a form that is a principle of practical knowledge since we call exemplar ideas the forms of things. Nevertheless, we also call "contemplating ideas" *(ideae contemplantes)* the forms of things. Hence, Thomas reiterates his position that ideas are also principles of speculative knowledge.[12]

In this brief passage, we see Thomas employ a broad understanding of what constitutes an idea, describing ideas as belonging equally to these two modes of cognition. However, he does imply that there is a distinction between exemplars and other types of ideas: his mention of exemplars within the context of common parlance suggests that exemplar ideas belong only to practical knowledge (see figure 1-1 below, p. 11).

Thomas provides further insight into the character of exemplarism in d. 38, q. 1, a. 1. There he considers whether God's knowledge is the cause of things, and in the course of this consideration, he makes several observations regarding the causality of art. He notes first that an artisan's knowledge manifests an end. Second, he notes that the will of the artisan *intends* that end. Third, he notes that the artisan's will commands the act through which the work is produced, a work for which the artisan had a preconceived form. Thomas thus presents both will and intention as essential elements in defining an idea as productive.[13]

---

12. *In I Sent.,* d. 36, q. 2, a. 1 (Mandonnet ed., vol. 1.839–40).
13. *In I Sent.,* d. 38, q. 1, a. 1 (Mandonnet ed., vol. 1.899).

De veritate, q. 3 (1256–1257)

A more extensive consideration both of ideas and of exemplar causality appears in *De veritate,* q. 3. In a. 1 of this question, Thomas examines whether ideas exist in God. He begins by quoting Augustine's observation from the *De diversis quaestionibus LXXXIII* that the word "idea" can be translated into Latin as either *forma* or *species.*[14] But the form of a thing can be understood in three different ways. In the first way, form is that "by which" *(a qua)* a thing is formed, as the formation of an effect proceeds from the form of an agent. However, Thomas explains, such a form is not what is meant by the term "idea." The second way that we may understand form is as that "according to which" *(secundum quam)* something is formed. In this way, the soul is the form of man and the figure of a statue is the form of copper. Such a form is part of a composite and, as such, is truly said to be the form of the thing.[15] Thomas maintains, however, that neither is this form to be called an idea since the name "idea" seems to signify a form that is *separate* from that which it forms. The third way in which we may understand form is as that "in regard to which" *(ad quam)* something is formed. And *this* is the exemplar form in imitation of which something is made. It is in this sense, Thomas concludes, that the name "idea" is commonly understood, namely, as a form that something imitates.[16]

Something can imitate a form, however, in one of two ways. The first way is according to the intention of an agent, as when an artist paints a picture that depicts someone's likeness. The second way

14. Augustine's influence on Thomas's doctrine of the divine ideas will be examined in more detail in chaps. 3 and 4.

15. What Thomas elsewhere terms a *forma partis* (*In VII Meta.,* lect. 9, n. 1469 [Cathala ed., (Turin: Marietti, 1935) 432]; *De ente,* c. 2 [Leonine ed., vol. 43.373:274–91]).

16. *De ver.,* q. 3, a. 1 (Leonine ed., vol. 22.1.99:159–82): "Tertio modo dicitur forma alicuius ad quam aliquid formatur, et haec est forma exemplaris ad cuius imitationem aliquid constituitur, et in hac significatione consuetum est nomen ideae accipi ut idem sit idea quod forma quam aliquid imitatur."

occurs when such an imitation results accidentally *(per accidens)*—not according to the artist's intention, but simply by chance. Thus, for example, an artist might paint a portrait that shares an unintended likeness to someone. When a form is imitated in this way, we would not say that the product is formed "in regard to" that form because the phrase "in regard to" seems to signify order toward an end. Since an exemplar (or idea) is "that in regard to which something is formed," Thomas concludes that it is necessary that an exemplar form (or idea) be imitated intentionally and not accidentally.[17]

Having identified intentionality as essential to the character of an exemplar, Thomas makes a distinction regarding how an end is intended. Something acts on account of an end in one of two respects. In one respect, an agent is able to determine the end for himself. Such is the case with all agents acting through intellect. In another respect, however, an agent acts for an end because the end has been determined *for* it by another principal agent. Thomas gives an example from archery to illustrate this point: an arrow that is set in flight seeks a goal, but this goal is an end that has been determined for it by the archer.[18]

Given this distinction, Thomas argues that when something is made in imitation of another by an agent that has not *itself* determined the end, then the imitated form will not have the character *(ratio)* of an exemplar, or idea. Thus, we do not say that the form of a man who generates is the idea, or exemplar, of the child who is generated since the end is determined instead by nature (and, as we shall see, ultimately by God). Rather, we only say that a form is the exemplar of another when an agent, acting for an end, determines that end *himself*. In this way, we say the form of art that exists within the mind of the artisan is an "exemplar," or "idea," of an artifact. So, too, Thomas adds, we say the form that is *external* to

17. *De ver.,* q. 3, a. 1 (Leonine ed., vol. 22.1.99:183–96).
18. *De ver.,* q. 3, a. 1 (Leonine ed., vol. 22.1.99–100:196–204).

him, in imitation of which he makes something, is an "exemplar." From the foregoing discussion concerning form, imitation, and intentionality, Thomas concludes that "This, therefore, seems to be the character *(ratio)* of an idea: that an idea is a form that something imitates because of the intention of an agent who predetermines the end for himself."[19]

This passage from the *De veritate* provides us with a more detailed consideration of the general character of ideas than is offered in *In I Sent.* In both works, Thomas presents ideas as forms in the mind of the artisan. But whereas in his *Sentences* commentary he reserves his discussion of the role of the agent's intention and will for a future article on God's knowledge, in the *De veritate* he presents this discussion within his very consideration of the ideas themselves. Hence, the agent's will and intention are now clearly made part of the very definition of exemplar ideas. Given these elements of the definition, however, we are faced with a question: does Thomas now consider ideas to belong solely to practical knowledge?

He addresses this question in a. 3. There, he begins by quoting Aristotle's *De anima* 3.10.433a14 to the effect that the speculative intellect differs from the practical by means of its end—the end of the former being absolute truth, the end of the latter being action. Consequently, some knowledge is called practical because it is directed to a work, and this occurs in two ways. In the first way,

19. *De ver.*, q. 3, a. 1 (Leonine ed., vol. 22.1.100:209–23): "Haec ergo videtur esse ratio ideae, quod idea sit forma quam aliquid imitatur ex intentione agentis qui praedeterminat sibi finem." Here, Thomas is careful to draw the limits of the analogy between human art and the divine ideas: unlike the human artisan, God does not act on account of any exemplars outside of himself (*De ver.*, q. 3, a. 1 [Leonine ed., vol. 22.1.100:254–61]).
Elements of this definition can already be found in the earlier *In I Sent.* Referring specifically to the character of divine ideas, Thomas explains in d. 36, q. 2, a. 3, that "Sicut ex auctoritate Dionysii, cap. V *De div. nom.*, §8, col. 823, t. I, inducta patet, idea dicitur similitudo vel ratio rei in Deo existens, secundum quod est productiva ipsius rei et praedeterminativa" (Mandonnet ed., vol. 1.844). Despite following Dionysius here in emphasizing an idea's predeterminative character, Thomas does not present that character in terms of the agent's predetermining the end for himself.

knowledge is directed to a work in act, as when an artisan intends to introduce a preconceived form into matter. Thomas describes such knowledge as being actually practical *(actu practica)*, and he describes such a form as being a form of understanding *(forma cognitionis)*. He notes, however, that sometimes knowledge that is *capable* of being ordered to act nevertheless is not so ordered. Thus, an artisan can think out the form of the work of art and know the way that it can be made and, yet, still not intend to make it. This sort of knowledge Thomas describes as being not actually practical, but *habitually* or *virtually* practical *(habitu vel virtute practica)*.[20]

In contrast to both of these modes of cognition, purely speculative knowledge is not ordered to act in any way. Here, too, Thomas describes two modes of knowledge. In one way, speculative knowledge occurs in regard to those things whose natures cannot be produced through the knowledge of the knower, an example is man's knowledge of natural things. But in another way, speculative knowledge occurs when the thing that is known is *capable* of being produced but is simply not considered in that respect—for while a thing is produced in being *(esse)* through an operation, some things that can be separated according to the intellect do not exist separately according to an act of existence. To make this point clear, Thomas gives the example of an artisan who considers the genus, species, and properties *(passiones)* of a house separately from each other even though they are not found separately in the thing. Such knowledge is neither actually nor virtually practical but, rather, speculative. By contrast, he notes, when a thing is considered as it is capable of being produced, then every element of the thing that is required for its existence is considered at the same time.[21]

After outlining these four modes of cognition, Thomas considers to which one ideas properly belong. Following Augustine, he observes that according to the proper meaning of the word, an "idea" is called a "form." In this sense, an idea includes only a

---

20. *De ver.,* q. 3, a. 3 (Leonine ed., vol. 22.1.107:85–100).
21. *De ver.,* q. 3, a. 3 (Leonine ed., vol. 22.1.107:100–21). Wippel, *Divine Ideas,* 21.

knowledge of that which can be formed and, hence, is practical—either actually or virtually so.[22] If we consider what an idea itself is, however, then it can be understood in a broader sense as the notion *(ratio)* or likeness *(similitudo)* of a thing. Considered in this respect, an idea can also pertain to purely speculative knowledge. Thomas concludes, therefore, that properly speaking, the terms "notion" and "likeness" belong as much to speculative knowledge as to practical whereas the term "idea" belongs only to practical knowledge (whether actual or virtual).[23]

Where, then, does the term "exemplar" fit into this schema? We find an answer to this question in Thomas's reply to the third objection. In this objection, it is argued that an idea is nothing other than an exemplar form. The objector maintains that since an exemplar is that in imitation of which something is made, it must belong to practical knowledge and, hence, so too must all ideas.[24] In reply, Thomas grants that an exemplar does express a relation to something that is outside of the mind. Nevertheless, he notes that something can be called an exemplar simply from the fact that another thing *can* be made in imitation of it even though that other thing is never so made. Thus, Thomas concludes that properly speaking, the term "exemplar" belongs both to knowledge that is actually practical *and* to knowledge that is virtually practical. Moreover, the same is true regarding the term "idea" (see figure 1-2).[25]

In the *De veritate,* then, we see a development as regards Thomas's division of the modes of knowledge. His distinction between the two types of practical and two types of speculative knowledge is one that is not present in his *Sentences* commentary. This new di-

---

22. Thomas grants, furthermore, that the latter mode of practical knowledge "quodam modo speculativa est" *(De ver.,* q. 3, a. 3 [Leonine ed., vol. 22.1.108:167–68]).

23. *De ver.,* q. 3, a. 3 (Leonine ed., vol. 22.1.108:163–74); Wippel, *Divine Ideas,* 21–22; Boland, *Ideas in God,* 251–53.

24. *De ver.,* q. 3, a. 3, obj. 3 (Leonine ed., vol. 22.1.106.25–29).

25. *De ver.,* q. 3, a. 3, ad 3 (Leonine ed., vol. 22.1.108:185–94).

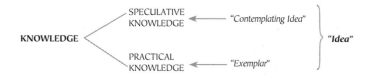

FIGURE 1-1. Terminology in *In I Sent.*

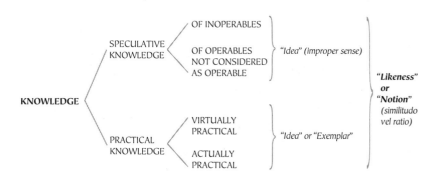

FIGURE 1-2. Terminology in the *De veritate*

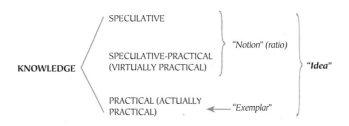

FIGURE 1-3. Terminology in *Summa theologiae I*

vision allows for a refinement regarding his doctrine of ideas. As we have seen, in the *Sentences* commentary, Thomas argues that ideas belong equally to practical and to speculative knowledge. The primary characteristic of an idea that he identifies there is that it is the form of a thing, a characteristic that is just as applicable to both types of knowledge. We see in the *De veritate,* however, that an idea is more than merely the formal likeness of a thing: it is something that is *imitated.* For this reason, Thomas concludes there that an idea properly belongs to practical knowledge, either actual or virtual. His reply to obj. 3 of a. 3, furthermore, describes exemplars in the same way, indicating that he considers exemplars to be coterminous with ideas, taken in the strict sense. Hence, they belong only to practical knowledge. In this last respect, we see a continuity with the *Sentences* commentary.[26]

In De divinis nominibus (1261–1265 or 1265–1268)

It is in *In librum beati Dionysii De divinis nominibus expositio* that we find the next discussion of the divine ideas, according to one possible dating of the manuscript (1261–65 or 1265–68).[27] Thomas's

26. Thomas's next treatment of the divine ideas is a brief consideration provided in *Quodlibet* 8, q. 1, a. 2, in 1257, around the same time as the *De veritate* passage or shortly thereafter (Leonine ed., vol. 25.1, preface, 1). There, Thomas makes his usual observation that an exemplar is that in imitation of which something is made. For this reason, he explains, the character *(ratio)* of an exemplar requires that an agent intend the assimilation of a work to its exemplar. Without this intention, the assimilation would happen by chance rather than by exemplarity. The definition of an exemplar, therefore, must include an agent's intention (Leonine ed., vol. 25.1.54:42–59). This passage thus offers continuity with Thomas's treatment of exemplarism in the *De veritate:* central to the notion of an exemplar is the intention of an agent. Although he does not mention here to what mode of knowledge exemplars belong, Thomas again presents the term "idea" as coterminous with "exemplar" as he had in the *De veritate.*

27. The dating of this work remains uncertain, having been written either during Thomas's sojourn in Orvieto or during the following period in Rome (Torrell, *The Person and His Work,* 346). Pseudo-Dionysius's influence on Thomas's treatment of exemplarism is apparent in *Summa theologiae I* (1266–68). However, given the uncertain dating of *In De div. nom.,* it is also uncertain whether that work predates Thomas's consideration of the divine ideas in the *Summa.*

commentary on Pseudo-Dionysius's *De divinis nominibus* marks a turning point in his treatment of exemplarism. To get a sense of the implications that this work has for his doctrine of exemplarism in general, it will be beneficial for us this time briefly to examine what he has to say about *divine* exemplarism.[28] In chapter V, lect. 3 of his commentary, Thomas observes that God knows the things that proceed from him according to "notions" *(rationes)* that are exemplars. However, not all notions can be called exemplars. The reason is that an exemplar is that in imitation of which something is made, and God does not make everything that he knows. "Therefore," Thomas concludes, "only those notions *(rationes)* understood by God in imitation of which he *wills* to produce a thing in existence *(esse)* can be called 'exemplars', just as an artisan produces works of art in imitation of the forms of art that he conceives in his mind. And these [forms] are also called 'exemplars' of artifacts."[29]

In this passage, then, we find Thomas departing from the description of exemplars that he had provided in the *De veritate.* Not all notions *(rationes),* or ideas, are exemplars but only those that are *productive.* In the language of the *De veritate,* he now holds that only "actually practical" ideas can be termed exemplars. This new position is emphasized by the role of the will that he describes. Indeed, following Pseudo-Dionysius (hereafter Dionysius), Thomas goes so far as to refer to the divine exemplars as God's "willings" *(voluntates).*[30] His use of the analogy from art, furthermore, suggests that

---

28. Pseudo-Dionysius's influence on Thomas's doctrine of the divine ideas will be discussed in more detail in chaps. 2 and 3.

29. *In V De div. nom.,* lect. 3, n. 665 (Marietti ed., 249): "Non autem omnes huiusmodi rationes exemplaria dici possunt: exemplar enim est ad cuius imitationem fit aliud; non autem omnia quae scit Deus ex Ipso posse prodire, vult in rerum natura producere; illae igitur solae rationes intellectae a Deo exemplaria dici possunt, ad quarum imitationem vult res in esse producere, sicut producit artifex artificiata ad imitationem formarum artis quas mente concepit, quae etiam artificialium exemplaria dici possunt." Emphasis added in translation.

30. *In V De div. nom.,* lect. 3, n. 666 (Marietti ed., 249): "Hoc est ergo quod dicit,

the same understanding applies to the ideas of any artisan, that is, that only those ideas that are actually productive can be termed "exemplars." As we shall presently see, this new understanding of exemplarism that Thomas gets from Dionysius is one that he employs in his future writings.

Summa theologiae I (1266–1268)

The next significant treatment of exemplarism that Thomas offers appears in the *Prima Pars* of the *Summa theologiae*.[31] There, Thomas presents two separate considerations of exemplarism. The first appears in q. 15, which is dedicated to examining the divine ideas. The second appears in q. 44, which addresses how creatures proceed from God, who is their first cause.

---

quod *exemplaria dicimus esse* non res aliquas extra Deum, sed *in* ipso intellectu divino quasdam existentium *rationes* intellectas, quae sunt substantiarum factivae, et praeexistunt in Deo *singulariter,* idest unite et non secundum aliquam diversitatem; et huiusmodi rationes sacra Scriptura *vocat praediffinitiones* sive praedestinationes, secundum illud Rom. 8: '*Quos praedestinavit hos et vocavit*' et vocat etiam eas, *divinas et bonas voluntates,* secundum illud Psalm. 110: '*Magna opera Domini, exquisita in omnes voluntates Eius*'. Quae quidem praediffinitiones et voluntates sunt distinctivae entium et effectivae ipsorum, quia et *secundum* huiusmodi *rationes,* supersubstantialis Dei *essentia* praedeterminavit *et omnia produxit.*" For Dionysius's use of the term *voluntates* (θελήματα), see *In V De div. nom.,* lect. 3, Textus Dionysius, n. 8.282 (Marietti ed., 248).

Thomas's interpretation here of Dionysius marks a departure, not only from his earlier position in the *De veritate,* but also from an earlier interpretation of Dionysius in that same work. In q. 3, a. 6, obj. 3, of the *De veritate,* an objector argues precisely the position that Thomas is arguing in this Commentary, *viz.,* that since the divine exemplars are acts of God's will, exemplars only pertain to things that exist at some point in time. Thomas replies to this objection that "quamvis Deus numquam voluerit producere huiusmodi res in esse quarum ideas habet, tamen vult se posse eas producere et se habere scientiam eas producendi: unde et Dionysius *non* dicit quod ad rationem exemplaris exigeretur voluntas praediffiniens et efficiens sed *diffinitiva* et *effectiva*" (Leonine ed., vol. 22.1.113:60–67, emphasis added).

31. There are no major passages in the *Summa Contra Gentiles* dedicated to considering exemplar ideas. As I have noted, Thomas customarily presents his treatment of the ideas within a discussion of God's knowledge. However, such a treatment is not emphasized in the *Summa Contra Gentiles* (a fact that I will address in chap. 4). Thus, his discussion of divine exemplarism in book I, c. 54, does not present the customary analogy from art but instead examines the manner in which the divine intellect is the proper likeness of created things (Leonine ed., vol. 13.154–55).

In a. 1 of q. 15, Thomas addresses the question whether there are (divine) ideas. As in the *De veritate*, he begins with the observation that the Greek term "idea" is called "form" in Latin. "Hence," he notes, "through ideas the forms of other things are understood, existing apart from the things themselves."[32] The form of something can exist apart from the thing itself in two ways: either as the exemplar of that thing or as a principle of knowledge inasmuch as the forms of knowable things are said to be in the knower. In both respects, Thomas maintains, it is necessary to posit ideas.

As evidence, he observes that whenever a thing is not generated by chance, its form must be the end of generation. Furthermore, the agent that acts on account of form only does so because some likeness *(similitudo)* of that form exists in it—a likeness that can occur in one of two ways. In one way, a likeness is in a natural agent because the form of the generated thing preexists in the agent according to a natural being *(esse naturale),* as it does in things that act according to their nature. Thus, man generates man and fire, fire. In another way, the likeness of a generated thing can occur in the agent according to an intelligible being *(esse intelligibile);* such is the case with those agents who act by means of intellect. In this way, the likeness of a house preexists in the mind of the builder. "And this likeness," Thomas concludes, "can be called the 'idea' of the house since the artisan intends the house to be like the form that he conceived in his mind."[33]

We saw that at the beginning of the article, Thomas ascribed both an ontological and a cognitive function to ideas. As John Wippel notes, "In the rest of art. 1, however, Thomas bases his argumentation for divine ideas upon the need for divine exemplars, i.e., upon their *ontological* function."[34] Does this approach imply that

32. *ST* I, q. 15, a. 1 (Leonine ed., vol. 4.199): "*Idea* enim graece, latine *forma* dicitur: unde per ideas intelliguntur formae aliarum rerum, praeter ipsas res existentes."
33. *ST* I, q. 15, a. 1 (Leonine ed., vol. 4.199): "Et haec potest dici idea domus: quia artifex intendit domum assimilare formae quam mente concepit."
34. Wippel, *Divine Ideas,* 33. Emphasis added.

ideas are properly operative and, hence, that they belong only to practical knowledge? Thomas answers this question in a. 3, where he considers whether there are ideas of all things that God knows. There, in a rare moment when he cites Plato's authority, Thomas again observes that ideas are principles both of the knowledge and of the production of things.[35] Inasmuch as an idea is a productive principle, it is called an "exemplar" and belongs to practical knowledge. But inasmuch as an idea is a principle of knowledge, it is properly called a "notion" *(ratio)* and can also belong to *speculative* knowledge.[36]

In the *Summa theologiae*, then, we see a further refinement in Thomas's terminology. In the *De veritate*, he had reserved the proper sense of the term "idea" for practical knowledge, noting that the terms "notion" *(ratio)* and "likeness" *(similitudo)* could be applied equally to practical and speculative knowledge. Furthermore, as we saw, he described exemplars as being coterminous with ideas. In the *Prima Pars*, however, Thomas now presents the term "idea" as being more generic, including both species of knowledge, practical and speculative. The term "notion" *(ratio)* is now reserved for speculative knowledge alone, whereas "exemplar" is reserved for practical knowledge. In this last respect, then, there is continuity with the *De veritate* since Thomas presented exemplars in that work as belonging only to practical knowledge. Nevertheless, in the *De veri-*

35. *ST* I, q. 15, a. 3 (Leonine ed., vol. 204): "Cum ideae a Platone ponerentur principia cognitionis rerum et generationis ipsarum, ad utrumque se habet idea, prout in mente divina ponitur." It should be noted here that Thomas's observations in this article refer specifically to the *divine* ideas that exist within the mind of God. Nevertheless, in light of the analogy that he draws from human art in the prior articles of this *quaestio*, this observation is applicable to human ideas as well.

36. *ST* I, q. 15, a. 3 (Leonine ed., vol. 4.204): "Et secundum quod est principium factionis rerum, *exemplar* dici potest; et ad practicam cognitionem pertinet. Secundum autem quod principium cognoscitivum est, proprie dicitur *ratio*; et potest etiam ad scientiam speculativam pertinere. Secundum ergo quod exemplar est, secundum hoc se habet ad omnia quae a Deo fiunt secundum aliquod tempus. Secundum vero quod principium cognoscitivum est, se habet ad omnia quae cognoscuntur a Deo, etiam si nullo tempore fiant; et ad omnia quae a Deo cognoscuntur secundum propriam rationem, et secundum quod cognoscuntur ab ipso per modum speculationis."

tate he had described exemplars as belonging not only to actually practical knowledge, but to virtually practical knowledge as well. Hence, there could be exemplars of things that could be made but never are. Does Thomas reach the same conclusion in the *Summa?* To answer this question, we need to consider an article in the *Prima Pars* that appears prior to his consideration of the ideas.

Q. 14 concerns God's knowledge, and in a. 16 of that question Thomas considers whether God has speculative knowledge. As he had done in the *De veritate,* Thomas here presents a division of the different modes of knowing. He observes that some knowledge is only speculative, other knowledge only practical, while some is partly speculative and partly practical.

Regarding the first type of knowledge, it can be speculative in one of three ways. First, it may be speculative on the part of the *things* that are known, namely, things that are not operable by the knower. Regarding a human artisan, for example, knowledge of natural or divine things is speculative in this way because he simply cannot make such things. Second, knowledge may be speculative as regards the *manner* of knowing. So, for example, a house that a builder is otherwise capable of making can be considered by that builder apart from its operability if he focuses his attention simply on those elements that belong to a house in general. Third, knowledge may be speculative as regards the *end.* The end of the practical intellect differs from that of the speculative inasmuch as the practical intellect is ordered to the end of operation whereas the speculative intellect is ordered to the end of considering truth. Thus, if a builder were simply to consider *how* a house can be made without actually making it, such knowledge would be speculative as regards its end, even though it concerns an operable thing. From these observations, Thomas draws the following conclusions: (1) knowledge that is speculative by reason of the thing that is known is only speculative; (2) knowledge that is speculative according to either its mode or its end is partly speculative and partly practical; and (3) knowledge that is ordained to the end of operation is simply practical.[37]

To which of these three modes of knowledge would an exemplar belong? Clearly it does not belong to the first. But what of the second? Such knowledge would seem to correspond to what Thomas describes in the *De veritate* as being virtually practical: knowledge that is practical because it is operable, yet speculative because it is not directed toward the end of production. As will be recalled, in the *De veritate* he concludes that an exemplar *can* belong to such knowledge and, hence, that an exemplar can be of something that is never made. In the *Summa theologiae,* however, he now restricts the meaning of the term. This fact becomes clear if we consider what Thomas has to say about those ideas that are *divine* exemplars.

In a. 3 of q. 15, after describing an exemplar as belonging to practical knowledge, Thomas explains that "inasmuch as [an idea] is an 'exemplar', it is related to everything that is made by God *at any point in time.* But inasmuch as it is a 'notion' *(ratio),* it is related to all things that are known by God, even though they are *not* made at any point in time."[38] Unlike his treatment in the *De veritate,* where he had extended the meaning of "exemplar" to include ideas of things that can be made but never are, Thomas now clearly restricts the term to refer only to ideas of things that are in fact made. This more restricted use of the term "exemplar" corresponds with his interpretation of Dionysius in the commentary on *De divinis nominibus.* Thus, when an objection in the *Summa* cites the Areopagite for support of the position that God has no ideas of things that have not existed, do not exist now, and never will exist, Thomas replies that this reading is true only if the term "ideas" signifies exemplars, not inasmuch as it signifies notions.[39]

This refinement of the term "exemplar" occurs within a discussion of the divine ideas, but there is no reason to doubt that

---

37. *ST* I, q. 14, a. 16 (Leonine ed., vol. 4.196–97).

38. *ST* I, q. 15, a. 3 (Leonine ed., vol. 4.204). Emphasis added. For the Latin, see n. 36 above.

39. *ST* I, q. 15, a. 3, obj. and ad 2 (Leonine ed., vol. 4.204).

Thomas intends to use this restricted sense for exemplars in general, human or divine. We have seen him present a twofold role for ideas—either as productive principles or as cognitive ones. Regarding ideas of things that could be made but never are, he treats them as partly practical because they concern operable things. Nonetheless, such ideas are not productive, and so Thomas does not consider them to be exemplars since he now treats exemplars as belonging to purely practical knowledge. Or, to put it in the terminology of the *De veritate*, he now considers exemplars to belong to *actually* practical knowledge because their end concerns the actual production of a work (see figure 1-3 above, p. 11).

Thomas presents another consideration of exemplarism in the *Prima Pars* in q. 44, a. 3. There, in an effort to prove that God is the first exemplar cause of all things, he examines the character of exemplar causality. He observes that an exemplar is necessary in the production of a thing so that the effect can receive a determinate form. Thus, an artisan produces a determinate form in matter according to the exemplar that he considers. This exemplar can be one that is either external to him or one that is conceived within his mind.

Having made these observations about exemplarism in general, Thomas then explains that there must similarly be "notions" *(rationes)* of all things in the divine wisdom, "which we have previously called *ideas,* that is, exemplar forms existing in the mind of God." These ideas are multiplied according to their relations to things, but according to reality they are nothing other than the divine essence inasmuch as its likeness can be shared in different ways by different things. Furthermore, in created things, some can be called the exemplars of others because of their likeness to those other things, whether that likeness is according to the same species or according to the analogy of some imitation.[40]

40. *ST* I, q. 44, a. 3 (Leonine ed., vol. 4.460): "Oportet dicere quod in divina sapientia sunt rationes omnium rerum: quas supra diximus *ideas,* id est formas exemplares in

Thomas's discussion of exemplars in this passage reaffirms the meaning that he assigns to the term "exemplar" in q. 15. Although he makes no reference to practical knowledge here in q. 44, the entire article is addressing the causal relation that the divine exemplars have toward creation: not toward things that *could* be created, but toward things that *are*. Thus, he again presents exemplars as ideas that are actually productive.

What should we make, however, of his observation that an exemplar can exist outside of the artisan? As we shall see in coming chapters, Thomas is clearly not suggesting that God himself looks toward exemplars that are external to him.[41] But what are the implications for exemplarism in general? Does his observation suggest that an exemplar is not properly an idea? No. Rather, it reveals the analogous ways in which exemplarism can occur. As Thomas notes, an effect receives a determinate form from an exemplar; moreover, it receives that form because an agent first *considers* its exemplar. This element of consideration, then, indicates that even when an artisan looks to an external object as a model for his work, the exemplarism of that object is dependent upon the causality of the artisan's idea. For this reason, his idea is an exemplar primarily and properly speaking, whereas the external object is an exemplar only secondarily.

Quodlibet 4 (1271)

The latest and last text worth briefly considering occurs in *Quodlibet* 4 (1271).[42] In a. 1 of the first question, Thomas considers whether there is a plurality of ideas in God. He begins by observ-

---

mente divina existentes." In chap. 2, we will consider his argument from this article for the existence of divine exemplars.

41. As in prior passages, Thomas is careful to observe the limits of the analogy between human art and divine exemplarism. The human artisan might look toward objects that are outside of himself, but God does not since the divine ideas "non sunt realiter aliud a divina essentia." (*ST* I, q. 44, a. 3 [Leonine ed., vol. 4.460]).

42. The dating of this text is according to the Leonine edition (vol. 25.1, preface, 1).

ing that an idea is also called an exemplar form, and at the conclusion of his response he provides a definition of the term "idea." He explains that "The name 'idea' signifies this, namely, that it is a certain form understood by an agent in the likeness of which he intends to produce an external work, just as a builder preconceives a house's form in his mind, which is, as it were, the idea of a house coming to be in matter."[43]

This definition is very similar to the one that Thomas provides in the earlier *De veritate*. As in that work, an essential element of the definition here is the characteristic of the agent's intent. Still, this later text suggests that, properly speaking, exemplar ideas belong to actually practical knowledge and not to virtually practical knowledge. In this respect, the article appears to be more consistent with the later *Summa theologiae* rather than the earlier *De veritate*.[44]

Conclusions

In the texts we have considered, we find the general characteristic of an exemplar to be that it is something in the likeness of which another thing is made. What these texts also reveal is that exemplarism is an analogous notion. In one sense, it occurs when a natural agent causes an effect that shares the same species as itself, as when man generates man.[45] The substantial form of such an agent

43. *Quod.* 4, q. 1, a. 1 (Leonine ed., vol. 25.2.319:30–60): "Hoc enim significat nomen ideae, ut sit scilicet quaedam forma intellecta ab agente, ad cuius similitudinem exterius opus producere intendit; sicut aedificator in mente sua preconcipit formam domus, quae est quasi idea domus in materia fiendae."

44. If we consider that in this article, Thomas is speaking about the relation of the divine essence to things that are actually created, it is more likely that he is describing an exemplar form as a *type* of idea. In short, he is not considering the ideas here as principles of knowledge but rather as *productive* principles. See Wippel, *Divine Ideas*, 37n.75.

45. *ST* I, q. 44, a. 3 (Leonine ed., vol. 4.460). Thomas does not himself employ the term "natural exemplar," although he does describe such a form as exercising a type of exemplarism. Moreover, he also notes that this sort of (natural) exemplarism can occur when the effect shares an analogous likeness to the agent's nature. As we will see in

is what Thomas refers to in the *De veritate* as the "form by which" *(forma a qua)* a thing is made, and this form could be described as a sort of "natural exemplar" because the offspring is made in its likeness according to nature, not art. As we have seen, however, this sort of form is an exemplar only in an improper, extended sense, precisely because the natural agent does not itself determine its intended end, but rather nature does so.

In another sense, exemplarism occurs in art when an artisan employs a model for his work. Thus, the mother of painter James McNeill Whistler was the exemplar for the portrait commonly known as *Whistler's Mother.* Thomas refers to this sort of exemplar as an "external exemplar" since it exists externally both to the agent's mind and to his nature.[46] Since this sort of exemplarism does involve the agent himself determining the end, the external model to which he looks deserves the name "exemplar" more truly than does a natural agent's form. Nevertheless, this model is still not an exemplar according to the primary sense of the term because it is dependent for its exemplarism on the causality of a prior exemplar, namely, the artisan's idea. Because an idea is a form within the mind of an agent, we could call it an "intellectual exemplar," and Thomas considers it to be an exemplar properly and in the primary sense of the term—whether we are talking about human ideas or divine (see figure 1-4).[47]

As regards ideas, however, we find throughout these texts that Thomas presents them as having a twofold function: as cognitive and as productive principles. In this respect, the various texts are

---

the coming chapters, in addition to the exemplarism of the divine ideas, Thomas identifies an exemplarism of the divine nature—a sort of "natural exemplarism" by which created things share an analogous likeness to God's nature.

46. *De ver.,* q. 3, a. 1 (Leonine ed., vol. 22.1.100:209–23); *ST* I, q. 44, a. 3 (Leonine ed., vol. 4.460).

47. For a detailed consideration of the various types of exemplars in Aquinas and why the proper sense of the term applies to ideas, see Timotheus Sparks, *De divisione causae exemplaris apud S. Thomam* (River Forest, Ill.: Dominican House of Studies, 1936), esp. chap. 5. I have borrowed the terms "natural exemplar" and "intellectual exemplar" from Sparks, although my divisions of exemplarism do not follow his.

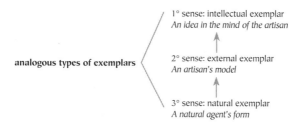

1° sense: intellectual exemplar
An idea in the mind of the artisan

↑

2° sense: external exemplar
An artisan's model

↑

3° sense: natural exemplar
A natural agent's form

analogous types of exemplars

FIGURE 1-4. Analogous Types of Exemplars

as a whole consistent. Where there is variation is in the breadth of his definition of the terms. Over the course of his writings, Thomas tends to employ the term "exemplar" in a stricter sense, applying it only to those ideas that are actually productive. This tendency first appears in his commentary on Dionysius's *De divinis nominibus* and is continued in the *Summa theologiae,* where the influence of the Areopagite is apparent.

Is this development in terminology simply a matter of semantics? Inasmuch as the substance of Thomas's theory of ideas remains the same, the answer would seem to be yes. Whether he calls them "ideas," "notions," or "exemplars," in each work he concludes that forms exist both as cognitive and as productive principles within the mind of intelligent agents. Nevertheless, this development poses a difficulty: when discussing Thomas's doctrine of exemplarism, should we take the term "exemplar" in the broad sense, as in his earlier writings? Or should we take it in the strict sense, as in his later ones?

Since he does move toward a stricter application of the term in his later works, it seems reasonable for us to address his doctrine of exemplarism in light of this refined, mature understanding of the term "exemplar." For this reason, in the pages that follow, I will employ this term following Thomas's strict sense of the word. The reader should presume, therefore, that my use of "exemplar," unless otherwise noted, will refer to actually practical ideas, that is, to ideas in the likeness of which effects are actually made.[48]

Another difficulty posed by this development becomes apparent when we attempt to discern what definition should be given for the term "exemplar." In the *Summa theologiae,* where Thomas most explicitly presents exemplar ideas as belonging only to actually practical knowledge, he does not provide a strict definition, but instead merely offers a general description of an exemplar as "a principle of the making of things" *(principium factionis rerum).*[49] His most complete definition appears in the earlier *De veritate.* As we have seen, there he defines an idea as "a form that something imitates because of the intention of an agent who predetermines the end for himself."[50]

Keeping in mind that in this work Thomas originally employed the terms "idea" and "exemplar" synonymously and also in a broad sense to include the two types of practical knowledge, we ourselves can nevertheless adopt this definition to refer exclusively to exemplars in the later strict sense of the term. In fact, the very phrasing of the *De veritate* definition presents exemplars as belonging to actually practical knowledge. Hence, it is to this definition (or variations thereof) that scholars commonly turn when discussing Thomas's doctrine of exemplarism, because it presents those characteristics that are essential to exemplar ideas: characteristics that we see him identify time and again in other texts.[51] For this reason,

48. I will take care when discussing exemplars in Thomas's earlier works to avoid a misreading of the text. When treating a passage that employs the term "exemplar" in the broad sense, I will make explicit to the reader where it is important to acknowledge that the text is referring to virtually practical ideas as well as to actually practical ones.

49. *ST* I, q. 15, a. 3 (Leonine ed., vol. 4.204).

50. *De ver.,* q. 3, a. 1 (Leonine ed., vol. 22.1.100:220–23): "Haec ergo videtur esse ratio ideae, quod idea sit forma quam aliquid imitatur ex intentione agentis qui praedeterminat sibi finem."

51. Giulio Girardi sees the *De veritate* definition as the most explicit one offered of the intellective exemplar. Giulio Girardi, S.D.B., *Metafisica della causa esemplare in san Tommaso d'Aquino* (Turin: Scuola Grafica Salesiana, 1954), 41. Perret offers a variation of this definition, explaining that "*La cause exemplaire d'une chose, c'est la forme extrin-*

it is worth analyzing the *De veritate* definition in more detail to get a better understanding of how ideas act as exemplar causes.

THE ESSENTIAL CHARACTERISTICS OF AN EXEMPLAR IDEA

In the *De veritate* definition, the most general characteristic of an exemplar idea that Thomas presents is that it is a *form*. This trait is one that he consistently attributes to exemplars in each of the texts that we have considered. Still, the question arises: In what way is an exemplar a form? Inasmuch as it acts as a principle of knowledge, it informs the mind of the knower. But it is not in this respect that the definition calls an exemplar a form. Rather, it is as a principle of production. In this respect, the exemplar is the form of *the thing that is made.* Thus, as an operative form it is that "in regard to which" *(ad quam)* a thing is formed.[52]

Thomas does not intend, however, to identify this form with the substantial form that is part of the very nature of a composite thing. In the *Summa theologiae,* he describes exemplar ideas as the forms of things existing *apart from* the things themselves; thus, he implies a distinction between the substantial form that is intrinsic to a thing and the form that is the thing's exemplar.[53] Indeed, in several places throughout his writings, Thomas makes this distinction between inherent *(inhaerens),* or intrinsic *(intrinseca)* form and exemplar form.[54] As we have seen, in the *De veritate* he distinguish-

---

sèque de cette chose, telle qu'elle pré-existe éminemment dans l'intelligence pratique de l'agent informateur" (Perret, "Exemplarité," 465, emphasis in original). John Farthing follows Perret's definition, adding that "By 'exemplarism' I will mean the thesis that phenomenal realities are patterned after ideas, whether subsistent or in a transcendent intellect, which serve as their exemplars in this sense" (Farthing, "Divine Exemplarity," 187).

52. *In I Sent.,* d. 36, q. 2, a. 1 (Mandonnet ed., vol. 1.839–40), and *De ver.,* q. 3, a. 1 (Leonine ed., vol. 22.1.99:177–82).

53. *ST* I, q. 15, a. 1 (Leonine ed., vol. 4.199).

54. See, e.g., *In III Sent.,* d. 27, q. 2, a. 4, *quaestiuncula* 3, obj. 1 and solutio 3, ad 1 (Moos ed., vol. 3.884.153 and 889–90.176–77); *De ver.,* q. 14, a. 5, obj. 4 (Leonine ed., vol. 22.2.451:27–35); *ST* I, q. 5, a. 2, ad 2 (Leonine ed., vol. 4.58).

es the substantial form *(forma secundum quam)* from the exemplar form *(forma ad quam)* insofar as the former is not separate from the thing whereas the latter is.[55]

If an exemplar *is* separate from the thing that it forms, however, in what way can it be said to be the form of that thing? Thomas explains that whereas an intrinsic form forms a thing by way of inherence, an exemplar form does so by way of imitation *(per modum imitationis)*.[56] Here we find the second element of his definition. As we have already had occasion to note, his most common observation regarding the character of an exemplar is that it is "that in imitation of which something is made." An exemplar thus acts as the form of a thing because the thing is assimilated to it, and the thing is assimilated to it by means of its own intrinsic form. Indeed, likeness occurs because of a communication in form. Hence, a thing receives a determinate form *from* its exemplar.[57]

Moreover, when an idea acts as an exemplar, the thing that it forms is in a certain respect also assimilated to the agent who possesses the idea. Thomas explains that this assimilation must be in the line of will and understanding since it is an assimilation to a being who wills and understands.[58] Thus, we find the third element in his definition of the term "exemplar," namely, that this assimilation occurs because of an agent's *intention*. If assimilation does not occur according to an agent's intention, then it occurs merely by chance. Hence, the intentionality of an agent is an essential characteristic of exemplar causality. And what the agent intends is that the work of art be like the form that he conceives in his mind.[59] This implies that the agent both *knows* and *wills* what he intends to produce.

55. *De ver.,* q. 3, a. 1 (Leonine ed., vol. 22.1.99:170–77).

56. *De ver.,* q. 3, a. 3 (Leonine ed., vol. 22.1.108:155–160).

57. *ST* I, q. 4, a. 3 (Leonine ed., vol. 4.53–4); q. 44, a. 3 (Leonine ed., vol. 4.460). Cf. *Quod.* 8, q. 1, a. 2 (Leonine ed., vol. 25.1.54:42–59).

58. *In XII Meta.,* lect. 7, n. 2535 (Marietti ed., 715).

59. *De ver.,* q. 3, a. 1 (Leonine ed., vol. 22.1.99:183–96); *Quod.* 8, q. 1, a. 2 (Leonine ed., vol. 25.1.54:42–59); *ST* I, q. 15, a. 1. (Leonine ed., vol. 4.199).

As regards the agent's knowledge, we have seen that his ideas can be either speculative or practical.[60] In the commentary on Aristotle's *Metaphysics,* Thomas examines these two types of knowledge in terms of measure and the measured. Measure, he explains, is properly applied in the category of quantity. It can, however, be transferred in a figurative way to knowledge. Thus, in a sense, our knowledge is a measure of what we know because it is by means of our knowledge that we know things. Still, it is more correct to say that our knowledge is measured *by* the things that we know since we simply experience reality and do not determine it. But when our knowledge is the cause of the thing known, then it does act as the measure of that thing. Such is the knowledge of art, which measures its product, "for anything that is made by art is complete insofar as it attains a likeness to the art."[61]

Thomas explains, furthermore, that truth consists in the adequation of intellect and thing. Consequently, when things are the measure of the intellect, truth consists in the adequation of the intellect to the thing. In the case of art, however, where intellect is the measure, then truth consists in the adequation of the *thing* to the intellect. In short, since an exemplar is a productive idea that is known by an agent, it is the measure of the form of the work of art and, hence, is also the measure of its very truth.[62]

The intentionality of exemplarism, however, involves more than

60. On this point, of course, the texts vary regarding the precise terms to be applied, but they are nonetheless consistent in the position that some intellectual forms, whatever we may call them, belong to each sort of knowledge.

61. *In X Meta.,* lect. 2, n. 1959 (Marietti ed., 562–63): "Si qua vero scientia est quae est causa rei scitae, oportebit quod sit eius mensura. Ut scientia artificis est mensura artificiatorum; quia unumquodque artificiatum secundum hoc perfectum est, quod attingit ad similitudinem artis." As we will see in the coming chapters, unlike man's knowledge, God's knowledge is not measured in any way by the things that he knows.

62. *ST* I, q. 21, a. 2 (Leonine ed., vol. 4.259–60); *De ver.,* q. 1, a. 2 (Leonine ed., vol. 22.1.9:49–120). Because a human artisan works with a presupposed matter that he does not make, the artifact that he produces is only assimilated to his idea due to its form. The *divine* exemplars, however, correspond not only to the forms of created things but to their matter as well (*De ver.,* q. 8, a. 11 [Leonine ed., vol. 22.2.256:204–17]). See the section "The Divine Ideas and the Production of Form" in chap. 5.

the mere possession of an idea on the part of the agent. A form that is in the intellect is not productive of anything except through the mediation of the will. The reason is that an intelligible form in and of itself does not denote a principle of action but rather a principle of knowledge. Only when an inclination toward producing an effect is added to such a form can it become productive. And this inclination is through the will.[63]

For the artisan's intention to come to fruition, then, he must both know and will that the thing come to be. It is through the mediation of his will (as well as through his motive powers and tools) that an external work is assimilated to the exemplar. Because this assimilation is in the line of will and understanding, the conformity of a work of art to the artisan differs from the conformity of a natural effect to a natural cause. The effect of a voluntary agent is said to conform to its cause, "not because it [the effect] is of the same nature as the art that is in the mind of the artisan, but because the form of the art is fulfilled in the work."[64]

Thus, we see that intentionality is a central characteristic of exemplarism. Furthermore, we find in the fourth and final element of the *De veritate* definition that this intentionality is that of an agent who predetermines the end for himself. Unlike the prior elements that we have considered, this one is unique to the *De veritate.* There is mention of the end in other texts but not in the same respect. Since an exemplar idea is a productive idea, it is presignative *(praesignativa),* or predeterminative *(praedeterminativae)* of the

---

63. *De pot.,* q. 6, a. 3, ad 3 *(Quaestiones Disputatae,* Marietti ed. [Turin and Rome: 1949], vol. 2.137); *In VI Meta.,* lect. 1, n. 1153 (Marietti ed., 353–54); *ST* I, q. 14, a. 8 (Leonine ed., vol. 4.179).

64. *De ver.,* q. 23, a. 7 (Leonine ed., vol. 22.3.670:165–78): "Conformitas autem effectus ad causam aliter invenitur in naturalibus et in voluntariis causis.In naturalibus enim causis attenditur conformitas secundum similitudinem naturae, sicut quod homo generat hominem et ignis ignem; sed in voluntariis dicitur effectus causae conformari ex hoc quod in effectu impletur sua causa, sicut artificiatum assimilatur suae causae non quia sit eiusdem naturae cum arte quae est in mente artificis, sed quia forma artis in artificiato impletur; et similiter etiam conformatur voluntati effectus eius, quando hoc fit quod voluntas disposuit."

thing that is made in its likeness. In this sense, the artisan's idea manifests an end, an end that the will can then intend. Thus, as Thomas observes, "intention is guided and aroused and strengthened from the consideration of some exemplar in which the end precedes in reality."[65]

Nevertheless, when he speaks of the agent "predetermining the end for himself," Thomas is not referring only to the end that the exemplar presents to the will. To get a sense of the full meaning of this element of the definition, we must consider that an end can be understood in two respects. As he explains in the *De principiis naturae*, the end may refer to the end of production *(generatio)* or to the end of the thing that is produced. To illustrate this point, he gives the example of a knife. An artisan intends to make a knife, and he actually does so by giving it its form. That form is consequently an end: the end of the production. But while it is the end of the production, it is not the end of the knife itself; rather, the end of the knife itself is the operation of cutting.[66] If we consider the exemplar idea that is in the mind of the artisan, it is true that it too manifests an end since it arouses the artisan's intention. In this respect, it acts in a sense as the end of production—not in reality, since it is not the form of the thing that is produced, but in *intention* since it is the formal likeness of that thing.

When the *De veritate* definition speaks of the agent predetermining the end for himself, the end to which it refers is both the end of production and the *end of the very product*. As we have seen, Thomas gives the example of the archer who sets an arrow in flight. This example clearly illustrates an occasion where an agent predetermines the end of his own operation. But it also illustrates an occasion where an agent predetermines the end of a product's opera-

65. *In IV Sent.*, d. 8, q. 2, a. 1, *solutio* 4, ad 1 (Moos ed. [Paris: Lethielleux, 1947], vol. 4.334.169–70); *In I Sent.*, d. 38, q. 1, a. 1 (Mandonnet ed., vol 1.899); *In III Sent.*, d. 21, q. 2, a. 2, ad 1 (Moos ed., vol. 3.644–45.73): "Intentio autem et dirigitur et excitatur et roboratur ex inspectione alicuius exemplaris, in quo finis secundum rem praecedat."
66. *De prin. nat.*, n. 4 (Leonine ed., vol. 43.45:104–8).

tion: the arrow tends toward its end only because this goal has been determined for it.[67]

Of course, even though the archer determines the end of the arrow by putting it in flight, he does not himself produce the arrow. So, let us consider another object, such as a watch. A watchmaker who produces his work does so according to a form within his mind by which he designs an instrument that will keep time. In making the watch, he determines the end of his own operation, but in giving the watch the form that he had in mind, he determines the watch's end as well. The watch acts for the end of telling time only because the watchmaker has himself predetermined that it act for this end. So, too, with the example of the knife in the *De principiis naturae:* it performs its function of cutting in accordance with the end that its maker has predetermined for it. So it is with everything that is made in the likeness of an exemplar.

Thomas explains that "if something is made in imitation of another through an agent who does *not* determine the end for himself, the imitated form as a result will not have the character *(ratio)* of an exemplar." He gives as an example the generation of a man, explaining that we would not say that the form of the man who generates is, properly speaking, the exemplar of his offspring because we only say this when the agent, acting for the sake of an end, determines that end for himself.[68] That Thomas uses man as an example is not insignificant. Unlike the other animals, man *can* predetermine the end in generating man in the sense that he can determine his own operation, freely choosing whether and when he will procreate. What man *cannot* predetermine, however, is the end of his offspring: that end is predetermined according to na-

---

67. *De ver.,* q. 3, a. 1 (Leonine ed., vol. 22.1.99–100:196–209).

68. *De ver.,* q. 3, a. 1 (Leonine ed., vol. 22.1.100:209–17): "Si ergo aliquid fiat ad imitationem alterius per agens quod non determinat sibi finem, non ex hoc forma imitata habebit rationem exemplaris vel ideae." Emphasis added in translation. As we have seen, the terms "idea" and "exemplar" are used here synonymously, unlike in the later *Summa theologiae*'s consideration of the divine ideas.

ture.[69] This example, therefore, reinforces the position that unlike a natural form, an exemplar not only predetermines the end of the agent's operation, but it predetermines the end of the effect as well. Thus, Thomas notes that "the operation of a nature that is for a determined end presupposes an intellect that has predetermined the end of that nature and ordered it to that end."[70]

As Giulio Girardi observes, this characteristic of the agent's predetermining the end for himself constitutes the specific difference of the definition that we have considered, distinguishing the intellectual exemplar from the more general sense of an exemplar as "that in imitation of which something is made."[71] This final element of the definition, however, only appears in the *De veritate*. Other texts address the end of the agent's operation, but none makes mention of the agent's predetermining the end of his work. Should we then conclude that Thomas abandons this characteristic as belonging to the *ratio*, or character, of an exemplar? No. Even though he does not explicitly mention it in his other considerations, this characteristic is nonetheless implicitly present.

An agent's ability to predetermine the end for himself is dependent upon his intellectually knowing that end. The most general trait of an exemplar identified in each and every passage that we have considered is that it is a form—a form that resides in the intellect. Hence, the agent who is possessed of an exemplar idea is possessed of knowledge: he not only produces the thing by means of that exemplar, but he does so knowingly. It is in fact due to his faculties of will and reason that an intellectual agent is said to have dominion over his actions. By contrast, Thomas notes, "those things that lack reason tend to the end through a natural inclination, as being moved by another and not by themselves since they

---

69. And, as we shall see in future chapters, according to God's intention.

70. *De ver.,* q. 3, a. 1 (Leonine ed., vol. 22.1.100:204–9): "operatio naturae quae est ad determinatum finem praesupponit intellectum praestituentem finem naturae et ordinantem ad finem illum naturam."

71. Girardi, *Metafisica della causa esemplare,* 41.

do not know the nature *(ratio)* of an end. Consequently, they cannot ordain anything to an end but are only ordered to an end by another."[72]

Thus, even though the characteristic of the agent's predetermining the end for himself may not be explicitly enunciated in Thomas's other considerations of exemplarism, it is nonetheless implicit: because the agent is possessed of will and reason, and because he produces an external work according to a practical idea, he is able to determine the end of that work. Why, then, does Thomas only draw out this characteristic of exemplarism in the *De veritate?* One possible explanation rests simply in the very scope of his treatment of the divine ideas in that work. The extent of his consideration of any topic in the *Quaestiones disputatae* exceeds that of his consideration in a work like the *Summa theologiae.* Thus, in the *De veritate,* Thomas dedicates eight articles to examining the divine ideas, as opposed to a brief three in the *Summa.* It is not surprising, then, that he should investigate the topic in more detail there than he does elsewhere.

From these considerations regarding the character of exemplars, we get a sense not only of Thomas's doctrine of ideas but also of how it differs from Plato's.[73] Ideas (whether human or divine) are

---

72. *ST* I-II, q. 1, a. 2 (Leonine ed., vol. 6.9): "Illa ergo quae rationem habent, seipsa movent ad finem: quia habent dominium suorum actuum per liberum arbitrium, quod est *facultas voluntatis et rationis.* Illa vero quae ratione carent, tendunt in finem per naturalem inclinationem, quasi ab alio mota, non autem a seipsis: cum non cognoscant rationem finis, et ideo nihil in finem ordinare possunt, sed solum in finem ab alio ordinantur." Emphasis added in translation.

73. At least, of how it differs from Thomas's understanding of Platonism. In the thirteenth century, only three of Plato's works were available to the Latin West: the *Meno, Phaedo,* and *Timaeus* in the partial translation of Calcidius (Raymond Klibansky, *The Continuity of the Platonic Tradition During the Middle Ages* [London: The Warburg Institute, 1939; reprint with new prefaces and supplement, Kraus International Publications, 1982], 27–28). Although Thomas makes reference to each of these three works in his own writings, it is almost certain that he never read either the *Meno* or the *Phaedo,* and it is unclear whether he even read the *Timaeus* (Robert J. Henle, S.J., *Saint Thomas and Platonism* [The Hague: Martinus Nijhoff, 1956], xxi n. 41).

Aquinas was indebted to a number of authors for his understanding of Plato's exemplarism, including Augustine, Macrobius, William of Auvergne, and Proclus. But

not separate entities but are principles that exist within a mind.[74] It is a mind, furthermore, that belongs to an agent. Ideas are not productive principles in and of themselves, as Plato had argued, but are so rather through the agent's will, which brings his intended goal to fruition.[75] Only through this agency can exemplars act as causes. But that they *do* act as causes raises the next question that we need to consider, namely, what is their manner of causality?

EXEMPLARISM AND THE FOUR CAUSES

From the texts examined above, it is clear that Thomas considers an exemplar to be a form—a fact suggesting that it exercises formal causality. Indeed, in some places he distinguishes the ex-

---

as R. J. Henle illustrates, perhaps the most important single source for Thomas is Aristotle's *Metaphysics* (Henle, *Thomas and Platonism*, 422). His reliance upon this source was both beneficial and detrimental to his understanding of Platonism: beneficial because it provided an account of Plato's exemplarism from one of Plato's own students, yet detrimental because this account is limited to what Plato said on the matter in the *Phaedo* (ibid., 363).

74. For Plato's theory of Ideas, see *Phaedo,* 100a–101d; *Cratylus,* 439c–440b; *Phaedrus,* 246a–250a; *Symposium,* 210a–212a; and *Republic,* 5.478a–e, 6, 7.508c–517c. Following Aristotle, Thomas understands Plato's Ideas to be subsistent universals. See, e.g., *In I Meta.,* lect. 10, nn. 151-70 (Marietti ed., 45-49); lect. 14 n. 209 (ibid., 74); *In VII Meta.,* lect. 13, n. 1570 (ibid., 458); *De ver.,* q. 21, a. 4 (Leonine ed., vol. 22.3.601–2:150–79); *ST* I, q. 85, a. 3, ad 1 and ad 4 (Leonine ed., vol. 5.336–37); q. 76, a. 3, ad 4 (ibid., vol. 5.221); *In II De an.,* c. 12, (Leonine ed., vol. 45-1.116:111–13).

Joseph Owens argues that, contrary to Thomas's interpretation, the Ideas of Plato's dialogues do not correspond with the Thomistic notion of the universal, but rather with the Thomistic notion of common nature, despite some profound differences between the two theories (Owens, "Thomistic Common Nature and Platonic Idea," *Mediaeval Studies* 21 [1959]: esp. 218–21).

75. Thomas understands Plato to have neglected the role of efficiency when discussing exemplarism. Looking to Aristotle, he interprets Platonism as positing the Ideas as formal causes of both being and becoming (*In I Meta.,* lect. 15, n. 237 [Marietti ed., 82]). Although Thomas at times refers to the role of the Demiurge in Plato's philosophy, he never does so when discussing Plato's doctrine of exemplarism (See, e.g., *ST* I, q. 66, a. 2 [Leonine ed., vol. 5.156]). Rather, he consistently interprets the Platonic exemplars as being self-sufficient causes whose effects are the result of a formal participation rather than of efficient causality (*In VII Phys.,* c. 3, lect. 6 [Leonine ed., vol. 2.344.8]; *In VII Meta.,* lect. 6, n. 1381 [Marietti ed., 409–10]). For Plato's discussion of the Demiurge, see *Timaeus,* 28a ff.

emplar cause from the efficient and final cause by explicitly referring to it as an "exemplar form" *(forma exemplaris)*. In other places,
however, he refers to the "efficient exemplar cause" *(causa efficiens
exemplaris)* or the "effective exemplar principle" *(principium effectivum exemplare)*, suggesting that an exemplar is a type of efficient
cause.[76] Moreover, the very reference to the agent's intention in the
De veritate definition seems to indicate that an exemplar's causality
possesses characteristics of efficiency.

We have seen in this definition, furthermore, that finality is another element essential to the character of an exemplar since an exemplar exerts an attracting influence upon the will of the agent.
For this reason, Thomas notes that an exemplar has in a certain
sense the characteristic *(ratio)* of an end.[77] That the character of an
exemplar should manifest the aspects of these three causes is not
surprising when we consider Thomas's observation that the formal, efficient, and final cause can coincide in one thing.[78]

Given this unique causal status of the exemplar, it might be
tempting to conclude that Thomas considers exemplarism to be a
fifth type of cause. Nevertheless, his writings do not lead to such a
conclusion. He always remains true to Aristotle's fourfold division
of the causes. What then are we to conclude? As one writer aptly
puts it, "Unless we wish to claim that the exemplar forms a fifth

76. For references to the *forma exemplaris*, see In I Sent., d. 18, q. 1, a. 5 (Mandonnet
ed., vol. 1.445); *De ver.*, q. 3, a. 1 (Leonine ed., vol. 22.1.99:179); *Quod. 4*, a. 1 (Leonine ed.,
vol. 25.2.319:33); *ST* I, q. 44, a. 3 (Leonine ed., vol. 4.460); *Quod. 8*, a. 2 (Leonine ed., vol.
25.1.54:24–25). For references to the expressions *causa efficiens exemplaris* and *principium
effectivum exemplare*, see In I Sent., d. 1, q. 4, a. 2, expositio (Mandonnet ed., vol 1.49); d. 8,
q. 1, a. 3, ad 2 (ibid., 200); d. 10, q. 1, a. 5, ad 4 (ibid., 272); d. 19, q. 5, a. 2 and ad 3 (ibid.,
492 and 493); d. 38, q. 1, a. 1 (ibid., 898). Interestingly, these expressions appear only in
the early commentary on the *Sentences*. I read this as evidence that if Thomas did at
one time view exemplarism as being, at least in part, a type of efficient causality, it is a
youthful view that he comes to abandon. Regarding the relationship between exemplar
causality and efficient causality, see immediately below.

77. *De ver.*, q. 3, a. 1 (Leonine ed., vol. 22.1.100:254–55): "Forma exemplaris vel idea
habet quodam modo rationem finis et ab ea accipit artifex formam qua agit si sit extra ipsum."

78. See, e.g., *De prin. nat.*, n. 4 (Leonine ed., vol. 43.44–5:95–103); *De ver.*, q. 3, a. 1,
sed contra 3 (Leonine ed., vol. 22.1.98:101–6). See Aristotle, *Physics* 2.7.198a24–27.

class of cause all on its own, we are forced, it would seem, to reduce it to one of the four causes."[79]

To which of the four types of causality, then, should exemplarism be reduced? We can immediately rule out material causality. Material causality is not suggested by the *De veritate* definition, nor does Thomas ever associate it with exemplarism. Furthermore, an effect's material cause is intrinsic to it, whereas its exemplar cause is extrinsic. We can again quickly conclude that exemplarism is not properly reduced to efficient causality either. As we have seen, in and of itself, an idea is not productive. Because it is in the intentional order, an idea does not have *esse reale* but only *esse intelligibile.* Hence, it is incapable of acting efficiently. It is only when conjoined to the will that an idea is disposed to act. Still, it might be objected that since the causality of an exemplar idea depends upon the action of an efficient cause, exemplarism is at least in part a type of efficient causality. To see why this view is problematic, however, it is helpful to consider what Thomas says about the relationship between efficient causality and final causality.

In the *De principiis naturae,* Thomas notes that the final cause is, in a sense, the cause of the efficient cause. To illustrate in what respect this is true, he gives the example of the doctor's concern with health: health does not cause the doctor to be a doctor, but it does cause him to engage in doctoring. Thus, "the end is the cause of efficient causality since it makes the efficient cause to be an efficient cause."[80] This passage is significant because it reveals that one cause can depend upon another for its causality without either cause losing its distinct identity. Final causality is the cause of efficient causality, but efficiency is not for that reason a type of fi-

79. David L. Greenstock, "Exemplar Causality and the Supernatural Order," *The Thomist* 16 (1953): 4–5.

80. *De prin. nat.,* c. 4 (Leonine ed., vol. 43.44:25–31): "Finis autem non est causa illius quod est efficiens, sed est causa ut efficiens sit efficiens; sanitas enim non facit medicum esse medicum—et dico sanitatem quae fit operante medico—, sed facit ut medicus sit efficiens. Unde finis est causa causalitatis efficientis, quia facit efficiens esse efficiens."

nal causality. Similarly, we can conclude that, *mutatis mutandi,* efficient causality is the cause of exemplar causality, but exemplarism is not for that reason a type of efficient causality.[81]

The efficient cause (i.e., the artisan) is the cause of exemplar causality through his will and operative power. By employing his idea to produce an effect, the artisan causes it to measure that effect. As we have seen, the artisan's idea measures the effect inasmuch as the effect conforms to his idea. But, as Thomas explains, "a work of art is assimilated to its cause . . . because the form of the art is fulfilled in the work of art."[82] In short, an exemplar measures its effect as the formal cause of that effect.

As Gaston Isaye has shown in his work *La Théorie de la mesure et l'existence d'un maximum selon saint Thomas,* for Aquinas measure has its foundation in similitude and is always of the formal order.[83] This is not to say that the effect conforms to the exemplar exactly; indeed, it is impossible for the effect to imitate the exemplar according to its mode of being *(esse)* since the form in the mind of the artisan has only an intentional existence. As Thomas notes, however, an effect need not imitate its exemplar in every respect; but this much is always the case: "The exemplified thing must conform to the exemplar according to the order *(ratio)* of form."[84]

81. While the exemplars found in the mind of the human artisan are not necessarily efficient causes, Thomas notes that in God the exemplar cause and the efficient cause coincide *(De ver.,* q. 7, a. 1, ad 13. [Leonine ed., vol. 22.1.200:265–67]). As we shall see in the coming chapters, this is because he identifies the divine exemplars with the divine essence. Nevertheless, even though he identifies these two modes of causality in God according to reality, Thomas holds that they can still be distinguished according to reason.

In contrast to the position that exemplar causality cannot be identified with efficient causality, both Godfrey of Fontaines and Duns Scotus hold that it can be so identified in the case of intelligent agents. On this point, see John F. Wippel, *The Metaphysical Thought of Godfrey of Fontaines* (Washington: The Catholic University of America Press, 1981), 138–40.

82. *De ver.,* q. 23, a. 7 (Leonine ed., vol. 22.3.670:163–76). See n. 64.

83. Gaston Isaye, S.J., *La Théorie de la mesure et l'existence d'un maximum selon saint Thomas,* Archives de Philosophie, vol. 16, bk. 1 (Paris: Beauchesne et Ses Fils, 1940), 20.

84. *ST* III, q. 24, a. 3, ad 3 (Leonine ed., vol. 11.274): "Non est necessarium quod exemplatum exemplari quantum ad omnia conformetur: sed sufficit quod aliqualiter

Still, as we have seen, Thomas describes an exemplar as an *extrinsic* form; hence, its causality as a form must also be extrinsic—unlike the causality of an accidental or substantial form. Theodore Kondoleon views such a reading of Aquinas's exemplarism as problematic. As he notes, when Thomas divides the four causes, he commonly identifies the formal and material causes as intrinsic to an effect and the final and efficient causes as extrinsic to it. To reduce exemplar causality to the genus of formal causality, therefore, appears to be incompatible with Aristotle's division of the four causes.[85]

To avoid this problem, Kondoleon maintains that exemplar causality should instead be reduced to the genus of final causality. As a preconceived form that exists within the intentional order, an exemplar idea represents the end of the agent's work. Consequently, Kondoleon sees a twofold causal function for the exemplar: one of attracting the agent in his act of production, the other of measur-

---

exemplatum imitetur suum exemplar." *ST* I, q. 18, a. 4, ad 2 (Leonine ed., vol. 4.230): "Exemplata oportet conformari exemplari secundum rationem formae, non autem secundum modum essendi. Nam alterius modi esse habet quandoque forma in exemplari et in exemplato: sicut forma domus in mente artificis habet esse immateriale et intelligibile, in domo autem quae est extra animam, habet esse materiale et sensibile. Unde et rationes rerum quae in seipsis non vivunt, in mente divina sunt vita, quia in mente divina habent esse divinum." Commenting on this passage, Greenstock notes that "This brings out even more clearly the close connection between the notions of formal cause and exemplar" (Greenstock, "Exemplar Causality," 16).

85. Kondoleon, *Exemplary Causality*, 146–54. Regarding this division of the causes, see, e.g., *De prin. nat.,* n. 3 (Leonine ed., vol. 43.42:42–52).

Addressing this division, Fernand Van Steenberghen explains that "The name extrinsic cause properly belongs to the efficient cause, since this cause exercises a *real influence* on another reality. The exemplary cause and final cause are termed causes only in a *wider* and *less proper* sense. Thus when an intelligent efficient cause exercises its influence to produce a determined effect, we call the object which serves as a model for the realization of that effect the 'exemplary cause,' and we call the goal which the intelligent agent wishes to realize by his causality, the 'final cause.' Consequently, the exemplary and final causes have no direct influence on the effect. Their influence on the mind of the efficient cause belongs to the intentional order." Emphasis added. Canon Fernand Van Steenberghen, *Ontology,* trans. Martin J. Flynn (New York: Joseph F. Wagner, Inc., 1952), 97–98. Van Steenberghen's position that exemplar causes do not exercise a real influence on their effects may be true of human exemplars regarding the being *(esse)* of their effects, but it is not true of the effects' coming-into-being *(fieri)* (this distinction will be examined in more detail in chap. 3). Moreover, as regards the divine ideas, creatures *are* dependent upon these exemplars for their very being.

ing that action inasmuch as the exemplar measures the form of the thing that is produced. But the primary role of the exemplar, he insists, is that of attracting the agent's action since this characteristic is prior. Hence, he concludes, exemplar causality is fundamentally the same as final causality: there may be justification for speaking of it as an extrinsic formal cause logically considered, but ontologically an exemplar is nothing other than a final cause.[86]

Although this reading of Aquinas's doctrine is intriguing, it is problematic. It is true that Thomas commonly divides the four causes in terms of intrinsicism versus extrinsicism and that when he does so he lists the formal cause as being intrinsic. Nevertheless, this division alone does not suggest that an exemplar's extrinsic character prevents it from being a formal cause. When Thomas divides the four causes in this way, he generally does so within the context of discussing natural generation, not artistic production. Granted that in nature there is no such thing as an extrinsic formal cause, that does not mean that intrinsicism is essential to the *ratio,* or character, of form. Indeed, contrary to Kondoleon's assumption, Thomas does not even consider the intrinsic-extrinsic division to be the primary division of the causes.

In his commentary on Aristotle's *Metaphysics,* Thomas observes that causes can be divided in two ways: either (1) by the kind *(species)* of causality; or (2) by the mode *(modus)* of causality. As he explains, the division of causes by *kind* is based upon different characteristics of their causality *(rationes causandi),* the way essential differences constitute species. But the division of causes by *mode* is in terms of the different relationships *(habitudines)* that causes have to their effects.[87]

Commenting on this passage, Francis Meehan observes that "Here we have definite indication that in the opinion of St. Thomas, the *first immediate division* of the genus, cause, is the fourfold division into material, formal, final, and efficient, and not, as some

86. Kondoleon, 158–60.
87. *In V Meta.,* lect. 3, n. 783 (Marietti ed., 259).

would maintain, the twofold division into intrinsic and extrinsic, and only through this, mediately, into material and formal on the one hand, and efficient and final on the other."[88] Only the former division, then, is based upon the *ratio causandi.* The division of the causes into intrinsic and extrinsic is based instead upon a *mode* of causality, that is, upon the way in which the four causes are related to their effects, not the way they are in themselves. Consequently, this division is not the primary division of the causes. Since the division of the causes by their mode is secondary, there can be both intrinsic *and* extrinsic formal causes. Hence, positing an extrinsic formal cause does not violate the Aristotelian division of causality.

This fact is confirmed by a discussion earlier within the commentary on the *Metaphysics* regarding the placement of the exemplar cause within the division of the causes. There, Thomas divides the causes in terms of the *ratio causandi,* examining each of the four causes in turn. Following Aristotle's text, he begins by observing that the material cause is "that from which something comes to be" *(ex quo fit aliquid).* But a thing can be said to come to be from privation and from a contrary as well. For this reason, Aristotle describes matter as an intrinsic principle, in order to distinguish it from these other sources of coming to be.[89] Thus, we find that intrinsicism is part of the very character of a material cause.

Thomas next notes that Aristotle describes another sense of cause which is the "species" *(species,* in Greek, εἶδος) or "pattern" *(exemplum)* of a thing; clarifying this, Thomas adds, "in other words, the exemplar." This cause, he explains, is the formal cause of a thing. Going beyond a literal reading of the text, he then notes that the formal cause can be related to a thing in one of two ways. A formal cause can be intrinsic to a thing, in which case it is the thing's species; but it can also be extrinsic to a thing and, despite this extrinsicism, still be a cause inasmuch as the thing is said to

88. Francis X. Meehan, *Efficient Causality in Aristotle and St. Thomas* (Washington: The Catholic University of America Press, 1940), 179n40.

89. *In V Meta.,* lect. 2, n. 763 (Marietti ed., 254).

be made in its likeness. "And in *this* way," Thomas explains, "an exemplar is called a thing's form."[90] Thus, intrinsicism is not an essential characteristic of formal causality, as it is with material causality. Indeed, neither is extrinsicism an essential characteristic of formal causality. This is because such characteristics do not concern the formal cause as a cause, but, rather, they concern the mode or manner in which it is related to its effect.

Thomas next goes on in the text to consider efficient and final causality, but what concerns us here is his treatment of formal causality. From this passage, it is clear not only that he views an exemplar as exercising formal causality but that this view does not violate the primary division of the causes. The fundamental characteristic of form is that it is the *pattern* of a thing, making that thing to be the kind of thing it is. A form can thus be extrinsic to a thing without violating the intrinsic-extrinsic division of the causes precisely because that division is a secondary division. Hence, Thomas himself sees no difficulty in holding that a formal cause can be either intrinsic or exemplary, that is, extrinsic.[91]

But what of Kondoleon's position that the primary role of an exemplar idea is to attract the agent's will in his act of production? If this is true, then the exemplar is primarily a final cause. Here, we need to recall that when Thomas speaks of an exemplar as a final cause, he does so with qualification, noting that it has the character of an end only "in a certain way" *(quodam modo)*. This is because an exemplar idea acts as a final cause with respect to the agent, not

---

90. *In V Meta.,* lect. 2, n. 764 (Marietti ed., 254–55): "Alio modo dicitur causa, species et exemplum, id est exemplar; et haec est causa formalis, quae comparatur dupliciter ad rem. Uno modo sicut forma intrinseca rei; et haec dicitur species. Alio modo sicut extrinseca a re, ad cujus tamen similitudinem res fieri dicitur; et secundum hoc, exemplar rei dicitur forma." Emphasis added in translation.

91. See, e.g., *In III Sent.,* d. 27, q. 2, a. 4, *quaestiuncula* 3, obj. 1 (Moos ed., vol. 3.884.1); *In IV Sent.,* d. 1, q. 1, a. 1, *quaestiuncula* 3, obj. 2 (Moos ed., vol. 4.10.2); *De ver.,* q. 14, a. 5, obj. 4 (Leonine ed., vol. 22.2.451:27–35). Although these references appear in the context of objections, in his replies Thomas implicitly accepts the position that form is always either intrinsic or exemplary-extrinsic, taking issue with the objections on other accounts. Cf. *ST* I, q. 5, a. 2, ad 2 (Leonine ed., vol. 4.58).

the effect. But as Thomas explains, "[the term] 'exemplar', when taken in the proper sense, conveys a causality with respect to *exemplified things,* for an exemplar is [that] in imitation of which another thing is made."[92] In this sense, it is a formal cause.

What we find, then, is that an exemplar idea exercises two types of causality: as a final cause, it arouses the artisan's will to produce an effect, and as a formal cause, it measures the effect that he produces.[93] Only in the latter sense, however, can an exemplar be said to act *as* an exemplar. It does not act as an exemplar in its role of motivating the agent precisely because it does not act as a formal cause. To say this is not to deny the significance of an exemplar's teleological role: if such an idea did not motivate the agent's intention in the first place, its likeness would never come about. But motivating an agent is not what is proper to it as an exemplar, for even ideas of merely possible works can act as final causes in this way. Thus, Leonardo da Vinci was motivated by his idea of the *Gran Cavallo* to sculpt a giant horse, but because of a lack of bronze, the statue was never made.

If exemplars were primarily and properly final causes, then even such ideas of mere possible works would be exemplars. As we have seen, however, Thomas comes to reject this view, insisting in his later works that only actually productive ideas are exemplars because only such ideas actually exemplify something. Hence, he explains that "the work of an exemplar (in other words its use) seems to be this: that in looking to an exemplar, an artisan introduces a likeness of form *in* his work of art."[94] In this way, the exemplar acts in its proper role as a formal cause.

92. *De ver.,* q. 8, a. 8, ad 1 (Leonine ed., vol. 22.1.): "Ad primum igitur dicendum, quod exemplar, si proprie accipiatur, importat causalitatem respectu exemplatorum quia exemplar est ad cuius imitationem fit aliud." Emphasis added in translation. Regarding Thomas's qualification of an exemplar's role as final cause, see n. 77 above.

93. Even so, as Greenstock points out, "the exemplar is not desired or willed for itself, but rather with a view to the effect" (Greenstock, "Exemplar Causality," 6).

94. *In I Meta.,* lect. 15, n. 232 (Marietti ed., 81): "Hoc enim videtur esse opus exemplaris, idest utilitas, quod artifex respiciens ad exemplar inducat similitudinem formae in suo artificio." Emphasis added in translation. Cf. *ST* I, q. 36, a. 3 (Leonine ed., vol. 4.382): "In omnibus locutionibus in quibus dicitur aliquis per aliquem operari,

SUMMARY

In this first chapter, we have focused on the role of ideas in human art. Since Thomas holds that the ideas in the mind of God are analogous to those in the mind of the artisan, this study has provided us with a frame of reference to examine the causality of the divine ideas better. What we found is that Thomas considers ideas, whether human or divine, to be principles both of cognition and of production. It is in the latter role that they act as exemplar causes. This is not to claim that an idea is the only type of exemplar cause that he identifies. Nevertheless, for Thomas, the primary and proper sense of the term "exemplar" refers to the intellectual exemplar: the *idea* as exemplar cause.

Such an idea exercises a unique mode of causality: it exists separately from the thing that it causes, yet it does not have a separate existence in itself. Rather, since it is an idea, it exists only within a mind. Properly speaking, therefore, exemplar causality (or exemplarism) is exercised solely by intelligent agents. Although unique in its mode of causality, exemplarism is not a unique *kind* of causality. Thomas does not consider the exemplar to constitute a fifth type of cause; rather, he holds that it falls within Aristotle's fourfold division of the causes. As we have seen, it is a formal cause, even though it is an *extrinsic* form.

When we describe an exemplar in this way, however, we must keep in mind two points. First, although an exemplar is an extrinsic formal cause, not every extrinsic formal cause is, properly speaking, an exemplar.[95] The form of an agent can be regarded as

haec praepositio *per* designat in causali aliquam causam seu principium illius actus. Sed cum actio sit media inter faciens et factum, quandoque illud causale cui adiungitur haec praepositio *per,* est causa actionis secundum quod exit ab agente. Et tunc est causa agenti quod agat; sive sit causa finalis, sive formalis, sive effectiva vel motiva: finalis quidem, ut si dicamus quod artifex operatur *per cupiditatem lucri;* formalis vero, ut si dicamus quod operatur *per artem suam;* motiva vero, si dicamus quod operatur *per imperium alterius.*"

95. Girardi, *Metafisica della causa esemplare,* 98.

the extrinsic form of its effect (the *forma a qua*), but it is an exemplar only in an extended sense. In short, the term "exemplar" is not properly defined as an extrinsic form, as though "extrinsic" were its specific difference. Rather, for Thomas, the term is properly defined as "a form that something imitates because of the intention of an agent who predetermines the end for himself."

This definition raises the second point that we need to keep in mind, namely, that the intellectual exemplar, or exemplar idea, is not *solely* a formal cause.[96] Following Thomas's mature use of the term "exemplar," we saw that only actually practical ideas should be called "exemplars." Inasmuch as an exemplar is properly a productive idea, then, its causality necessarily entails efficient and final causality: it entails efficient causality because the exemplar's causality is caused by the efficient cause; it entails final causality because the exemplar must first motivate the intention of the agent for him to produce his work. Nevertheless, we found that an exemplar idea, in its capacity *as* an exemplar, is reduced to the order of formal causality since the characteristic that is proper to it as an exemplar is its imitability.

As David Greenstock observes, "One look at any work of art will be more than sufficient to prove to us that the exemplar undoubtedly fulfills all the conditions necessary for a real cause."[97] Indeed, one look at any work of art is sufficient to prove to us simply that, within the mind of the artisan, some exemplar must *exist* for that work to have come into being. Since Thomas does draw an analogy between human art and divine exemplarism, the question that we will need to answer next is, what evidence is there that such ideas exist within the mind of God? In short, how does Thomas prove the existence of *divine* exemplars?

96. Ibid.
97. Greenstock, "Exemplar Causality," 4–5.

TWO

THE EXISTENCE OF
DIVINE IDEAS

Thomas's analogy between human art and divine exemplarism is a useful one for understanding the metaphysical role that he assigns to the divine ideas. Taken alone, however, the analogy presumes two things: first, that God does in fact exist and second, that he indeed possesses ideas. Regarding the first point, we find in Thomas's *ex professo* treatments of the divine ideas that the existence of God is either taken for granted or has already been proven earlier in the relevant work. As regards the divine ideas themselves, however, he is not content in these treatments merely to presume their existence. Rather, he also presents a variety of philosophical arguments to *prove* that they exist.

THOMAS'S CRITIQUE OF THE
PLATONIC APPROACH

It might strike the reader as surprising that Aquinas affirms the existence of ideas as formal causes of things: it is well known that, following Aristotle, he is strongly critical of Plato's account of Ideas.[1] In numerous passages

---

1. When referring to this Platonic doctrine, I have chosen to capitalize the first letter of the term "Ideas" to emphasize their self-subsistent na-

throughout his corpus, Thomas presents this account and then rejects it. To be more precise, what he rejects is his *understanding* of Plato's account. As scholarship has shown, it is likely that Thomas had little if any direct exposure to Plato's writings, instead gathering his knowledge of Platonism from sources such as Aristotle's *Metaphysics*.[2]

It is in Thomas's commentary on that work that we find his most detailed presentation of Plato's doctrine of Ideas. Following Aristotle, Thomas explains that Plato was motivated to posit his doctrine out of a concern to find certainty. Like Cratylus and Heraclitus, Plato had believed that all sensible things are in a constant state of flux and, consequently, that there could be no scientific knowledge of particular, sensible things. It is for this reason that Socrates had turned his attention away from the natural world to focus on moral matters, seeking universals and definitions. Plato adopted this method and applied it to natural things, identifying in them universals that could be defined. Since only what is immutable can be defined, he concluded that these universals are immutable entities. The universal "man" that is predicated of both Socrates and Plato,

---

ture and to contrast them with the Thomistic divine ideas, which exist only within the mind of God. For a consideration of Aquinas's criticisms of Plato, see Henle's *Thomas and Platonism*. Despite this explicit opposition to Plato, Thomas is nonetheless *implicitly* influenced by Platonism and Neoplatonism. Scholarship since the mid-twentieth century has increasingly come to acknowledge this fact. See, e.g., Norris Clarke, "The Platonic Heritage of Thomism," *Review of Metaphysics* 8 (September 1954): 105–24; Luis Cortest, "Was St. Thomas Aquinas a Platonist?" *The Thomist* 52 (1988): 209–19; Cornelio Fabro, *La nozione metafisica di partecipazione,* 2nd ed. (Turin: Società Editrice Internazionale, 1963); id., *Participation et causalité selon s. Thomas d'Aquin* (Louvain: Publications Universitaires, 1961); id., "Platonism, Neoplatonism and Thomism: Convergencies and Divergencies," *The New Scholasticism* 44 (Winter 1970): 69–100; Louis B. Geiger, *La participation dans la philosophie de s. Thomas d'Aquin,* 2nd ed. (Paris:Librairie Philosophique J. Vrin, 1953); Wayne J. Hankey, *God in Himself: Aquinas' Doctrine of God as Expounded in Summa theologiae* (Oxford: Oxford University Press, 1987); Charles A. Hart, "Participation and the Thomistic Five Ways," *The New Scholasticism* 26 (1952): 267–82; id., *Thomistic Metaphysics* (Englewood Cliffs, N.J.: Prentice Hall Inc., 1959); Arthur Little, S.J., *The Platonic Heritage of Thomism* (Dublin: Golden Eagle Books, 1949); Rudi A. te Velde, *Participation and Substantiality in Thomas Aquinas* (New York: E.J. Brill, 1995); Wippel, *Metaphysical Thought,* chap. 4, 94–131.

2. See chap. 1, nn. 73–75.

therefore, would have a real existence independent of Socrates, Plato, or any other man. This universal "man" would be the essence of all individual men, and similarly, every other universal would be the essence of those particulars of which it is predicated.[3] In short, according to this account, Plato held that whatever is separated in thought is also separated in reality, existing apart from matter. For this reason, R. J. Henle has termed this approach to proving the existence of Ideas the *via abstractionis*.[4]

Thomas explains that Plato named these universal entities in the following way:

He called them "Ideas" and "Species" of existing sensible things: "Ideas" (i.e., forms) because sensible things were produced according to their likeness, "Species" because sensible things had their substantial being *(esse substantiale)* through a participation of them. Or he called them "Ideas" because they were a principle of being *(essendi)* but called them "Species" because they were a principle of understanding. And thus, all sensible things have being because of them and according to them. "Because of them" insofar as the Ideas are the causes of being for sensible things. "According to them" insofar as they are the *exemplars* of those things.[5]

Aristotle offers numerous criticisms of the Platonic Ideas, but perhaps his most derisive words are in response to Plato's view that the Ideas are exemplar causes. Commenting on the Ideas as they are presented in the *Phaedo,* Aristotle notes that "to say that they are patterns [παραδείματα] and the other things share them is to use empty words and poetical metaphors. For what is it that works,

---

3. *In I Meta.,* lect. 10, nn. 152–58 (Marietti ed., 54–55).

4. Henle, *Thomas and Platonism,* 384.

5. *In I Meta.,* lect. 10, n. 153 (Marietti ed., 54): "Et ideo huiusmodi entia universalia, quae sunt a rebus sensibilibus separata, de quibus definitiones assignantur, nominavit ideas et species existentium sensibilium: 'ideas quidem', idest formas, inquantum ad earum similitudinem sensibilia constituebantur: species vero inquantum per earum participationem esse substantiale habebant. Vel ideas inquantum erant principium essendi, species vero inquantum erant principium cognoscendi. Unde et sensibilia omnia habent esse propter praedictas et secundum eas. Propter eas quidem inquantum ideae sunt sensibilibus causae essendi. Secundum eas vero inquantum sunt eorum exemplaria." Emphasis added in translation.

looking to the Ideas? Anything can either be, or become, like an-other without being copied from it, so that whether Socrates ex-ists or not a man might come to be like Socrates; and evidently this might be so even if Socrates were eternal."[6] Examining this argument, Thomas explains that it concerns the induction of a likeness in the thing made. In the operations of natural beings, we commonly observe that like is generated by like, as man is generated by man. Now, this likeness either results from some agent looking toward Platonic-style Ideas, or it does not. If it does not, then there is no need to posit Ideas. What is implied in Thomas's reasoning here is that exemplarism cannot occur without an agent: if there is no agent to *use* Ideas, then they cannot possibly be causes, and if they cannot be causes, they serve no purpose.[7]

But what if there *were* an agent that looked to Ideas? Plato sug-gests as much in the *Timaeus* where he presents his Demiurge, a di-vine craftsman who employs Ideas that exist separately from him-self in order to make the sensible world.[8] Thomas responds to this possibility with a *reductio ad absurdum*. If the likeness in a natural effect were to result from an agent looking to Ideas, then the cause of that likeness would not be the form of some natural agent. For example, Socrates would not be the cause of his offspring's like-ness to himself, but rather the Idea "man" would be the cause of that likeness. The absurdity would result that someone similar to Socrates could be generated whether Socrates ever existed or not. Common experience, however, shows us that natural agents do play an active role in generation, otherwise their offspring would not share a likeness to them. Hence, Thomas concludes, "it is vain and superfluous to posit separate exemplars."[9]

---

6. *Metaphysics*, 1.9.991a20–31, trans. W. D. Ross, in vol. 2 of *The Complete Works of Ar-istotle*, ed. Jonathan Barnes (Princeton: Princeton University Press, 1991), 1566.

7. *In I Meta.*, lect. 15, n. 232 (Marietti ed., 81).

8. *Timaeus*, 28a ff. Aristotle does not acknowledge this agent in his critique quoted above but presents Plato's account of Ideas solely as it appears in the *Phaedo*, where the Demiurge is not mentioned.

9. *In I Meta.*, lect. 15, n. 232 (Marietti ed., 81): "Si igitur hoc est falsum, quod non

Having agreed with Aristotle's argument against exemplarism thus far, Aquinas next adds a careful qualification: "it must, however, be understood that even though that argument refutes the separate exemplars posited by Plato, it nevertheless does not deny that the *divine knowledge* is the exemplar of all things."[10] In short, the argument does not refute the existence of exemplars within the mind of God. Why Thomas holds this position is revealed in the various demonstrations he offers to prove the existence of the divine ideas.

These demonstrations appear in most of his *ex professo* treatments of the divine ideas. Prior to such treatments, Aquinas typically first provides an examination of the divine knowledge in general, offering evidence that God is intelligent and identifying *what* God knows.[11] To examine all of these arguments here would take us too far afield from the central question of this chapter: why Thomas concludes that there must be divine ideas. For this reason, I will focus below only on those arguments that either explicitly or implicitly conclude to their existence. Some of the arguments, therefore, will presume that God exists and that he is intelligent. Since Thomas's method of argumentation develops somewhat over time, I will again consider the relevant texts chronologically, providing a summary at the end of this textual analysis.

---

similitudo generatorum dependeat a proximis generantibus, vanum et superfluum est ponere aliqua exemplaria separata."

10. *In I Meta.,* lect. 15, n. 233 (Marietti ed., 81): "Sciendum autem quod illa ratio, etsi destruat exemplaria separata a Platone posita, non tamen removet divinam scientiam esse rerum omnium exemplarem." Emphasis added in translation.

11. According to Thomas, God only knows created things through ideas; he knows himself through his own essence (see *ST* I, q. 15, a. 1, ad 2 [Leonine ed., vol. 4.199]). We will discuss this point in more detail in chap. 3, n. 46). Many of the arguments Thomas offers to prove that God has knowledge merely conclude to that general point: they do not reveal whether he has knowledge of created things through ideas or even whether he has knowledge of himself (see, e.g., *In I Sent.,* d. 35, q. 1, a. 1 [Mandonnet ed., vol. 1.808–9]; *De ver.,* q. 2, a. 1 [Leonine ed., vol. 22.1.37–42]; *SCG* I, c. 44 [Leonine ed., vol. 13.129–42]; *ST* I, q. 14, a. 1 [Leonine ed., vol. 4.166–67]).

THOMAS'S ARGUMENTS FOR THE
EXISTENCE OF DIVINE IDEAS

In I Sententias (1252–1256)

Thomas's earliest *ex professo* treatment of the divine ideas occurs in d. 36 of this book of his commentary on the *Sentences*. He does not offer any proof of their existence here, but rather presumes it from his general treatment of God's knowledge in d. 35. In the first article of q. 1, Thomas provides arguments to prove that God has knowledge. He then proceeds in a. 2 to offer evidence that God has knowledge of things other than himself. There, he explains that whatever acts by a necessity of nature must be directed to its end by some knowing agent. But this direction is impossible unless the knowing agent knows (1) the things that it directs, (2) the operations of those things, and (3) the end toward which they are directed. A blacksmith *(faber)*, for example, could not make an axe unless he knew the act of cutting as well as those things that are needed for cutting. Similarly, God must know those things that are ordered toward himself since they have being *(esse)* from him and, hence, also have a natural order toward an end. Following Moses Maimonides, Thomas cites as scriptural evidence the words of Psalms 93:9, "He that formed the eye, doth he not consider?" It is as if the psalmist were saying, "Since God made the eye, would he not consider its act which is life and its object which is the visible particular?" In short, Thomas suggests that the order manifest in nature testifies to God's knowledge of things other than himself.[12]

---

12. *In I Sent.*, d. 35, q. 1, a. 2 (Mandonnet ed., vol. 1.814): "Unde Rabbi Moyses hanc rationem dicit intendisse David cum dixit psal. xciii, 9: *Qui finxit oculum non considerat? quasi diceret: cum Deus oculum faceret, numquid ipse non consideravit actum oculi qui est videre, et objectum ejus, quod est visibile particulare?*" See Maimonides, *The Guide of the Perplexed*, 3.19, trans. Shlomo Pines (Chicago: University of Chicago Press, 1963), 478–79.

As it is presented here, this argument, which I will call the "argument from natural teleology" (or the "teleology argument" for short), does not explicitly argue for the existence of divine ideas, but it does imply the need for them. Moreover, Thomas presents this argument shortly before his examination of the divine ideas in d. 36, suggesting that he indeed views the argument as implicitly proving the existence of what he will there term "ideas."

De veritate, qq. 2 and 3 (1256–1257)

In q. 2 of the De veritate, Thomas provides a consideration of God's knowledge, and he begins with the simple assertion that everyone attributes knowledge to God.[13] Although he sees no need to demonstrate the truth of this claim, Thomas does provide arguments in a. 3 to prove that God has knowledge of things other than himself. The article begins by enunciating the same teleological principle enunciated in his earlier commentary on the Sentences, namely, whatever naturally tends toward an end must have this tendency from something directing it to that end. If it did not, a thing would merely tend to that end by chance.

Natural things tend to their respective ends by what Thomas terms a "natural appetite." Given the teleological principle mentioned above, he concludes that there must be some (divine) intellect above all natural things which has ordered them to their ends and has implanted in them this appetite or inclination. Since a thing cannot be ordered to an end unless both the thing and its end are known, there must be in the divine intellect a knowledge of natural things, from which knowledge the nature and order of things originate. As before, Thomas quotes the Psalms regarding the formation of the eye, this time commenting that it is as if the psalmists were to have said that "He who made the eye as propor-

13. De ver., q. 2, a. 1 (Leonine ed., vol. 22.1.39:109–10).

tioned to its end which is its act (namely, vision), does he not consider the *nature* of the eye?"[14]

Having shown that God knows things other than himself, Thomas next proceeds to examine the manner in which God knows creatures, and in doing so he presents another argument for God's knowledge of created things—one that was not offered in the commentary on the *Sentences*. Since every agent acts inasmuch as it is in act, whatever is caused by an agent must in some way be in the agent; hence, every agent causes something similar to itself *(omne agens agit sibi simile)*.[15] But whatever is in another is in it according to the mode of the receiver. Hence, if the agent is immaterial, its effect must exist within it in an immaterial way.

At this point, Aquinas reminds us that a thing is known when it is received immaterially. For this reason, effects that are present in an immaterial cause are present in a knowable manner. Therefore, every immaterial active principle knows its own effect; as the author of the *Liber de causis* (prop. 8) notes, "an intelligence knows that which is below itself because it is its cause." Since God is the immaterial active principle of things, it follows, therefore, that he has knowledge of those things.[16]

---

14. *De ver.,* q. 2, a. 3 (Leonine ed., vol. 22.1.50–51:211–34): "Et hanc probationem innuit Psalmista cum dixit «Qui finxit oculum non considerat?» ut Rabbi Moyses dicit, quod idem est ac si diceret 'qui oculum fecit sic proportionatum ad suum finem qui est eius actus, scilicet visio, nonne considerat oculi naturam?'" Emphasis added in translation.

15. *De ver.,* q. 2, a. 3 (Leonine ed., vol. 22.1.51:235–40). Thus, Thomas presents a brief deductive justification for the principle of similitude. For a consideration of Thomas's justification for the principle of similitude, see John F. Wippel, "Thomas Aquinas on Our Knowledge of God and the Axiom that Every Agent Produces Something Like Itself," in *Proceedings of the American Catholic Philosophical Association* 74 (2000): 81–101. Regarding deductive justifications, see 91–95.

16. *De ver.,* q. 2, a. 3 (Leonine ed., vol. 22.1.51:240–61). "Et inde est quod in libro De causis dicitur 'quod intelligentia cognoscit id quod est sub se in quantum est causa ei.' Unde, cum Deus sit rerum immateriale principium activum sequitur quod apud ipsum sit earum cognitio." Regarding Thomas's reference to the *Liber de causis,* see the Saffrey edition of Thomas's commentary on that work, prop. 8, p. 54.

⟿

Thomas's *ex professo* treatment of the divine ideas appears in q. 3. It is in a. 1 that he first explicitly asks the question whether there are ideas in God.[17] He notes as in prior passages that some agents act for an end that they determine for themselves, namely, all agents who act through the intellect. By contrast, some agents are determined to the end by another and principal agent. Again the example from archery is offered: an arrow in flight tends toward a definite end, but one that has been determined for it by the archer. Similarly, the operation of natural things presupposes an intellect predetermining and ordering them to their ends. Hence, every work of nature is said to be the work of intelligence. In light of this observation, Thomas concludes, as we saw in chapter 1, that an exemplar idea is a form that something imitates because of the intention of an agent who predetermines the end for himself.[18]

Having defined an exemplar idea in this way, Thomas notes that those people who hold that everything happens by chance clearly cannot admit the existence of divine ideas. Their position is flawed, however, because chance happens only in a few instances, whereas nature proceeds in the same way always, or for the most part. Other people say that everything proceeds from God according to a necessity of nature rather than through an act of the will. They too cannot admit of divine ideas because any agent acting from a necessity of nature does not predetermine the end for itself; rather, such an agent has its end determined for it by something superior. Their position, however, is also flawed: since no cause is superior to God, it is impossible for anything to predetermine the end for which he acts.[19]

---

17. By contrast, in the commentary on the *Sentences* Thomas merely asks, "Quid nomine ideae importetur?" (*In I Sent.*, d. 36, q. 2, a. 1 [Mandonnet ed., vol. 1.839–40]).

18. *De ver.*, q. 3, a. 1 (Leonine ed., vol. 22.1.99–100:196–223). It should be recalled that in this text, Thomas treats the term "exemplar" as synonymous with the term "idea," each term referring to knowledge that is both actually practical *and* virtually practical.

19. *De ver.*, q. 3, a. 1 (Leonine ed., vol. 22.1.100:224–40).

It was to avoid these two flawed positions, Thomas tells us, that Plato posited the existence of Ideas in the first place. And Dionysius, in an effort to provide an account of the predetermination or predefinition *(praediffinitio)* of God's works, posits the *divine* exemplars as the "substantiating and singularly preexisting notions" *(rationes substantificas et singulariter praeexistentes)* of existing things, as well as "predefinitions" *(praediffinitiones)* and "divine and good willings" *(divinas et bonas voluntates)* by which God predefines and produces all things. It is this position to which Thomas subscribes.[20]

In these passages from the *De veritate,* we again find Thomas employing the argument from natural teleology. As in his commentary on the *Sentences,* he uses this argument to prove that God has knowledge of things other than himself. Now, however, he also employs it to demonstrate explicitly that *ideas* of these things must exist within the mind of God as their exemplars.

In addition to the teleology argument, Thomas offers another type of argument that was not present in the *Sentences* commentary. This argument is based upon (and attempts to justify) the causal principle that every agent causes something similar to itself *(omne agens agit sibi simile).* In light of this principle, he concludes that all of God's effects must preexist within him and must do so in an intelligible manner. Thomas employs this new argument which

---

20. *De ver.,* q. 3, a. 1 (Leonine ed., vol. 22.1.100:240–61). The Latin terms above are from Thomas's references to the *Divine Names* V, 8 *(Dionysiaca,* vol. 1.22.359–60: S). When working with Dionysius's texts, Thomas employed Latin renditions, relying principally on the Iohannus Sarracenus translation and amending it when necessary from his experience with Eriugena's translation *(In librum beati Dionysii De divinis nominibus expositio,* ed. C. Pera [Turin and Rome: Marietti, 1950], xxii, §11]); Jean Durantel, *Saint Thomas et le Pseudo-Denis* [Paris: Librairie Félix Alcan, 1919], 210). For some examples of Thomas's use of Eriugena's translation, see Fran O'Rourke, *Pseudo-Dionysius and the Metaphysics of Aquinas* [New York: E.J. Brill, 1992], 55, 88n255. For a history of the various Latin translations and commentaries of the Dionysian corpus up until Thomas's time, see Marietti (xi–xxii). For a concordance containing various Latin translations of these works, consult *Dionysiaca,* ed. Philippe Chevallier (Paris: Desclée, de Brouwer & Cie., 1937).

I will refer to as the "argument from divine similitude" (or the "similitude argument" for short) to prove that God has knowledge of things other than himself, but he does not offer it here as an explicit proof of the existence of divine ideas.

Summa Contra Gentiles (1259–1264)

In c. 44 of book I, Thomas offers several brief arguments to prove that God is intelligent, one of which is the argument from natural teleology. He reiterates the principle that whatever determinately tends to an end either determines that end for itself or has that end determined for it by another, otherwise it would not tend to *this* end rather than to *that* one. Since natural things do not determine the ends toward which they tend, they must have their ends determined for them by another, namely, by one who is the author of nature *(institutor naturae)*. This author is God, who must be intelligent in order to determine the end of nature.[21]

In c. 49, Thomas considers whether God knows things other than himself. Here he presents a version of the argument from divine similitude. The likeness of every effect preexists in some way in its cause and does so according to the mode of that cause. Since God is by his very nature intellectual, the likeness of his effects must exist in him intelligibly. Hence, God understands things other than himself.[22]

Thomas offers another style of argument here, one that proceeds from God's knowledge of himself as cause. As he explains, the knowledge of any effect is sufficiently known through a knowledge of its cause. God, however, is the cause of other beings through his essence. Since God knows his essence in the fullest sense, he must know other things as well. Immediately following this argument, another one is presented in the same vein. Thomas observes that whoever knows a thing perfectly knows everything that belongs

21. *SCG* I, c. 44 (Leonine ed., vol. 13.130).
22. *SCG* I, c. 49 (Leonine ed., vol. 13.142).

to the nature of the thing. Since God knows his nature perfectly, he must know that he is the cause of other things. But he could not know himself perfectly as their cause unless he understood the things that he causes, which are other than himself. Hence, God must know things other than himself.[23]

These arguments from the *Summa Contra Gentiles* offer both continuity with and development from Thomas's prior works. Both the teleology argument and the similitude argument are present, and there is also a new line of reasoning, what I will refer to as the "argument from divine self-knowledge" (or the "self-knowledge argument" for short). As it is presented here, this argument does not explicitly prove the existence of divine ideas. Indeed, none of the three types of arguments here does. I do not read this fact as suggesting that Thomas has changed his mind about the usefulness of the teleology argument in explicitly proving the existence of divine ideas. The absence of any explicit arguments for divine ideas in the *Summa Contra Gentiles* can be explained by the absence of any *ex professo* treatment of the ideas in this work. Why Thomas does not include such a treatment here will be examined in chapter 3.

In De divinis nominibus (1261–1265 or 1265–1268)

The self-knowledge argument appears again in the commentary on Dionysius's *De divinis nominibus,* and now it is used to prove explicitly the existence of divine ideas. In chapter 5, lect. 3 of that work, Thomas comments upon Dionysius's doctrine of the divine exemplars. He explains that divine exemplarism should be understood as follows: God knows both his unity and his power, and in so knowing them, he knows the diverse things that are able to proceed from himself. In this way, Thomas concludes, God knows the

---

23. *SCG* I, c. 49 (Leonine ed., vol. 13.142).

understood notions *(rationes intellectae)*, or ideas, that proceed from himself. In short, he knows things other than himself inasmuch as he knows both his power and what he is capable of producing. Thus, exemplars exist within the mind of God. Thomas is careful to note, however, that not all of God's ideas are properly called "exemplars"; rather, only those ideas in imitation of which another is made are properly so called.[24] In this text, then, the self-knowledge argument is used to prove explicitly the existence of divine ideas.

Summa theologiae I (1266–1268)

In the *Prima Pars* of the *Summa theologiae,* Thomas yet again employs the argument from divine self-knowledge. Q. 14 is dedicated to examining God's knowledge. Having established in a. 1 that God does indeed have knowledge and in a. 2 that God knows himself, Thomas considers in a. 5 whether God knows other things as well. As in the *Summa Contra Gentiles,* he explains that God knows his own power perfectly inasmuch as he knows himself perfectly. Since a thing's power can only be perfectly known by knowing to what that power extends, God must know things other than himself. The reason he must is that his power extends to other things because he is the first effective cause of all beings *(prima causa effectiva omnium entium).* This conclusion is still more evident when we consider that this first effective cause *is* his very act of understanding. Presenting the other version of the self-knowledge argument found in the *Summa Contra Gentiles,* Thomas notes that anything that is in another is in it according to the other's mode. God's effects, therefore, must preexist in him in an intelligible manner. Hence, God must know things other than himself.[25]

---

24. *In V De div. nom.,* lect. 3, n. 665 (Marietti ed., 249). Regarding the use of the term "exemplar" in this text, see the textual analysis section in chap. 1. As will be recalled, Thomas restricts the term "exemplar" here to refer to actually practical knowledge.

25. *ST* I, q. 14, a. 5 (Leonine ed., vol. 4.172).

⇁⇀

Q. 15 presents an *ex professo* treatment of the divine ideas, and a. 1 of that question examines whether there in fact are (divine) ideas. As we saw in chapter 1, Thomas notes in this article that the term "idea" denotes the form of a thing existing apart from the thing. But the form of a thing can exist apart from it in two ways: (1) either as the exemplar of the thing; or (2) as a principle of knowledge, since the forms of knowable things are said to be in the knower. Thus, ideas can serve either an ontological function or a cognitive one. Again, as we saw in chapter 1, Thomas reserves the term "exemplar" here for the former type of idea, choosing to call the latter, instead, a "notion" *(ratio)*. He contends that in both respects it is necessary to posit ideas. However, the argument offered in this article to prove the existence of divine ideas is based upon the need for ideas that serve an ontological function. In short, the argument that follows does not conclude to the existence of divine ideas simply speaking but rather to the existence of divine *exemplar* ideas.[26]

The argument begins by noting that in all things not generated by chance, the form is the end of the generation. An agent, however, only acts for the sake of a form because a likeness of the form exists in the agent. Now the form of an effect can preexist in the agent in two ways. In one way, it can preexist according to natural being *(esse naturale)*, as when an agent acts through nature. In this respect, we see that the agent gives its offspring the same type of form as its own, as when man generates man. The second way is according to intelligible being *(esse intelligibile)*. Such is the case with agents that act through intellect. Thus, the likeness of a house preexists in the mind of the builder. We would call this likeness an "idea" because the artisan intends his effect to be assimilated to this form that he mentally conceives. Since the world is not made by chance but rather by God's acting through intellect, Thomas concludes that there

26. *ST* I, q. 15, a. 1 (Leonine ed., vol. 4.199). On this point, see Wippel, *Divine Ideas*, 33.

must exist in the divine mind a form in the likeness of which he has made the world. And this form has the character *(ratio)* of an idea. To be more precise, as we have noted, this form has the character of an *exemplar* idea.[27] Although the principle of similitude is not explicitly stated in this argument, the line of reasoning nevertheless follows the same basic format of the similitude arguments that appear in both the *De veritate* and *Summa Contra Gentiles.* Unlike those earlier versions of the argument, however, this one explicitly proves the existence of divine (exemplar) ideas.[28]

The divine ideas are touched upon again in q. 44, which examines the production of creatures. In a. 3 of that question, Thomas considers whether God is the exemplar cause of things. He observes that an exemplar is needed in the production of something so that the effect can receive a determinate form. Thus, an artificial thing has a determinate form because an artisan produces his work according to the exemplar that he considers. Natural things also receive determinate forms in their production. Thomas argues that this determination must be reduced to the divine wisdom as to a first principle, for the divine wisdom has "thought out" *(excogitavit)* or discerned the order of the universe, which consists in the distinction of things.[29] Thus, he concludes that there must be ideas of all things in the divine wisdom, and these ideas are the exemplar

27. *ST* I, q. 15, a. 1 (Leonine ed., vol. 4.199).

28. As in the *De veritate,* Thomas offers a justification for the principle of similitude in this argument. The justification here, however, is inductive, whereas the justification in the *De veritate* is deductive. Regarding Thomas's inductive justifications for this principle, see Wippel, "The Axiom that Every Agent Produces Something Like Itself," 89–91.

29. As we will see in chap. 3, the divine ideas are nothing other than God's knowledge of his essence inasmuch as it is imitable. Therefore, Thomas's reference to "excogitation" here should not be taken to suggest that God somehow "comes up with" new ideas in the process of thinking. On this point I follow Wippel, who differs with Norris Clarke. Clarke contends that God "does not find them [the divine ideas] somehow ready-made in His essence (what could that possibly mean ontologically?) but literally 'invents,' 'excogitates' them . . ." (W. Norris Clarke, "What Is Really Real?" in *Progress in Philosophy,* ed. J. A. McWilliams [Milwaukee: Bruce, 1955], 85n45). Wippel responds that "I prefer to stress the fact that God, in knowing his own essence, also

forms existing in the mind of God.[30] As in q. 15, then, this argument concludes to the existence of ideas *as* exemplars.

With its emphasis on the production of a determinate form, this argument follows in the vein of Thomas's earlier arguments from natural teleology. It differs from them, however, inasmuch as it does not explicitly enunciate its dependence upon final causality. Rather than focusing upon an agent's intention and desire for the end, the argument here considers the end itself: the determinate form that is produced. The notion that some natural agent exists that is directed to this end is merely implied.

In *Summa theologiae* I, we see the by now three familiar types of arguments: the argument from divine self-knowledge (q. 14), the argument from divine similitude (q. 15), and the argument from natural teleology (q. 44). In this work, Thomas employs the self-knowledge argument only to prove that God knows things other than himself. He employs both the similitude argument and the teleology argument to prove explicitly the existence of divine ideas, and to be precise, of exemplar ideas.

In I Metaphysicam (1270?–1271?)

What is most likely the last explicit argument that Thomas offers to prove the existence of the divine ideas appears in his commentary on Aristotle's *Metaphysics*.[31] As we saw at the outset of

knows (or 'discovers') the many ways in which it is imitable and, therefore, the divine ideas and the possibles" ("Reality of Nonexisting Possibles," 738–39n19 [also in Wippel, *Metaphysical Themes in Thomas Aquinas* (Washington, D.C.: The Catholic University of America Press, 1984), 72–73n19]). Still, Wippel observes that his difference with Clarke seems to be "mainly a matter of emphasis" (ibid.).

30. *ST* I, q. 44, a. 3 (Leonine ed., vol. 4.460).

31. Torrell notes that the dating of this work poses numerous problems. He suggests that the beginning of the commentary (with which we are concerned) may date from the academic year 1270–71. "The only sure thing, in the current state of research," Torrell explains, "is that this text is earlier than the *De caelo et mundo,* probably composed in Naples, 1272–1273" (Torrell, *The Person and His* Work, 344).

this chapter, Thomas concurs with the argument Aristotle offers in the first book of the *Metaphysics* to refute the Platonic doctrine of Ideas. As we also saw, however, Thomas is careful to note that "even though that argument refutes the separate exemplars posited by Plato, it nevertheless does not deny that the *divine knowledge* is the exemplar of all things."[32] Thomas then proceeds to show why.

Since natural things intend to induce *(inducere)* likenesses *(similitudines)* into the things they generate, that intention must be reduced to some directing principle ordering things to every single end. This directing principle, moreover, must be an intellect since it needs to know the end and the relationship of things to that end. Thus, Thomas concludes that the likeness of effects to their natural causes is reduced to some intellect as to a first principle and that God's knowledge is the exemplar of all things.[33] Here, then, we see Thomas employing yet again the argument from natural teleology to prove explicitly the existence of divine exemplar ideas.

Summary

In the various texts considered above, we find three different types of arguments: what I have termed the arguments from natural teleology, from divine similitude, and from divine self-knowledge. Thomas begins by employing each to prove simply that God has knowledge. Over time, he also comes to employ each to prove explicitly that God has exemplar ideas. The teleology argument begins with the observation that natural things both desire and intend an end; from this premise it proceeds to the conclusion that an intelligent agent exists who directs those things to their end by means of exemplar ideas. The argument from divine similitude is founded upon the causal principle *omne agens agit sibi simile.* From the premise that God is an immaterial agent who is the cause of the universe, the argument proceeds to the conclusion that

---

32. *In I Meta.,* lect. 15, n. 233 (Marietti ed., 81). For the Latin, see above, n. 10.
33. *In I Meta.,* lect. 15, n. 233 (Marietti ed., 81).

his effects preexist in him in an immaterial way, namely, as ideas, or exemplary likenesses. Finally, the argument from divine self-knowledge begins with the premise that God has a perfect knowledge of himself and his power; from this premise it proceeds to the conclusion that he must therefore have a perfect knowledge of his effects, knowledge that consists of ideas in the divine intellect.

Of these three arguments, the one that reveals the most is the self-knowledge argument. Following its line of reasoning, Thomas concludes that God possesses ideas of anything that is within his power to create, whether or not he in fact creates it. By contrast, the other two arguments conclude only that God possesses ideas of things that he actually does create at some point in time. In short, these arguments conclude only to the existence of *exemplar* ideas.[34] Nevertheless, the argument that Thomas favors and employs most frequently is the one from natural teleology. This argument is structured as an *a posteriori* demonstration consisting of two basic stages. The first stage "ascends" from the teleological action of natural agents to prove the existence of a higher agent directing them to their end; the second stage then shows what is required for that agent to direct things in this way, namely, exemplar ideas.

The pivotal premise of the entire argument is the principle that whatever acts by a necessity of nature must be directed to its end by some knowing agent. In the versions of the argument that we have considered, Thomas offers little if any justification for this principle, treating it instead as axiomatic. This is unfortunate because the argument as presented is thus left open to the criticism of anthropomorphizing. Nevertheless, justification of this teleological principle can be made, and Aquinas offers just such a justification in the *De potentia.*

There, he explains that whatever acts of natural necessity cannot determine the end for itself because it is determined only to one effect and cannot act otherwise. Hence, its end must be deter-

---

34. Ideas that are actually practical, not ones that are either virtually practical or speculative.

mined by another since an action can only be suited to an end if some agent knows, not only (1) the end, but also (2) the nature of the end *as* an end and, moreover, (3) the proportion between that end and the means to it. Why, we might ask? Because only intellect is capable of adapting and making those means *proportionate* to the end. Thomas explains that if the sort of agent that acts out of natural necessity could reach the end without any direction from intellect, then the suitability of its actions to that end would be by chance, which is antithetical to the notion of final causality.[35] In this passage, then, he expresses in a more thorough way what is implied in the argument from natural teleology: final causality is ultimately inexplicable apart from intellect.[36]

At times in his writings, Thomas speaks of the teleological direction provided by the intelligent agent as a kind of "governance" *(gubernatio)* of things.[37] It is a governance that not only accounts for the static order of parts, but as Alice Ramos observes, it also accounts for the *"dynamic* order of subordination whereby there is a

35. *De pot.,* q. 1, a. 5 (Marrietti ed., vol. 2.19).

36. Regarding the strength of the argument from natural teleology, see Wippel, *Metaphysical Thought,* 480–85, 578–79; Fernand Van Steenberghen, *Le problème de l'existence de Dieu dans les écrits de s. Thomas d'Aquin,* Philosophes Médiévaux, vol. 23 (Louvain-la-Neuve: L'Institut Supérieur de Philosophie, 1980), 52–71. Concerning Thomas's treatment of the axiom *omne agens agit propter finem,* see George P. Klubertanz, "St. Thomas' Treatment of the Axiom, 'Omne Agens Agit Propter Finem'," in *An Etienne Gilson Tribute,* ed. Charles J. O'Neil (Milwaukee: The Marquette University Press, 1959), 101–17. For criticism of Thomas's arguments from finality, see Anthony Kenny, *The Five Ways* (Notre Dame: The University of Notre Dame Press, 1980), 96–120.

37. See, e.g., *ST* I, q. 103, a. 1 (Leonine ed., vol. 5, 453), where Thomas asks whether the world is governed by someone. In response to this question, we find him present an argument in the affirmative that is similar to the natural teleology argument used to prove the existence of divine exemplars: "Videmus enim in rebus naturalibus provenire quod melius est, aut semper aut in pluribus: quod non contingeret, nisi per aliquam providentiam res naturales dirigerentur ad finem boni, *quod est gubernare.* Unde ipse ordo certus rerum manifeste demonstrat gubernationem mundi: sicut si quis intraret domum bene ordinatam, ex ipsa domus ordinatione ordinatoris rationem perpenderet; ut, ab Aristotele dictum, Tullius introducit in libro *de Natura Deorum.*" Emphasis added. As I will discuss below, Thomas explicitly describes the Fifth Way in the *Summa theologiae,* which follows this same approach, as being *ex gubernatione rerum (ST* I, q. 2, a. 3 [Leonine ed., vol. 4.32]). See the concluding paragraphs of the section "The Fourth Way and Divine Exemplarism" in this chapter.

right arrangement of means to the end."[38] In the arguments that we have considered, dynamic ordering is illustrated in Thomas's repeated example of the arrow that has been loosed from the archer's bow. Such an arrow is clearly determined toward an end, but this determination is due to the intention of an agent ordering it *to* that end. Thomas argues that in an analogous way, natural things must also be dynamically ordered. But he does not simply provide us with the analogy from archery to illustrate this order, rather he provides a particular example in his discussion of the eye. In an eye, we find both static and dynamic ordering, the former oriented to the latter: the parts of the eye are ordered for the sake of the end toward which it acts, which is the act of seeing. Such ordering, Thomas concludes, must ultimately be the result of a governing intellect—it must be the result of divine exemplarism.

By means of the argument from natural teleology, Aquinas both responds to Aristotle's critique of exemplarism and provides a significant alternative to Plato's exemplarism. As discussed above, the Platonic *via abstractionis* asserts that anything that can exist as separated in thought exists also as separated in reality as a universal abstraction. The *via abstractionis* does not acknowledge the integral roles of efficient and final causality that are implicit in exemplarism, and that is why Plato arrives at the erroneous conclusion that the Ideas subsist independently of an intellect.[39] By contrast, Thomas's argument from natural teleology begins with the efficient causality of natural agents, "moves from this efficiency and the similitudes it involves to finality through finality to a first intelligence and the involvement of exemplar knowledge."[40]

---

38. Alice Ramos, "Ockham and Aquinas on Exemplary Causality," in *Proceedings of the PMR Conference*, vols. 19–20 (Villanova: Augustinian Historical Institute, 1994–96), 208–9. Emphasis added. For a discussion of the distinction between static and dynamic order, see Hart, *Thomistic Metaphysics*, 392.

39. Thomas is particularly critical of Plato for neglecting these two types of causes in his account of exemplarism. See, e.g., *In I Meta.*, lect. 11, nn. 178–79 (Marietti ed., 61); *In I Meta.*, lect. 17, n. 259 (Marietti ed., 90).

40. Henle, *Thomas and Platonism*, 366–67. The strongest example of this pattern occurs in the argument as it appears in the commentary on the *Metaphysics*, the only

EXISTENCE OF DIVINE IDEAS

This final move in the argument from natural teleology is a step that this argument shares in common with the other two arguments Thomas employs to prove the existence of divine ideas. That is, all three arguments ultimately deduce their existence from *God's* existence as the first cause. Whereas both the similitude argument and the self-knowledge argument presume God's causality, the teleology argument first proves it. Some scholars have proposed, however, that Thomas offers another path to proving divine exemplarism, a path that is best outlined in his famous Fourth Way argument of proving God's existence, presented in the *Summa theologiae.*

The contention by some is that the Fourth Way proves the existence of God as the exemplar cause of all things and, what is more to the point, that it does so *from* exemplarism.[41] According to this interpretation, the argument seeks to account for the distinction that is found in things by reasoning from the degrees of perfection that are found in them to the existence of an exemplar in which all finite things participate by various degrees of similitude. As Kondoleon has observed, if these scholars are correct, "then there would appear to be another way of establishing divine exemplarism than that of deducing it from the self-existing nature of the creator."[42] In light of this possibility, we will next examine the Fourth Way to see if it might be another route that Thomas offers for proving the existence of divine ideas.

---

work in which Thomas explicitly enunciates the natural agent's intention to induce its likeness. In the argument as it is presented there, we see most clearly what Henle describes as the "determined pattern of mutual involvement" among these three modes of causality (ibid.).

41. For a list of such scholars, see n. 60 below.

42. Kondoleon, *Exemplary Causality,* 162–63.

THE FOURTH WAY AND DIVINE
EXEMPLARISM

In order to discern whether exemplarism does indeed serve a role in the Fourth Way, it is worthwhile to begin by presenting the argument in its entirety. Having discussed three ways of proving God's existence, Thomas explains that

> The Fourth Way is taken from the grades that are found in things, for there is found in things something more and less good, true, noble, and so forth regarding other such [attributes]. But "more" and "less" are said of diverse things because they approach in diverse ways something that is a maximum, just as a hotter thing is that which approaches more to the hottest. Therefore, there is something that is the truest, and the best, and the most noble, and, consequently, maximally a being *(maxime ens)*, for those things that are truest are beings the most, as is said in *Metaphys.* II. But that which is called the "maximum" in some genus is the cause of all the things that are in that genus, just as fire, which is most hot, is the cause of all hot things, as is said in the same book. Therefore, there is something that is for all beings the cause of existence *(esse)*, and of goodness, and of every perfection, and this we call "God."[43]

The structure of the Fourth Way consists of two basic stages. In the first stage, Thomas argues from the grades of perfections that are found in things to the existence of a maximal being *(maxime ens)*. In the second stage, he demonstrates that this maximal being must be the cause of all perfection and of all existence *(esse)*. To un-

---

43. *ST* I, q. 2, a. 3 (Leonine ed., vol. 4.32): "Quarta via sumitur ex gradibus qui in rebus inveniuntur. Invenitur enim in rebus aliquid magis et minus bonum, et verum, et nobile, et sic de aliis huiusmodi. Sed *magis* et *minus* dicuntur de diversis secundum quod appropinquant diversimode ad aliquid quod maxime est: sicut magis calidum est, quod magis appropinquat maxime calido. Est igitur aliquid quod est verissimum, et optimum, et nobilissimum, et per consequens maxime ens: nam quae sunt maxime vera, sunt maxime entia, ut dicitur II *Metaphys.* Quod autem dicitur maxime tale in aliquo genere, est causa omnium quae sunt illius generis: sicut ignis, qui est maxime calidus, est causa omnium calidorum, ut in eodem libro dicitur. Ergo est aliquid quod omnibus entibus est causa esse, et bonitatis, et cuiuslibet perfectionis: et hoc dicimus Deum."

derstand why some scholars have described the Fourth Way as an argument from exemplarism, we will need to consider each of these two stages in some detail, as well as how each is related to the other.

The first stage begins with the observation that we have already noted, namely, that there are grades that are found in things: a more and a less. These terms "more" and "less" are commonly employed to describe quantitative differences—for example, some things are heavier while others are lighter; some are larger while others are smaller; and so forth. Nevertheless, we quickly discover from Thomas's presentation that he is in fact speaking about a different sort of gradation. It is true that the terms "more" and "less" are first employed to describe quantitative differences, but as Fernand Van Steenberghen notes, the sense of these terms can be enlarged and applied to other things as well, for example, to corporeal qualities such as light, color, and heat, which can be found in greater or lesser degrees of intensity. Similarly, these terms can be applied in an immaterial way to transcendental and simple perfections. It is in this sense that we find Thomas speaking of the grades that are found in things, grades of perfections such as goodness. Thus, for example, we commonly describe some things as being better than others.[44] This gradation of perfection in things reveals their nature as limited beings because each possesses the perfection in a limited way and none is equal to it.

Thomas next explains that the things of our experience can be said to possess perfections to a greater or lesser degree only because they approximate a maximum. Here we are presented with a difficulty: even though he provides the example of heat, Thomas offers no justification for this principle.[45] Does he consider it to be self-evident? He does not tell us.[46] For now at least, let us grant the truth of that principle: in light of it, we see that if things do possess

44. Van Steenberghen, *Le problème de l'existence de Dieu*, 208.

45. Wippel, *Metaphysical Thought*, 472–73.

46. For arguments that he does consider it to be self-evident, see Little, *Platonic Heritage*, 100; Van Steenberghen, *Le problème de l'existence de Dieu*, 209–10.

the described perfections to a greater or lesser degree, those things would not themselves be the maximum to which Thomas is referring. Hence, the starting point of this argument is really the notion of limited being.[47] This fact prompts Charles Hart to observe that the Fourth Way "is a direct appeal to consequences of the limitation of the perfections of existence as seen in the universe of our immediate experience."[48]

As we have already seen, these perfections are capable of existing according to various degrees of intensity. They are not, therefore, the univocal perfections of genera and species, since something cannot be, for example, more or less a triangle, an animal, or a man.[49] Rather, they are transcendental and simple perfections. Consider the perfection of cognition: whereas plants do not possess it, brute animals do; but human beings possess it in a more excellent way. In the Fourth Way, then, Thomas is not comparing individuals within a species but, instead, one type of being with another type of being.

He explains that such perfections can only be spoken of as "more" and "less" because they approach in varying degrees some maximum. There must be some real standard by which things are measured, by which it is true that men are more excellent than brute animals and plants.[50] For this maximum to be such a measure, it must possess the same perfection as the things it measures. Moreover, it cannot be merely a relative maximum: it cannot be simply the most perfect one in a series. Troy's Helen may well have been the most beautiful woman ever to live, but it is possible in principle to be more beautiful than she. The sort of maximum to which Thomas is referring in the Fourth Way is instead an *absolute* maximum, that is, it is the very perfection taken in its pleni-

47. Little, *Platonic Heritage,* 102–3.

48. Hart, "Participation," 270.

49. Van Steenberghen, *Le problème de l'existence de Dieu,* 209.

50. Joseph Bobik, "Aquinas' Fourth Way and the Approximating Relation," *The Thomist* 51 (1987): 35.

tude. Hence, all beautiful things are truly beautiful—not because they approach Helen's beauty, but because they approach beauty itself.[51] If the maximum of the Fourth Way were not an absolute maximum, it would itself require a standard. As Joseph Bobik notes, such a conclusion would be an absurdity, for "if there are standards for standards, then, it seems, there can be no standard at all."[52] Thus, Thomas concludes in the first stage of the argument that some standard really exists that is truest, best, most noble, and, moreover, most fully a being—what he terms the *maxime ens.*

All other beings, by contrast, are good, true, noble, and so forth only because they approach or imitate this maximal being. Thus, the *maxime ens* that Thomas describes appears to be an exemplar cause of the degrees of perfection found in limited beings.[53] If this being has indeed been shown to exist, then, in the first stage of the Fourth Way, "the mind passes *formally* from the *measured* to the *measure,* but the cause *measuring* the measured does not exist except [as] an *exemplar* cause," as François-Xavier Maquart observes.[54] Even though Thomas makes no explicit reference to exemplar causality in the Fourth Way, many scholars nonetheless conclude that exemplarism is implicitly present. Van Steenberghen, for one, offers evidence from some of Thomas's other works as background for interpreting the Fourth Way.

Van Steenberghen maintains that the Fourth Way is principally influenced, not by Thomas's Aristotelianism, but rather by his Neoplatonic thought. He thus looks to two of Thomas's Neoplatonic writings: the commentaries on the *De divinis nominibus* and on the *Liber de causis.*[55] These texts, he maintains, provide us with

---

51. Van Steenberghen, *Le problème de l'existence de Dieu,* 210.

52. Joseph Bobik, "Aquinas' Fourth Way" 35.

53. Ibid., 36.

54. François-Xavier Maquart, *Elementa philosophiae,* vol. 3, pt. 2 (Paris: Andreas Blot, 1938), 315. "Siquidem in *priori* parte argumenti mens transit *formaliter* de *mensurato* ad *mensuram,* sed causa *mensurans* mensuratum non est nisi causa *exemplaris.*"

55. Fernand Van Steenberghen, "Prolégomènes à la «quarta via»," *Rivista di Filosofia Neo-Scholastica* 70 (1978): 99. "Le problème de l'existence de Dieu n'est pas traité

an elaboration of the central notion of the Fourth Way, namely, that the limited perfections in things imply a reference to absolute perfections in which they participate. Van Steenberghen concludes that these commentaries reveal to us that the foundation of the Fourth Way is what he terms the "principle of participation."[56] In the commentary on the *Liber de causis,* for example, we find a language of participation that is reminiscent of the Fourth Way when Thomas notes that "the First Being is the measure of every being, since he has created all beings with the proper measure that is appropriate to every single thing according to the mode of its nature: indeed, [the fact] that some things approach him more or less *(magis vel minus),* is from [that thing's] disposition."[57] Here not only do we see the language of participation in Thomas's discussion of the more and the less approaching a most, but we also see the language of exemplarism in his discussion of measure and the measured. Indeed, one notion is seen to entail the other. This fact suggests that the Fourth Way is founded not merely upon the principle of participation but upon the notion of exemplarism as well.

Van Steenberghen is insistent that despite Thomas's references to Aristotle in the Fourth Way, the argument is fundamentally Neoplatonic.[58] He maintains that this fact is true, not merely as regards the first stage of the Fourth Way, but as regards the second as well. As he explains, the principle that Thomas enunciates in the second stage (viz., that the first in a genus is the cause of all that is found in that genus) is simply a formulation of the principle of

---

expressément dans ces deux écrits," Van Steenberghen explains, "mais ils méritent néanmoins de figurer au programme de cette enquête parce qu'on y trouve des éléments précieux pour l'exégèse de la *quarta via.*" Cf. Fabro, "Sviluppo, significato e valore della 'IV Via'," *Doctor* Communis 7 (1954): 84.

56. Van Steenberghen, "Prolégomènes," 112.

57. *In Lib. de caus.,* prop. 16 (Saffrey ed., 97:6–10): "Sed ipse exponit *ens primum esse mensuram* omnium *entium, quia creavit* omnia *entia* cum debita *mensura* quae convenit unicuique rei secundum modum suae naturae: quod enim aliqua magis vel minus accedant ad ipsum, est ex eius dispositione."

58. Van Steenberghen, "Prolégomènes," 99.

participation, and this genus principle is also found in the commentary on the *Liber de causis*.[59]

Having established to his satisfaction the existence of a *maxime ens*, Thomas proceeds in the second stage of the Fourth Way to argue that this being must be the cause of all the perfections mentioned in the first stage. He grounds the second stage upon the principle mentioned above, namely, that that which is the maximum in any genus is the cause of everything in that genus. The example of fire is offered to illustrate this principle: fire, it is claimed, is the maximum in the genus of heat and, as such, it is the cause of all hot things. The implication is that the *maxime ens* of the first stage is the maximum as regards all transcendental perfections such as goodness, truth, nobility, and even being itself. As such, not only is this being the standard by which all limited perfections are measured, but it is the very *cause* of their being *(esse)*; more precisely, it is because the *maxime ens* is the standard by which all such perfections are measured that this being is their agent cause.

In sum, the Fourth Way attempts to prove that God exists by proving that he is the cause of all transcendental and simple perfections, and it attempts to do this by focusing on two types of causality: exemplarism and efficiency. In the first stage of the Fourth Way, Thomas argues for the existence of a *maxime ens* that he presents as an exemplar for all the lesser degrees of perfection that approach it. In the second stage, he argues that this absolute max-

---

59. Ibid., 111. See *In Lib. de caus.*, prop. 16 (Saffrey ed., 97:3–6): "Primum in quolibet genere est mensura illius generis, in quantum, per accessum ad ipsum vel recessum ab ipso, cognoscitur aliquid esse perfectius vel minus perfectum in genere illo." Still we must recall that Thomas's explicit reference is not to the *Liber de* causis but to a text from *Metaphysics* 2 (993b25–31). However, it is a text that he misinterprets here by reversing its order. It should be noted that elsewhere Thomas presents this text in the correct order. For more on his usage of this text, see two articles by Vincent de Couesnongle, "La causalité du maximum. L'utilisation par S. Thomas d'un passage d'Aristote," *Revue des sciences philosophiques et théologiques* 38 (1954): 433–44, 658–80; "La causalité du maximum. Pourquoi Saint Thomas a-t-il mal cité Aristote?" *Revue des sciences philosophiques et théologiques* 38 (1954): 658–80.

imum must be the efficient cause of all of the perfections that approach it in likeness. It must be granted that he never explicitly mentions either of these two types of causality by name, but scholars are generally agreed that the argument is nonetheless referring to both. Where scholars differ, however, is in their interpretations of *how* these types of causality are present.

Some writers maintain that the first stage of the Fourth Way rests solely on exemplar causality. It is only in the second stage, they argue, that Thomas proceeds to show that the *maxime ens* is the efficient cause of all the limited perfections of which it is the exemplar. By contrast, others maintain that the first stage rests not only upon exemplar causality but upon efficient causality as well. They argue that things possessing transcendental perfections in a limited way could only receive such perfections from an efficient cause possessing them essentially.[60] This interpretation, however, is not supported by a literal reading of the text. Indeed, if we follow the text itself, the first stage of the argument appears to depend solely on exemplar causality with no reference either explicitly or implicitly to efficiency.[61] Nevertheless, both interpretations of the Fourth Way raise a peculiar question, namely, is the second stage of the argument a necessary part of this proof of God's existence?

60. For arguments in favor of the position that the first stage reasons from exemplar causality alone, see Van Steenberghen, *Le problème de l'existence de Dieu*, 241; Lucien Chambat, "La «Quarta Via» de Saint Thomas," *Revue Thomiste* 33 (1928): 421; Maquart, *Elementa*, 315; Wippel, *Metaphysical Thought*, 473; Louis Charlier, "Les cinq voies de saint Thomas: Leur structure métaphysique," in *L'existence de Dieu*, Cahiers de l'actualité religieuse 16 (Tournai and Paris, 1961), 181–227; Jules M. Brady, S.J., "Note on the Fourth Way," *The New Scholasticism* 48 (1974): 229; Little, *Platonic* Heritage, 62–80. For a discussion on this point, see Marion Wagner, *Die Philosophischen Implikate der "Quarta Via." Eine Untersuchung zum Vierten Gottesbeweis bei Thomas von Aquin (S. Th. I, 2, 3c)* (Leiden: E.J. Brill 1989), 29–37.

For arguments in favor of the position that the first stage argues from both exemplarism *and* efficient causality, see Maurice Corvez, "La quatrième voie vers l'existence de Dieu selon saint Thomas," in *Quinque sunt viae*, ed. Leo Elders (Vatican City, 1980), 75–83; Réginald Garrigou-Lagrange, *God: His Existence and His Nature*, vol. 1 (St. Louis and London: B. Herder, 1949), 301–17. For a summary of several recent authors who find both modes of causality present in the Fourth Way, see Bobik's article "Aquinas' Fourth Way."

61. Wippel, *Metaphysical Thought*, 473.

If the first stage of the Fourth Way proves the existence of an absolute maximum that measures all other things, it might seem as though the second stage is superfluous: why should Thomas continue a proof for the existence of God if he has already proven God's existence? Some commentators such as Cornelio Fabro attempt to resolve the apparent difficulty by maintaining that the argument in the first stage occurs in the formal order rather than in the real order of causal derivation.[62] Interpreted in this way, the Fourth Way would not be a proof *from* exemplarity since the first stage would not prove the actual existence of a *maxime ens*. According to this reading, it is only through the argument from efficiency in the second stage that the actual existence of this divine exemplar is demonstrated.

In response to this position, Van Steenberghen reminds us of the Neoplatonic influences on Thomas's argument. The principle of causality that is enunciated in the second stage of the proof, he maintains, is implied by the principle of participation that is enunciated in the first stage. Exemplarity and efficiency are two aspects of the same participation.[63] Van Steenberghen argues, therefore, that implicit in the first stage is the notion that the *maxime ens* is not only the measure of finite beings but is also their creative cause. According to this reading, the second stage of the argument is a development of the conclusion from the first.[64] For this reason, Van Steenberghen contends that the existence of God is already proven in the first stage by way of exemplarity. However, he insists that we should not thus consider the second stage superfluous; rather, we should view it as "facultative" (i.e., optional rather than necessary), an additional argument that reveals the full implications of the first stage.[65]

62. See, e.g., Fabro, "IV Via," 78, 84–85. R. Lavatori, "La quarta via di S. Tommaso d'Aquino secundo il principio dell'ordine," *Divinitas* 18 (1974): 62–87.

63. We will consider the role of exemplarity in Thomas's doctrine of participation in chap. 6.

64. Van Steenberghen, *Le problème de l'existence de Dieu*, 222.

65. Ibid., 211. As further evidence of the "facultative" nature of the second part of the Fourth Way, Van Steenberghen draws the reader's attention to the fact that this ad-

A similar conclusion is reached by Arthur Little. Little sees the second stage of the Fourth Way as a corollary to the first. The first stage, he argues, proves that the degrees of perfection found in limited beings necessitate the existence of an absolute maximum. From this conclusion, the second stage supposedly reveals a corollary, namely, that an analogy exists between that which is maximal and the less perfect things that imitate it—an analogy that always "prerequires" a relationship of efficient causality. He maintains, however, that the analogy itself can be known before this causal relationship is known. Little's view of the Fourth Way, therefore, is that "the proof is completed by exemplary causality alone before the reference to Aristotle's *Metaphysics.* In this way St. Thomas ascends from creatures to God."[66]

Although the Fourth Way makes no mention of either exemplar or efficient causality, it is clear from the text that both modes of causality are implicitly present. The Fourth Way argues from the limited perfections that are found in created things to the existence of an absolute standard that they imitate. As we saw in chapter 1, however, the notion of assimilation is central to the character of exemplarism. Indeed, the fundamental characteristic that Thomas repeatedly attributes to an exemplar is that it is "that in the likeness of which something is made." In light of this notion, the *maxime ens* of the Fourth Way bears the clear character of an exemplar in relation to the limited beings that approximate it.

Furthermore, as we also saw in chapter 1, implicit in the notion of exemplarism is the notion of efficient causality, for if something is made in the likeness of an exemplar, there must be a *maker* to make that thing—there must be an efficient cause. In short, with-

---

ditional argument is absent in a parallel text in the *Summa Contra Gentiles* I, c. 13 (Leonine ed., vol. 13.33–34).

66. Little, *Platonic Heritage*, 67. Linwood Urban offers a unique interpretation of the Fourth Way, arguing that it can be explicated in terms of both efficient and exemplar causality, as well as final causality ("Understanding St. Thomas's Fourth Way," *History of Philosophy Quarterly* 1 [1984]: 283 ff.).

out efficient causality there can be no exemplarity. Hence, the second stage of the Fourth Way illustrates the fact that the *maxime ens* acts, not only as an exemplar for the limited beings that approximate it, but also as their efficient cause. Indeed, not much later in the *Prima Pars,* we find Thomas acknowledging the interrelationship of exemplar and efficient causality in discussing the perfection of goodness. In answer to the question "Whether all things are good by the divine goodness?" Thomas explains that "Everything is called good from the divine goodness, as from the first exemplar, effective, and final principle of all goodness."[67]

But is the Fourth Way an argument from exemplarity, or is it an argument from efficient causality? Van Steenberghen's textual evidence from Thomas's Neoplatonic commentaries provides strong evidence that it is the former. Although the Fourth Way does make explicit mention of Aristotle, it is nonetheless founded upon a Neoplatonic principle of participation that reveals the exemplarist character of the proof.[68] Indeed, Van Steenberghen's interpretation is supported by the very text on the perfection of goodness that we have just considered. Presupposing his earlier proofs of God's existence, Thomas explains in this article that "From the First, through its essence [as] Being and Good, every single thing can be called good and a being, *inasmuch as it participates in it by way of a certain assimilation,* although remotely and deficiently."[69]

In this article considering the perfection of goodness, then, we find not only the notion of exemplarity, but that of participation as

---

67. *ST* I, q. 6, a. 4 (Leonine ed., vol. 4.70): "Sic ergo unumquodque dicitur bonum bonitate divina, sicut primo principio exemplari, effectivo et finali totius bonitatis."

68. One possible reading is that these texts from the *Metaphysics* are themselves Platonic in inspiration.

69. *ST* I, q. 6, a. 4 (Leonine ed., vol. 4.70): "Et quamvis haec opinio irrationabilis videatur quantum ad hoc, quod ponebat species rerum naturalium separatas per se subsistentes, ut Aristoteles multipliciter probat; tamen hoc absolute verum est, quod aliquid est primum, quod per suam essentiam est ens et bonum, quod dicimus Deum, ut ex superioribus patet. Huic etiam sententiae concordat Aristoteles. A primo igitur per suam essentiam ente et bono, unumquodque potest dici bonum et ens, inquantum participat ipsum per modum cuiusdam assimilationis, licet remote et deficienter, ut ex superioribus patet." Emphasis added in translation.

well, supporting Van Steenberghen's reading. Still, his interpretation suggests difficulties regarding the validity of the Fourth Way. One difficulty that Van Steenberghen himself observes concerns the principle that where there is a more and a less there must be a maximum; this principle is borrowed from a doctrine of participation that in fact concerns a unique relationship found only in a creature's total dependence upon God. There is no commensurate example in nature; the one that Thomas offers of fire is an outdated notion. The principle can only be established once the existence of God has already been proven.[70]

Another difficulty that arises from reading the Fourth Way in light of Thomas's doctrine of participation concerns the types of causality that are involved. As we have seen, the first stage of the Fourth Way concludes to a maximum being without any appeal to efficient causality. Thomas's doctrine of participation, however, posits that participated being is efficiently caused.[71] It would be impossible, therefore, to justify the first stage of the argument in light of participation without bringing in efficient causality. But to bring in efficient causality to defend the first stage would involve a serious reinterpretation of the Fourth Way. For these reasons, I find that the first stage of the argument does not succeed in its attempt to prove that such an exemplar exists.[72]

Even though the Fourth Way does not successfully prove the existence of God as exemplar cause, this much is true: Thomas himself sees it as a route to proving that there is such a thing as divine exemplarism. The methodology of the Fourth Way, moreover, differs from that of the three arguments for the existence of divine ideas that we considered above. All three of those arguments attempt at one stage or another to deduce the existence of the divine ideas from God's nature. By contrast, the Fourth Way attempts to

70. Van Steenberghen, *Le problème de l'existence de Dieu*, 225.
71. We will discuss Thomas's doctrine of participation in more detail in chap. 6.
72. For Wippel's criticisms of the first stage, see his *Metaphysical Thought*, 474–79.

deduce the existence of a divine exemplar from the limited perfections found in finite beings.[73]

Furthermore, the exemplar whose existence the Fourth Way proves is a different sort of exemplar than those presented in the arguments from natural teleology, divine similitude, and divine self-knowledge. This fact becomes apparent when we consider the manner of exemplification described in the Fourth Way. As we have seen, this exemplarism concerns perfections that can be possessed in diverse degrees. Consequently, as Van Steenberghen observes, "this excludes *univocal* perfections, genera and species: something is not more or less triangle, animal, man, *etc.*"[74] But such univocal perfections are precisely what the divine ideas exemplify.[75] How, then, do we account for this difference in divine exemplarism?

The answer lies in a distinction that Thomas provides in book I of his commentary on the *Sentences.* In d. 19, q. 5, a. 2, he considers whether all things are called true by an uncreated truth. An objector argues that if we say that the exemplar form that makes all things true exists in God, we are presented with an absurdity: just as the exemplar of truth would be in God, so too would the exemplar of color. Hence, if all things should be called true because they are exemplified by a form that is in God, it would seem that all things should also be colored, which is clearly false.[76]

73. The methodology of the Fourth Way also differs from that of the *via abstractionis* of which Thomas is critical. Although Neoplatonic in character, Thomas's argument does not move from the mental order to the real order but from limited perfections to absolute perfections. Thus, the absolute perfections to which it concludes are not subsisting universals. As Henle explains, the maximum described by Thomas in the Fourth Way is not a logical concept but, instead, is "an ontological fullness that outreaches any possible human conception" (Henle, *Thomas and Platonism*, 356).

74. Van Steenberghen, *Le problème de l'existence de Dieu,* 209. "Quelles sont ces autres perfections du même genre? Il s'agit des perfections qui peuvent exister à *des degrés divers* (ceci exclut les perfections *univoques,* genres et espèces: on n'est pas plus ou moins triangle, animal, homme etc.)." Cf. Van Steenberghen, "Prolégomènes," 106.

75. See, e.g., *ST* I, q. 15, a. 3, obj. and ad 3 (Leonine ed., vol. 4.204). We will consider in more detail in chap. 4 whether the divine ideas properly exemplify genera, species, or singulars.

76. *In I Sent.,* d. 19, q. 5, a. 2, obj. 4 (Mandonnet ed., vol. 1.491).

To this objection, Thomas replies that the exemplar of things exists in God in two ways. In the first way, an exemplar is in him as that which is in his intellect. His ideas are thus the exemplars of all the things that he makes, just as the exemplars of works of art exist in the mind of the artisan. In the second way, however, the exemplar of things is in God as that which is in his nature (in natura sua), as his goodness is the exemplar of everything that is good. It is in this sense that the exemplar of truth is in him. Thus, Thomas responds to his objector, God is not the exemplar of color and truth in the same way.[77] With this distinction, we see that God is the exemplar form of things both as regards his ideas (rationes ideales) and as regards his attributes (attributa), that is, all the transcendental and simple perfections that he possesses.[78]

That there could be two types of divine exemplarism is not surprising if we recall the three different types of exemplars Thomas identifies. As we saw in chapter 1, he mentions (1) intellectual ex-

---

77. In I Sent., d. 19, q. 5, a. 2, ad 4 (Mandonnet ed., vol. 1.493).

78. In I Sent., d. 2, q. 1, a. 2 (Mandonnet ed., vol. 1.62–63). For a detailed consideration of the distinction between these two modes of divine exemplarism, see Federico Balmaceda, "La Doble Causalidad Ejemplar Divina en Santo Tomás de Aquino," Philosophica 9–10 (1986–87): 155–66. In his later works, Thomas does not explicitly refer to the exemplarism of the divine attributes as much, although he acknowledges it implicitly. For example, in the Summa theologiae, when he considers whether the image of God is to be found in irrational creatures, Thomas explains that the word "image" (imago) can be used in two respects. According to the first respect, it refers to the likeness by which a work of art imitates the species in the mind of the artisan. In this sense, every creature is an image of an exemplar (imago rationis exemplaris) that is in the mind of God. According to the second respect, "image" refers to a likeness in nature (similitudinem in natura). In this respect, Thomas explains, "all things are alike to the First Being inasmuch as they are beings; and to the first Life inasmuch as they are living things; and to the Highest Wisdom inasmuch as they are intelligent beings" (ST I, q. 93, a. 2, ad 4 [Leonine ed., vol. 5.403]: "Sic autem non loquimur nunc de imagine: sed secundum quod attenditur secundum similitudinem in natura; prout scilicet primo enti assimilantur omnia, inquantum sunt entia; et primae vitae, inquantum sunt viventia; et summae sapientiae, inquantum sunt intelligentia.").

Here, then, Thomas draws a distinction between the divine ideas and the divine attributes but this time considered in the context of the image rather than of the exemplar itself. What becomes apparent is that he now tends to reserve the term "exemplar" principally for intellectual exemplars, or ideas. This could explain why in the later Summa he does not mention exemplarism by name in the Fourth Way.

emplars, which are the ideas in the mind of an artisan; (2) external exemplars, which are the models, or real beings, in imitation of which the artisan produces his works; and (3) natural exemplars, which are the forms of natural agents in likeness of which their effects are made. In their role as ontological principles, the divine ideas are clearly intellectual exemplars, but what about the divine attributes? We can quickly conclude that Thomas does not consider them also to be intellectual exemplars since he contrasts these attributes with the divine ideas. We can also quickly conclude that he does not consider them to be external exemplars since he notes that they are *in* the divine nature. By a process of elimination then, we are left with the conclusion that Thomas considers the divine attributes to be natural exemplars of a sort.

Still, this conclusion seems to raise a problem. From what we saw in chapter 1, a natural exemplar is nothing other than the form of the agent. Thomas, however, identifies a multiplicity of divine attributes. Does this mean that the exemplarism of the divine attributes entails multiple exemplars? If so, then it would seem that there would have to be several agents involved for the attributes to be "natural exemplars." Thomas provides an answer to this question in the *De veritate*. There, he notes that the divine ideas signify God's knowledge of his essence inasmuch as it is imitable; by contrast, the divine attributes signify the divine essence *itself*. Whereas the divine ideas signify a multiplicity of things (viz., the different proportions that creatures have to the divine essence), the divine attributes signify only *one* thing even though they are conceptually distinct. In short, the divine attributes are nothing other than the divine nature: God is his goodness, his truth, his unity, and so forth.[79] The exemplarism of the divine attributes, therefore, is simply the exemplarism of the one divine essence acting as a "natural exemplar."[80]

79. *De ver.*, q. 3, a. 2, ad 2 (Leonine ed., vol. 22.1.105:229–43). We will discuss the multiplicity of divine ideas and their relationship to the divine essence in more detail in chap. 3.

80. The fact that effects imitating the divine nature would not share an exact like-

The distinction between these two types of divine exemplar-ism provides an insight into the type of exemplar presented in the Fourth Way. There Thomas is proving the existence of a God whose essence is a natural exemplar of the transcendental and simple perfections in all finite beings. Regardless of whether the Fourth Way is a valid proof, therefore, it is not intended to prove the existence of divine ideas.

If we are to consider the Five Ways, it is the Fifth Way, rather than the Fourth, that proves the existence of divine ideas—at least implicitly. In the Fifth Way, we find the key elements that are present in Thomas's *De veritate* definition of the term "idea":

The Fifth Way is taken from the governance of things. We see that some things that lack cognition (viz., natural bodies) act for an end, which is clear from the fact that they act always or more frequently in the same way in order to attain what is best. Hence, it is clear that they attain the end, not by chance, but from intention. But those things that do not have cognition do not tend to an end unless directed by something knowing and intelligent, as the arrow [is directed] by the archer. Therefore, there is some intelligence by which all natural things are ordered to an end. And this we call God.[81]

---

ness to it does not contradict the notion that the divine nature is a type of natural ex-emplar. Here we can draw an analogy between the created order and the uncreated order. As Thomas explains, "In created things, some can be called the exemplars of others because they are in the likeness of others, either according to the same species or according to the analogy of some imitation." (*ST* I, q. 44, a. 3 [Leonine ed., vol. 4.460]: "Possunt etiam in rebus creatis quaedam aliorum exemplaria dici, secundum quod quaedam sunt ad similitudinem aliorum, vel secundum eandem speciem, vel se-cundum analogiam alicuius imitationis"). Thus, the form of a man is the natural ex-emplar of his offspring, which is of the same species; by contrast, the sun is the natural exemplar of all the things it illuminates "according to the analogy of imitation" (see, e.g., *ST* I, q. 4, a. 2 [Leonine ed., vol. 4.51–52]). Thomas considers the divine nature to be an exemplar in the latter sense.

We will examine the exemplarism of the divine nature in more detail in chaps. 4 and 6.

81. *ST* I, q. 2, a. 3 (Leonine ed., vol. 4.32): "Quinta via sumitur ex gubernatione rerum. Videmus enim quod aliqua quae cognitione carent, scilicet corpora naturalia, operantur propter finem: quod apparet ex hoc quod semper aut frequentius eodem modo operantur, ut consequantur id quod est optimum; unde patet quod non a casu, sed ex intentione perveniunt ad finem. Ea autem quae non habent cognitionem, non

As with the Fourth Way, there is no explicit mention of the divine exemplars in this argument. Nevertheless, given Thomas's definition of what constitutes exemplar ideas, their existence is implicitly proven. As we have seen, he defines an exemplar as a form that something imitates because of the intention of an agent who predetermines the end for himself. In the Fifth Way, we find the same argument from natural teleology that we considered above: the directedness of natural bodies points to the need for a governor who provides them with their intention toward an end.[82] And this governor can only do so if he is intelligent. As with the Fourth Way, however, Thomas's principal concern here is to prove, not the existence of divine exemplars, but the existence of God himself. Hence, he does not draw the consequent conclusion that is implied by this argument, namely, that God could only direct things to an end in light of exemplar ideas. Nevertheless, if we follow Thomas's reasoning from his other teleological arguments, the Fifth Way implicitly acknowledges exemplar ideas to account for the directedness of things.[83]

---

tendunt in finem nisi directa ab aliquo cognoscente et intelligente, sicut sagitta a sagittante. Ergo est aliquid intelligens, a quo omnes res naturales ordinantur ad finem: et hoc dicimus Deum."

82. This similarity between the Fifth Way and what I have termed the argument from natural teleology is acknowledged by Fabro, although he does not comment upon its significance for Thomas's doctrine of the divine ideas ("IV Via," 74).

83. In commenting on the Fifth Way, Van Steenberghen recognizes this implicit role of the divine ideas in Thomas's argument. The Fifth Way, he explains, considers the good of the universe, "auquel chaque être de la nature concourt selon sa nature: des textes fort clairs de S. Thomas le montrent, celui-ci par exemple: *Illud quod est optimum in rebus existens est bonum ordinis universi.*" The text that he cites as evidence is *ST* I, q. 15, a. 2 (Leonine ed., vol. 4.201–2), in which Thomas demonstrates that there must be a plurality of divine ideas to account for the order of the universe (Van Steenberghen, *Le problème de l'existence de Dieu*, 231). Although the Fifth Way argues for the existence of an intelligence that we call God, it is not until q. 14 that Thomas explicitly proves that God is intelligent.

THE DIVINE IDEAS AS INTENTIONAL
SIMILITUDES

What remains consistent in all of the arguments Thomas offers to prove the existence of divine ideas is not only the conclusion that they exist, but also that they exist within the mind of God. This latter conclusion prompts Norris Clarke to observe that with Thomas's doctrine of exemplarism, there is a clear break from Platonism: "The die is cast. The divine ideas are no longer the very forms, the true being, of creatures, but their *intentional similitudes,* whose only being is that of the one divine act of knowing."[84] Thomas makes this point clear whenever he discusses the divine ideas.

Considering the nature of exemplar ideas, Thomas maintains that it is impossible for them to exist in any way other than in a mind: an idea is that which is understood *(intellectum),* but that which is understood must exist in an intellect. Since the forms of natural things cannot exist without matter, neither are they understood without matter. Hence, contrary to Plato's position, exemplar ideas cannot be self-subsistent.[85] Considering the divine nature, Thomas reminds us that God does not act for any end other than himself. Since an exemplar idea has, in a certain sense, the nature of an end, the divine ideas could only exist within God's mind.[86] If God *were* to consider external exemplars, the perfection of his understanding would be dependent upon something other than himself and so would his being *(esse)* since his being is his act of understanding. Thus, his intellect would be in potency and would require something to reduce it to act. But this is impossible, Aquinas concludes, for it would imply that there is something that is prior to God, which is absurd.[87]

Thomas is confident, furthermore, that this doctrine of ideas is not contrary to the teachings of Aristotle. He asserts (without sup-

---

84. Clarke, "Reality and Multiplicity," 122. Emphasis added.
85. *SCG* I, c. 51 and c. 52 (Leonine ed., vol. 13.148).
86. *De ver.,* q. 3, a. 1 (Leonine ed., vol. 22.1.100:254–61).
87. *SCG* I, c. 51 and c. 52 (Leonine ed., vol. 13.148).

porting evidence) that the Stagirite did not intend to deny the existence of ideas in the mind of God but only the notion of natural forms existing in themselves without matter, as had been posited by Plato.[88] Thomas maintains that even though the doctrine of divine ideas also posits forms existing apart from matter, it does not contradict this Aristotelian position: natural forms cannot exist immaterially of themselves, but they can acquire an immateriality from the one in whom they exist. This is evident with our own intellects in which they exist in an immaterial way, and so such forms can also exist in an immaterial way in the divine intellect.[89]

Josef Pieper thus observes that for Aquinas, "The essence of things is that they are creatively thought. . . . It was, as it seems, St. Thomas's view that the notion that things have an essence cannot be separated from the other notion: that this essential character is the fruit of a form-giving thought that plans, devises, and creates."[90] Returning to Thomas's artistic analogy, we can observe that works of art attest not only to the existence of the artisan but also to the presence of ideas within his mind; so too, we have seen in this chapter that the existence and nature of finite beings reveal in turn the existence of a divine artisan and ideas within *his* mind. Unlike the human artisan, however, whose ideas are originally derived in some way from the external world, God's ideas are not derived from anywhere other than himself. The divine ideas, therefore, must somehow be present in his very essence. Given the simplicity of that essence, we will need to consider next how Thomas is able to account for a multiplicity of ideas within the mind of God.

88. *In I Sent.,* d. 36, q. 2, a. 1, obj. 1 and ad 1 (Mandonnet ed., vol. 1.838 and 840). Cf. *ST* I, q. 15, a. 1, obj. 1 and ad 1 (Leonine ed., vol. 4.199).

89. *De ver.,* q. 3, a. 1, ad 4 (Leonine ed., vol. 22.1.101:301–9).

90. Josef Pieper, *The Silence of St. Thomas,* trans. John Murray, S.J. and Daniel O'Connor (New York: Pantheon Books, Inc., 1957), 51. Pieper goes on to observe that "This interrelation is foreign to modern Rationalism. Why, it would argue, can we not think of the 'nature' of plants and the 'nature' of men without needing also to consider that these 'natures' are called into being by thought? Modern thinking habits can make nothing of the suggestion that there could be no such 'nature' unless it were thus creatively thought" (ibid., 51–52).

THREE

THE MULTIPLICITY
OF DIVINE IDEAS

⌒

The arguments that we considered in the last chapter present the divine ideas as principles accounting for the order of the created universe. As we saw, Thomas argues that from the ideas, the diverse things of our experience receive their determinate forms. That there *is* a diversity of formed beings suggests that there must also be a corresponding diversity of divine ideas. Indeed, this is Thomas's very position. It is a position, however, that presents a philosophical problem: If God is a perfectly simple being (as Aquinas holds), how can a multiplicity of ideas exist within his mind?[1]

From his earliest works, Thomas recognizes that this problem requires a solution. It is a problem to which he

1. Regarding God's simplicity, see, e.g., *In I Sent.*, d. 8, q. 4, a. 1 (Mandonnet ed., vol. 1.218–20); *SCG* I, c. 16 (Leonine ed., vol. 13.44–45); *ST* I, q. 3, a. 7 (Leonine ed., vol. 4.46–47). Christopher Hughes, *On a Complex Theory of a Simple God* (Ithaca, N.Y.: Cornell University Press, 1989), esp. 107–50; Norman Kretzmann, *The Metaphysics of Theism* (Oxford: Clarendon Press, 1997), 169–73; Wippel, *Metaphysical Thought,* 486–87; Garrigou-Lagrange, *God*, vol. 1, 43 ff.; Brian Davies, "Classical Theism and the Doctrine of Divine Simplicity," in *Language, Meaning and God,* ed. Brian Davies (London: Geoffrey Chapman, 1987), 51–74; David B. Burrell, "Distinguishing God from the World," in Davies, ed., *Language, Meaning and God,* 75–91.

returns time and again over the course of his career, and his general approach to resolving it varies little from work to work. Nevertheless, variations do occur in his presentations, so it is worth our while to look at the historical development in the relevant texts. At the conclusion of the textual analysis that follows below, I will provide a summary of how he resolves this problem regarding the multiplicity of divine ideas.

TEXTUAL ANALYSIS

In I Sententias (1252–1256)

In the commentary on the *Sentences,* the issue of the unity of God's knowledge is raised before Thomas even begins to address the divine ideas. In d. 35, q. 1, a. 2, he considers whether God knows things other than himself. Concluding that he does, Thomas then explains how this is possible by presenting an analogy from sight. The first object of sight is the species of the visible thing that exists in the pupil of the eye. This object is the perfection of the person who sees and is a principle of the act of seeing, as the medium by which the thing outside the eye is seen. The second object of sight is the extra-ocular thing. Similarly, with intellectual cognition the first intelligible object is the likeness of the thing as it exists in the intellect, whereas the second object is the external thing that is understood through this likeness.[2]

Regarding the first object of the intellect, Thomas explains that God understands nothing other than himself since he does not receive the species of things that he knows; rather, he knows his own essence, which is the likeness of all things. If, however, we consider the second object of the intellect, then God has knowledge not merely of himself but of other things as well.[3] In reply to an ob-

---

2. *In I Sent.,* d. 35, q. 1, a. 2 (Mandonnet ed., vol. 1.814–15). Wippel, *Divine Ideas,* 3–4.

3. *In I Sent.,* d. 35, q. 1, a. 2 (Mandonnet ed., vol. 1.814–15). Regarding this passage,

jection that follows, Thomas notes that God's essence thus acts as one simple medium through which he knows all things.[4] In a subsequent article considering whether the things that are known by God exist in God, Aquinas explains that the creatures God knows can be in him without causing diversity precisely because they exist in him through his likeness.[5]

In d. 36, Thomas reiterates his position that the divine essence is the medium of God's knowledge. There, in q. 2, a. 1, he asks what the name "idea" signifies. In the course of this consideration, he observes that divine ideas exist both as exemplars and as contemplating forms (contemplantes formas): the former belonging to God's practical knowledge, the latter to his speculative knowledge.[6] In reply to the third objection, Thomas tells us that God knows created things through these ideas rather than through the very essences of created things. As he explains, the medium through which a thing is known is united to the knower. Since the essences of created things are separate from God, they cannot be the medium by which he knows those things; rather, he knows them through a nobler medium, namely, his own essence. God thus knows in a more perfect and nobler manner than we do because nothing other than his essence is the principle of his knowing.[7]

In a. 2 of the same question, Thomas considers whether there is a multiplicity of divine ideas. In his *sed contra,* he affirms that there is indeed such a multiplicity, citing the authority of Augustine's *83 Diverse Questions.*[8] He then proceeds in his reply to defend this position.

Wippel observes that "While the emphasis here is on God's knowledge, the reference to his essence as a likeness of things at least adumbrates the theme of exemplarity" (Wippel, *Divine Ideas,* 3–4).

4. *In I Sent.,* d. 35, q. 1, a. 2, ad 4 (Mandonnet ed., vol. 1.815).

5. *In I Sent.,* d. 36, q. 1, a. 3, ad 1 (Mandonnet ed., vol. 1.836).

6. *In I Sent.,* d. 36, q. 2, a. 1, ad 1 (Mandonnet ed., vol. 1.839–40).

7. *In I Sent.,* d. 36, q. 2, a. 1, ad 3 (Mandonnet ed., vol. 1.840).

8. See *De div. qq. 83,* 46 (Corpus Christianorum. Series Latina [hereafter abbreviated CCSL], vol. 50.1.70). As the title of this work indicates, it consists of eighty-three different questions. Augustine composed it between 388 and 396, later editing the work in book form. It addresses both theological and philosophical questions that originat-

Since God has a proper knowledge of singular things, his essence must be the likeness of those things. Created things imitate God's essence in different and particular ways according to the capacity of the divine essence. Although that essence is fully imitable in itself, however, it is not imitated perfectly by any one creature; rather, it is imitated in a manifold manner *(difformiter)*, due to the diversity and deficiency of creatures, as Dionysius observes.[9] The name "idea" is thus applied to God's essence inasmuch as his essence is an exemplar imitated by creatures, for it acts as the proper idea of each thing according to that thing's determined mode of imitation.

Thomas explains that since the divine essence *is* imitated differently by different creatures, a man is said to be created by a different idea or notion *(idea vel ratio)* than is a horse. Thus, although God's essence is one, there are nevertheless many ideas since it is imitated by different things in different ways. There are many ideas, moreover, because God understands his essence as imitable in *this* way or *that* way. Indeed, it is the very understanding of these ways that constitutes the ideas, for a form is an idea—not simply as it exists in the knower, but as it is understood by him.[10]

If the divine ideas can be reduced to the one divine essence, we might ask why we should speak of many ideas at all. Thomas tells us in his replies to objections. Responding to the first objection, he explains that the term "idea" does not refer simply to God's essence, which is indeed one, but to that essence *as imitable*. Since there is a manifold imitability in the divine essence according to

---

ed in conversations with friends. The forty-sixth of these questions, entitled *De Ideis,* addresses the divine ideas (Boland, *Ideas in God,* 39, 45). The influence of this work on Thomas's doctrine of divine ideas will be discussed in more detail below. See the summary at the end of this section as well as n. 60.

9. *The Divine Names,* II, 6,644B–D, in *Pseudo-Dionysius: The Complete Works,* trans. Colm Luibheid, with notes by Paul Rorem (New York: Paulist Press, 1987), 63.

10. *In I Sent.,* d. 36, q. 2, a. 2 (Mandonnet ed., vol. 1.841–42). As Wippel notes, "The notion that a divine idea expresses God's understanding of his essence as imitable is crucial, just as is the point that the divine essence is imitated in different ways by different creatures and therefore bears a different relationship to each" (Wippel, *Divine Ideas,* 9).

the fullness of its perfection, there are accordingly many ideas. Responding to the third objection, he explains that even though this multiplicity is discerned from the relationships that the divine essence has to diverse things, the diversity of things is not the cause of the diversity of ideas; rather, the contrary is the case: it is because God knows his essence as imitable in diverse ways that there are diverse things.[11]

The fourth objection claims that there is only one idea because God has only one knowledge *(scientia)*. Thomas responds by drawing a distinction between various terms. Whatever signifies the divine essence itself cannot be diverse. Hence, there is only one knowledge in God because the term "knowledge" *(scientia)* refers more to the knower than to that which is known. By contrast, the term "notion" *(ratio)* refers more to that which is known; hence it can be used in the plural. But the term "idea" holds a middle position between these other two terms since it signifies both God's essence *and* the characteristic of imitation *(ratio imitationis)*. Hence, it too can be used in the plural.[12]

In this early work, then, we see that Thomas clearly defends the multiplicity of the divine ideas. It is a multiplicity that involves God's knowledge of his essence as imitable in different respects. The ideas, therefore, are not really distinct either from God or from one another. They are not really distinct from God precisely because they are his very essence. Yet, they are logically distinct from him because they signify something in addition to the divine essence. Again, the ideas are not really distinct from one another precisely because they have no reality apart from the divine essence. Yet, they are logically distinct from each other because one idea signifies something different than does another, as Thomas illustrates regarding the idea of a man versus that of a horse.

11. *In I Sent.,* d. 36, q. 2, a. 2, ad 1 and ad 3 (Mandonnet ed., vol. 1.842–43).
12. *In I Sent.,* d. 36, q. 2, a. 2, ad 4 (Mandonnet ed., vol. 1.843). On this point, see Boland, *Ideas in God,* 203.

De veritate, q. 3 (1256–1257)

In the *De veritate,* Thomas addresses the multiplicity of the divine ideas again in q. 3, a. 2. He begins by rejecting the position of certain Islamic philosophers that God intends and causes only one thing, what Thomas refers to as "creature in general." According to this view, all distinction between creatures would be brought about by secondary causes. Hence, God would have only one idea common to all creation while the proper ideas for individual things would exist in their secondary causes.[13] Aquinas responds that if God had only the idea of creature in general, he could intend to create only in a general way. The consequence would be that all distinction between creatures would occur by chance. It is impossible, however, for creatures to be related only accidentally to the first cause. Thus, all distinction between them must be predefined by God, each thing in light of its proper notion *(propria ratio).* For this reason, there must be many ideas.[14]

Having established the existence of a plurality of ideas in the divine mind, Thomas proceeds to explain why this plurality does not contradict the divine simplicity. He begins by drawing a distinction between two modes by which a form can exist in the intellect. According to the first mode, a form can exist there as the *principle* of the act of understanding. In this respect, the form is present in the one who understands precisely insofar as he does understand; taken in this way, the form is the likeness of the thing that is understood. According to the second mode, a form can exist in the intellect as the *terminus* of understanding. In this respect, the form

---

13. *De ver.,* q. 3, a. 2 (Leonine ed., vol. 22.1.103:108–24). See Avicenna, *Philosophia prima* IX, c. 4, in *Avicenna Latinus: Liber de philosophia prima sive scientia divina V–X,* ed. Simone Van Riet (Louvain: Peeters and Leiden: Brill, 1980), 481–84; Algazel, *Algazel's Metaphysics: A Medieval Translation,* ed. Rev. J. T. Muckle, C.S.B. (Toronto: The Institute of Medieval Studies, 1933) I, 5 (119–29:44v–48v); Averroes, *Destructio Destructionum philosophiae Algazelis,* ed. Beatrice H. Zedler (Milwaukee: The Marquette University Press, 1961), III (175–80:23ra–24ra).

14. *De ver.,* q. 3, a. 2 (Leonine ed., vol. 22.1.103–4:124–57).

is not a principle of the act of understanding (since it is itself produced by such an act), but is rather that which is understood; it is
by means of such a form that the knower makes something.

To clarify this distinction, Thomas gives the example of the
form of "house" as it exists in the mind of an artisan: according to
the first mode of thinking, this form is the principle "by which" *(a
quo)* the artisan understands what a house is; according to the second mode, it is "that which" *(quod)* the artisan understands, and
it is by means of the latter type of form that he makes the house.
Thomas adds as an aside that if it were possible for an artisan to
produce a work according to the likeness of his very intellect, his
intellect would *itself* be an idea—not as an intellect, however, but
as understood by the artisan.[15]

As regards the work that is produced by the artisan, sometimes
it perfectly imitates his ideas. When it does, his productive intellect has as an idea of the very form of the thing imitated precisely
as the form of that thing. But sometimes the work does not perfectly imitate the artisan's idea. When that happens, his productive intellect does not understand *(acciperet)* the form of the thing made
as an idea or exemplar in an absolute way; rather, it understands
that form together with a determined relation according to the degree to which the thing imitates and falls short of its exemplar.[16]

Thomas next applies all of these observations to the divine intellect. In making things by means of his intellect, God makes
them according to the likeness of his essence. In this way, the idea
of things *is* God's essence—but not without qualification. Rather,
his essence is an idea inasmuch as it is known. (Although Thomas does not explicitly state it, one can infer from what he said ear-

15. *De ver.,* q. 3, a. 2 (Leonine ed., vol. 22.1.104:158–83). In this passage, Thomas also
explains how these two modes are found in an analogous sense in the speculative intellect (on this point, see Wippel, *Divine Ideas,* 17). The aside mentioned above foreshad-
ows his account of the way God's intellect is the idea of the things he makes, as we will
discuss immediately below.

16. *De ver.,* q. 3, a. 2 (Leonine ed., vol. 22.1.104:183–200). On this point, see Branick,
"Unity of the Divine Ideas," 179.

lier that the divine essence is presented to God's intellect in this respect as the terminus of his act of understanding rather than as the principle of that act.)[17] Having drawn this distinction, Thomas then notes that created things do not perfectly imitate the divine essence. In knowing them, therefore, God does not understand his essence unqualifiedly, but rather according to the proportion, or relationship, that creatures have to it—that is, according to the degree that creatures fall short of perfectly imitating him.[18]

Thomas concludes from the foregoing that there must be a diversity of ideas to account for the diversity of creatures. As he explains, different things imitate the divine essence in different ways, for each thing has its own being (esse) distinct from that of every other thing. Hence, each thing imitates the divine essence according to its proper manner. The one divine essence thus acts as the idea for everything that God makes, but it does so differently for different things according to the relationship that each thing bears to it. Since there is a diversity of such relationships, there must also necessarily be a diversity of ideas. If we consider the divine essence as it is in itself, then it is true that there is only one idea imitated by all things; but if we consider the various relationships that creatures have to that essence, there are many ideas.[19]

Thomas develops this account further in his replies to objections. In response to the second objection, he draws a key distinction between God's essential attributes and his ideas. As we saw in chapter 2, attributes such as goodness, wisdom, and power in God refer in their primary context to nothing other than the one divine essence, even though they are logically distinct from each other. For this reason, Thomas explains, these attributes are not plural—although by means of them, God can be referred to creatures. Thus, with reference to his goodness, God produces creatures that

17. Wippel, Divine Ideas, 18–19.

18. De ver., q. 3, a. 2 (Leonine ed., vol. 22.1.104–5:200–209).

19. De ver., q. 3, a. 2 (Leonine ed., vol. 22.1.105:209–19). Cf. De ver., q. 2, a. 4, ad 2 (Leonine ed., vol. 22.1.57–58:192–223).

are good, and with reference to his wisdom, he produces ones that are wise. By contrast, an idea principally signifies something *in addition to* the divine essence, namely, the relationship that creatures have to it. Thomas emphasizes that it is *this* notion that formally completes the character of what constitutes an idea, and it is for this reason that there are said to be many ideas.[20] In response to the sixth objection, he acknowledges that all created things are reduced to the one first form that is the divine essence. Nevertheless, there is still a multiplicity of ideas in this sense: in considering his essence, God "discovers" *(adinvenit),* as it were, the different ways in which that essence can be imitated.[21]

In the ninth objection, it is argued that the sort of intellect that understands by means of many things is composed and moves from one thing to another. These traits, however, are far removed from the divine intellect; hence, it seems that there cannot be many ideas in God. In response to this objection, Thomas again employs his distinction between the first and second acts of understanding, observing that an idea (presumably either divine or human) is not "that by which" *(a quo)* a thing is first understood but rather is "that which" *(quod)* is understood as it exists in the intellect. The uniformity of understanding, however, follows the unity of *that by which* a thing is first understood, just as the unity of action follows

20. *De ver.,* q. 3, a. 2, ad 2 (Leonine ed., vol. 22.1.105:229–43).

21. *De ver.,* q. 3, a. 2, ad 6 (Leonine ed., vol. 22.1.105:277–82): "Una prima forma ad quam omnia reducuntur est ipsa divina essentia secundum se considerata, ex cuius consideratione intellectus divinus adinvenit, ut ita dicam, diversos modos imitationis ipsius in quibus pluralitas idearum consistit."

Commenting on Thomas's choice of the term "discover" here, Wippel notes that "To me this does not mean that God 'thinks up' or invents out of thin air the various ways in which his essence can be imitated, or the various divine ideas. It means that he eternally contemplates all the ways in which his essence can be imitated and freely chooses to produce creatures which imitate him in some of these ways, though not in others. On this point Thomas is not a voluntarist" (Wippel, *Divine Ideas,* 20). For arguments that Thomas is a voluntarist, see James F. Ross, "Aquinas' Exemplarism; Aquinas' Voluntarism," 171–98. For responses to Ross's arguments, see Armand A. Maurer, "Divine Ideas: A Reply," 213–20. See also Dewan, "Exemplarism: A Reply," 221–34. For Ross's reply to these two articles, see Ross, "Response to Maurer and Dewan," 213–20. For more on this debate, see chap. 4, n. 43.

the unity of the form of an agent, which is its principle. For this reason, even though the relations understood by God are many (in which consists the plurality of ideas), his understanding is nevertheless not multiple but one since he understands all those things through his one essence.[22]

Thomas's consideration here of the multiplicity of divine ideas shares much in common with his earlier treatment of the topic in *In I Sent.* He again notes that all things imitate the one divine essence and that an idea is not simply that essence taken as such, for an idea implies understanding. Rather, a divine idea entails God's understanding of his own essence. Still, that understanding alone does not fully constitute the character of a divine idea. Its full character involves God's knowledge of the particular relationship that a particular creature bears (or can bear, as regards possible creatures) to his essence.[23] Hence, it is his knowledge of the divine essence as imitable that is the central characteristic of a divine idea.[24] And it is because the divine essence admits of diverse imitations that we can speak of many divine ideas.[25]

What is new in the *De veritate* is Thomas's distinction between a form considered as the first principle of an act of understanding and one considered as the terminus of such an act. Applied to the divine understanding, the former is nothing other than the divine essence as it is understood by God, whereas the latter is that essence understood as the exemplar for producing something else. This distinction provides a foundation for reconciling the plurality

<hr/>

22. *De ver.,* q. 3, a. 2, obj. 9 (Leonine ed., vol. 22.1.103:73–78); ibid., ad 9 (Leonine ed., vol. 22.1.106:302–13).

23. The status of ideas of pure possibles will be examined in chap. 4. See the section "Ideas of Possibles."

24. Thomas is careful to note that even though creatures are related to God in this way, they nevertheless involve no real relations in God. God does know, however, the relations that creatures have (or can have) to his essence, and these relations do exist in him as *known* by him (*De ver.,* q. 3, a. 2, ad 8 [Leonine ed., vol. 22.1.107:58–64]).

25. Cf. *De ver.,* q. 8, a. 10, ad 3 (Leonine ed., vol. 22.2.253:113–37).

of ideas with the simplicity of the divine essence. According to the first mode of understanding, God knows himself; according to the second, he knows himself as imitable—a knowledge that involves a plurality of ideas because it embraces all the diverse relationships that creatures can have to his essence.[26]

A further development in the *De veritate* follows from this first one. As we have seen, in his commentary on the *Sentences*, Thomas presents the ideas as being the medium by which God knows creatures. In the *De veritate*, however, he clearly emphasizes that an idea it is not "that by which" *(a quo)* a thing is understood but is rather "that which" *(quod)* is understood.[27] This distinction follows from the fact that Thomas now treats an idea as the terminus of knowledge.

Summa Contra Gentiles (1259–1264)

Thomas's next significant consideration of the divine knowledge appears in *Summa Contra Gentiles* I, c. 51 and c. 52 examine the philosophical difficulty posed by God's knowledge of a multiplicity of things. Thomas notes that a solution must be found that (1) does not introduce a multiplicity into the divine essence, (2) does not add anything accidental to God, or (3) does not posit ideas subsisting outside of the divine mind.[28] After discussing why each of these three

---

26. Wippel notes that in this way, "the plurality of divine ideas joins with the ontological unity of the divine essence to form two essential parts of Thomas's effort to account for the derivation of the many (creatures) from the one (their divine source)" (Wippel, *Divine Ideas,* 19–20). Louis Geiger maintains that the distinction presented in the *De veritate* between form as principle and form as terminus of knowledge is only to show how the artisan uses a model to produce his work. Geiger argues that it is not until the *Summa Contra Gentiles* that Thomas applies this distinction in order to resolve the problem regarding the multiplicity of divine ideas (Geiger, "Les idées divines," 194–97, 200–204). As Boland notes, however, *De ver.,* q. 3, a. 2, is precisely concerned with this problem. It is only reasonable to conclude, therefore, that Thomas is drawing this distinction in order to resolve the problem (Boland, *Ideas in God,* 208–9; cf. Wippel, *Divine Ideas,* 20n43).

27. *De ver.,* q. 3, a. 2, ad 6 (Leonine ed., vol. 22.1.106:302–13). Farthing, "Divine Exemplarity," 204–5.

28. *SCG* I, c. 51 and c. 52 (Leonine ed., vol. 13.148).

approaches is inadequate, he proceeds in c. 53 to present his own account of how God's knowledge of a multiplicity of things does not
compromise the divine simplicity.

Aquinas begins by looking at the human intellect to draw an
analogy with God's. The external things that we understand exist in us, not according to their proper nature, but rather as species that inform and actualize our intellect. The intellect is able to
understand an external thing because an intelligible species is the
likeness (*similitudo*) of that thing. Once the intellect has been informed by the species as by a proper form, it then in turn forms
a certain intention (*intentio*) of the thing, an intention that is understood in itself through the intellect's act of understanding. This
intention is the notion (*ratio*) of the thing as expressed in its definition, and forming such an intention accounts for the intellect's
ability to understand an external thing apart from its absence or
presence and apart from its material conditions. Indeed, it is impossible to understand in this way unless the intellect forms such
an intention.

Thomas then explains that this intention is distinct from the
intelligible species that first actualizes the intellect: whereas that
species is the *principle* of the intellect's operation, the subsequent
intention is the *terminus* of its operation. Nevertheless, both are
likenesses (*similitudines*) of the thing that is understood. This is
clear when we consider that the intention formed by the intellect
is formed from the intelligible species, which is itself the likeness
of the thing. Hence, the intention must also be such a likeness.
And since the understood intention *is* like the external thing, it follows that the intellect, in forming that intention, understands that
thing.

Having drawn this distinction between these two intellectual
forms, Thomas then turns to consider God's understanding. The
intelligible species of the divine intellect by which God understands is his very essence, which is also the likeness of all things;
the conception (*conceptio*) of the divine intellect by which he un-

derstands himself, however, is his Word. This Word is the likeness not only of God's intellect, but also of all the things of which the divine essence is a likeness. Therefore, by means of the one intelligible species that is the divine essence, and by means of the one understood intention that is the divine Word, God understands many things.[29]

Thomas acknowledges that despite this account, someone might still think it difficult or even impossible for one and the same thing (viz., the divine essence) to be the proper notion *(propria ratio)* or likeness of many things. Thus, to avoid the conclusion that God has only a general or universal knowledge of things, Thomas considers in c. 54 how he can have a proper understanding of them. As in the prior chapter, this one begins with an analogy drawn from human understanding. Aquinas explains that our intellect is able to consider in a distinct way things that are not separated in reality. In considering the number ten, for example, the mind can grasp the proper notion of the number nine by subtracting one unit; similarly, from the notion of "man" it can grasp the notion of "irrational animal" by subtracting, as it were, the specific difference "rational" and considering only what is included in "sensible being."[30]

As regards God's understanding, the divine essence comprises within itself the perfections *(nobilitates)* of all beings—not in a composite manner, but in a perfect one.[31] Now, every form, whether proper or common, is a certain perfection and includes imperfection only insofar as it falls short of true being *(esse).* The divine intellect, therefore, can grasp what is proper to every single thing by understanding both the way in which it imitates the divine essence and the way in which it falls short of the perfection of that

---

29. *SCG* I, c. 53 (Leonine ed., vol. 13.150–51). Regarding the divine essence as the likeness of all things, see *SCG* I, c. 29 (Leonine ed., vol. 13.89–90).

30. *SCG* I, c. 54 (Leonine ed., vol. 13.154). On this point, see Wippel, *Divine Ideas,* 26. For a consideration of the Aristotelian influences in Thomas's arithmetic example, see Jordan, "Intelligibility of the World," 25–26.

31. See *SCG* I, c. 30 (Leonine ed., vol. 13.92).

essence. For example, God grasps the proper form of "plant" by understanding his essence as imitable in respect to life but not to cognition; he grasps the proper form of "animal" by understanding his essence as imitable in respect to cognition but not to intellect; and so forth. Moreover, since the divine essence is absolutely perfect, it can be viewed as the proper notion even of individual things. In this way, God can have a proper knowledge of all things.[32]

This account of God's understanding not only preserves the integrity of the divine simplicity but also simultaneously affirms the plurality of his notions. As Thomas explains next, the proper notion of one thing is distinct from the proper notion of another, but distinction is the principle of plurality (because distinction occurs between things that are not the same and, hence, not one).[33] There must, therefore, be a certain distinction and plurality of understood notions in the divine intellect since what is in the intellect serves as the proper notion of different things. Still, these notions are not really diverse in God's intellect. Rather, their diversity follows from his understanding the various particular relationships of imitation that creatures bear to himself. Thus, Augustine can say that God has made a man and a horse according to different notions and that there are many notions in the divine mind. In this qualified sense, Thomas notes, Plato's theory of ideas can be saved.[34]

These passages from the *Summa Contra Gentiles* show continuity with Thomas's earlier works in several respects. To begin with, he reaffirms the plurality of God's notions: the multiplicity of created things is dependent upon a diversity that preexists in the mind of

32. *SCG* I, c. 54 (Leonine ed., vol. 13.154–55).

33. On Thomas's views regarding distinction and plurality or multitude, see, e.g., *De pot.*, q. 9, a. 7, where he examines whether numeral terms can be predicated of the divine Persons.

34. *SCG* I, c. 54 (Leonine ed., vol. 13.155): "In quo etiam aliqualiter salvatur Platonis opinio ponentis *ideas*, secundum quas formarentur omnia quae in rebus materialibus existunt."

God, yet it is a diversity that is logical, not real. Once again, Thomas attributes this diversity to God's knowledge of himself as imitable in diverse ways—a knowledge of the particular relationship of similitude that each creature bears to his essence. In order to reconcile this diversity with God's simplicity, Thomas again employs the distinction presented in the *De veritate* between form as the principle of knowledge and form as the terminus of knowledge.

Although the *Summa Contra Gentiles* shows continuity with the earlier works in these respects, in other respects it shows a departure from them. The most significant difference is the absence of the very word "idea," at least until the final sentence of c. 54, and even then it is used only in reference to Plato. If Thomas were to have directly addressed the divine ideas in this work, c. 53 and c. 54 would have been the most logical place for him to have done so. Nor is there any evidence that he omitted such a consideration in that section in order to reintroduce the ideas in subsequent chapters.[35] Their absence could thus be read to suggest that he no longer found it necessary to speak about the divine ideas in order to address the question of God's knowledge. Lending to such a reading is the discovery that Thomas in fact suppressed earlier redactions of these chapters in which he *had* explicitly referred to the divine ideas.[36]

This absence of the ideas has prompted some scholars to conclude that "the doctrine of divine ideas is logically peripheral to Saint Thomas' treatment of the question of God's knowledge."[37]

35. Boland, *Ideas in God,* 224.

36. For a consideration of the development of these redactions, see Louis B. Geiger, "Les rédactions successives de *Contra Gentiles,* I, 53 d'après l'autographe," in *Saint Thomas d'Aquin aujourd'hui* (Paris: Desclée de Brouwer, 1963), 221–40. Cf. René-Antoine Gauthier, *Somme contre les gentils, introduction* (Paris: Éditions universitaires, 1993), 109 ff.

37. Farthing, "Divine Exemplarity," 214. See also Henle, *Thomas and Platonism,* 359; Étienne Gilson, *Christian Philosophy: An Introduction,* trans. Armand Maurer (Toronto: Pontifical Institute of Mediaeval Studies, 1993), 103–4, 107–8. The latter work originally appeared in French in 1960 as *Introduction à la philosophie Chriétienne* (Paris: Librairie Philosophique J. Vrin, 1960). Armand Maurer provides an exposition of this text in

Nevertheless, even though the term "idea" is absent from these two chapters, the same issues are raised as in earlier works.[38] As Wippel notes, it seems clear that Thomas's various references in the *Summa Contra Gentiles* to God's "notions" *(rationes intellectae, rationes propriae, rationes rerum)* is nothing other than the use of a different term for the same divine ideas.[39]

Like Wippel, Louis Geiger sees the divine ideas as present in the *Summa Contra Gentiles,* but he sees them instead in the discussion of the divine Word, which refers to the second Person of the Trinity. The introduction of the Word into this consideration marks another departure from Thomas's earlier works because it adds a theological note that does not appear in any of his other *ex professo* treatments of the divine ideas. That he is indeed referring to the Son of God in this passage is confirmed later in book IV when Thomas discusses the Divine Word. In c. 11, which examines the generation of the Son, we find Aquinas defining the very terms that he had used earlier in book I, c. 53.[40] When he considers in c. 13 whether there is only one Son, he employs the same language of *rationes* as he had in bk I, c. 54.[41] Geiger sees this latter point as suf-

---

"James Ross on the Divine Ideas: A Reply," *American Catholic Philosophical Quarterly* 65 (Spring 1991): 213–20.

38. Boland, *Ideas in God,* 221.

39. Wippel, *Divine Ideas,* 26n56.

40. Geiger, "Les idées divines," 203. *SCG* IV, c. 11 (Leonine ed., vol. 15.32). Although Thomas does not employ the language of the *verbum mentis* in his *ex professo* considerations of human knowing, this passage and others reveal that neither does he limit his use of such language to discussions of divine cognition. See Lonergan, *Word and Idea,* esp. 11n48.

41. Geiger, "Les idées divines," 203n74. *SCG* IV, c. 13 (Leonine ed., vol. 15.49): "Cum vero Deus, intelligendo seipsum, omnia alia intelligat, ut dictum est, oportet quod Verbum in Deo conceptum ex eo quod seipsum intelligit, sit etiam Verbum omnium rerum. Non tamen eodem modo est Verbum Dei, et aliarum rerum. Nam Dei quidem Verbum est ex eo procedens: aliarum autem rerum, non sicut ex eis procedens, non enim Deus a rebus scientiam sumit, sed magis per suam scientiam res in esse producit, ut supra ostensum est. Oportet igitur quod Verbum Dei omnium quae facta sunt, ratio perfecta existat.—Qualiter autem singulorum ratio esse possit, ex his quae in primo libro tractata sunt, manifestum est, ubi ostensum est quod Deus omnium propriam cognitionem habet. Quicumque autem facit aliquid per intellectum, operatur per

ficient evidence, not only that the Word mentioned in bk I, c. 53 is identical to the second Person of the Trinity, but also that it is identical to the divine ideas.[42]

But why, then, does Thomas abandon the term "idea" that he had embraced in his earlier works, and why does he employ it again (as we shall see) in future ones? Rather than answer these questions now, I will reserve doing so until the end of this chapter when I will consider the claim of some scholars that the doctrine of divine ideas is not a genuine part of Thomas's philosophy.[43] For now, it is simply worth noting that this difference between the *Summa Contra Gentiles* and Thomas's other works does exist.[44]

---

rationem rerum factarum quam apud se habet: domus enim quae est in materia, fit ab aedificatore per rationem domus quam habet in mente."

42. Geiger, "Les idées divines," 203n74: "Que le verbe dont il s'agit dans notre chapitre est bien identique aux idées, il suffit, pour s'en convaincre, de comparer avec le chapitre 13 du 4e livre." As Geiger explains, reference to the Word appears only in the third and final redaction of c. 53 (ibid., 203).

43. See the section below, "The Divine Ideas in *SCG*."

44. Shortly following the *Summa Contra Gentiles,* Thomas briefly addresses the question of multiplicity in the divine intellect in the *De potentia* (1265–66). In q. 16, a. 3, he considers whether a multitude of things can proceed from one first thing. In reply to the twelfth objection, he explains that there can be one exemplar of all created things because each thing imitates that exemplar imperfectly and in a different way. In reply to the thirteenth objection, he explains that although there cannot be a real multiplicity in God's intellect, there can be one according to reason since God understands these different ways that creatures imitate his intellect. In reply to the fourteenth objection, he explains that there are thus many things in the divine intellect *as understood* by God. Thomas is insistent that even though the diversity of things in the divine intellect is according to reason, this diversity is not simply a way for us to make sense of God's knowledge: it is in fact *in* God's very understanding (Marietti ed., vol. 2.89–90).

As in the *Summa Contra Gentiles,* this consideration of the divine knowledge does not explicitly mention ideas. Still, it should be kept in mind that the article is not even dedicated to the topic of God's knowledge. Moreover, Thomas does acknowledge the divine ideas elsewhere in the *De potentia* (see, e.g., q. 1, a. 5, ad 11 [Marietti ed., vol. 2.20]; q. 3, a. 1, ad 13 [ibid., vol. 2.41]; q. 4, a. 2, ad 27 [ibid., vol. 2.124]).

Around the same time period as the *De potentia,* Thomas explicitly employs the language of ideas in another work. John of Vercelli, the master of the Dominicans at the time, requested Thomas's expert opinion on a series of propositions. He replied with his *Responsio de 108 articulis* (1265–66/67). The sixty-sixth of these propositions states that the ideas are many on the part of what is connoted according to a manifold (*plurificatum*) relationship that is eternal. Thomas replies that God has understood a

Summa theologiae I (1266–1268)

In his next major systematic work, Thomas returns to the language of ideas and addresses the topic of their multiplicity in q. 15, a. 2. The article begins with an argument to prove that there are in fact many ideas. In any effect, the ultimate end is the proper intention of the principal agent, just as the order of an army is intended by its general. Similarly, the order of the universe is the proper intention of God. If God had created only the first creature (which created the second, and so forth, resulting in the multitude of things), then the order of the universe would be merely accidental. He would thus have only one idea, an idea of the first creature, because that is all that he would have intended. But since he does intend the order of the whole universe (insofar as he has created it), he must have an idea of how it is ordered.

Now, God could not have a proper notion *(propria ratio)* of the whole unless he had proper notions *(propriae rationes)* of those things that constitute the whole, just as a builder would be unable to conceive the nature of a house unless he had a proper notion of each of its parts. There must, therefore, be proper notions of all things in the divine mind, as Augustine noted in his *83 Different Questions.* Hence, many ideas exist within the mind of God.

Having demonstrated the plurality of divine ideas, Thomas then proceeds to consider how such a plurality is possible without compromising the simplicity of the divine essence. He observes that the idea of a produced thing does not exist in the mind of the

---

multitude of creatures from eternity and, hence, a multitude of relationships of creatures to himself. There can thus be a multiplicity of ideas without multiplying the divine essence. The sixty-seventh proposition states that the plurality of ideas exists in God according to reason, *viz.,* the *divine* reason, and not that of a human or angelic intellect. Thomas grants the truth of this proposition: the divine ideas are not really distinct in God, but they are distinct as understood by him (*Resp. de 108 art.,* 66–67 [Leonine ed., vol. 42.289:7776–95]). Although Thomas employs the term "idea" here out of a need to reply to someone else's use of it, his responses reveal that he does not shy away from the term, but rather openly embraces it.

producer as a species "by which" *(a quo)* that thing is understood since a species actualizes the intellect. Rather, an idea exists in the mind as "that *which" (quod)* is understood. For example, the form of a house in the mind of a builder is something understood by him, and in likeness to this, he forms a house in matter. Regarding the mind of God, Thomas observes that it would be contrary to the simplicity of his intellect to be informed by many species, but it is not contrary to its simplicity that the divine intellect *understand* many things. Thus, the plurality of ideas does not compromise God's simplicity.

Thomas then proceeds to explain how the divine mind can possess many such understandings. Since God knows his essence perfectly, he knows every way in which it can be known. Now, it can be known not only as it is in itself but also as it can be participated by creatures according to any manner of likeness. Every single creature has a proper nature *(speciem)* because it participates in some way in a likeness of the divine essence. Since God knows his essence as it is imitable by a creature, he knows it as the proper notion and idea of that creature. So it is in regard to all creatures. In this way, God has many proper notions of many things, and, hence, there are many ideas.[45]

Thomas further develops his position in his replies to objections. The first objection argues that since the divine essence is only one, there is only one idea. He responds by noting that an idea is not called an "idea" simply because it is the divine essence but rather because it is the likeness or notion of this or that thing. Since there are several understood notions from the one divine essence, there are also said to be several "ideas."[46]

45. *ST* I, q. 15, a. 2 (Leonine ed., vol. 4.201–2); cf. *ST* I, q. 47, a. 1, ad 2 (Leonine ed., vol. 4.486).

46. *ST* I, q. 15, a. 2, ad 1 (Leonine ed., vol. 4.202). In the prior article, Thomas had noted that although God knows both himself and other things through his essence, his essence is the operative principle only of other things, not of himself. For this reason, the divine essence has the character *(ratio)* of an idea only with respect to other things:

In reply to the second objection, Thomas further refines the meaning of what constitutes an idea. The objection states that just as there are not several arts or wisdoms in God, so too there are not many ideas. In response, Thomas repeats his distinction from the corpus of the article, noting that wisdom and art signify "that by which" *(a quo)* God understands, whereas an idea is "that which" *(quod)* he understands. Now, God not only understands many things by his essence, but he "understands that he understands" through his essence. It is *this* understanding that constitutes an idea. Such an understanding, however, is of many things, so there must be many ideas as things understood by God.[47]

In the remaining replies to objections, Thomas goes on to explain that although the ideas are many because of their relationships to created things, these relationships are not caused by things but rather by the divine intellect comparing itself with them. These relationships thus exist in God and not in creatures, but they do not exist in him as real relationships like those among the Divine Persons; rather, they exist in him only as understood.[48]

Thomas directs his attention again to the issue of the plurality of divine ideas in q. 44, a. 3. The article considers whether the exemplar cause is anything other than God. As we saw in chapter 2, Thomas begins this article by demonstrating the existence of the divine ideas. The determination of forms in natural things must be reduced to the divine wisdom, and there must be notions *(rationes)* of all things *in* the divine wisdom. These notions we call ideas. Although the ideas are multiplied according to their relationships to things, in terms of reality they are nothing other than the divine essence since its likeness can be shared in different ways by differ-

---

God does not have an idea of himself (*ST* I q. 15, a. 1, ad 2 [Leonine ed., vol. 4.199]). Wippel notes, "I take this as meaning that there are divine ideas for other things because exemplars are needed for them. But since exemplars are not needed for God, there is no divine idea for God himself" (Wippel, *Divine Ideas*, 33–34).

47. *ST* I, q. 15, a. 2, ad 2 (Leonine ed., vol. 4.202).

48. *ST* I, q. 15, a. 2, ad 3 and ad 4 (Leonine ed., vol. 4.202).

ent things. In this sense, God himself is the first exemplar of all things.[49]

᷾

In these passages from *Summa theologiae* I, we see the same themes as in Thomas's earlier works: (1) the distinction between form as principle and as terminus of the act of understanding; (2) God's knowledge of the imitability of his essence; and (3) the plurality of ideas as objects of the divine intellect. As in works prior to the *Summa Contra Gentiles*, Thomas employs the language of ideas to describe this aspect of God's knowledge. Again, as in those works, he presents his consideration of the issue independently of any theological discussion of the divine Word.[50]

Quodlibet 4 (1271)

Thomas's final consideration of the plurality of divine ideas appears in *Quodlibet* 4. In q. 1, a. 1, he notes that a plurality can exist in two different ways. According to the first way, it can be a real plurality, and in this sense there are not many divine ideas. The reason is that the term "idea" refers to an exemplar form, and there is only one such form of all things, namely, the divine essence. According to the second way, a plurality can exist in the order of understanding *(ratio intelligentiae),* and in this sense there *are* many ideas. Such a plurality is possible because the divine essence admits of different imitations according to different degrees *(gradus).* There are thus as many ideas as there are relationships that things have to the divine essence—relationships that God knows and has

49. *ST* I, q. 44, a. 3 (Leonine ed., vol. 4.460).

50. In the *Prima Pars,* Thomas saves his discussion of the Word for a future article dedicated to examining the second Person of the Trinity (*ST* I, q. 34, a. 3 [Leonine ed., vol. 4.370]). In that article, he examines how the name "Word" signifies a relationship to creatures. Even there, however, he wishes to draw a distinction between the role of ideas and that of the Word in God's knowledge. See the section below, "Philosophy, Theology, and the Divine Ideas." Regarding the relationship of Thomas's doctrine of divine exemplarism to his doctrine of the Word, see Boland, *Ideas in God,* 235–48.

known from eternity. Hence, a plurality of ideas has existed in the divine mind from eternity as the proper reasons *(rationes propriae)* of the things that he understands.[51]

Thus far, the article reads much like Thomas's earlier writings on the matter. When we turn to the objections, however, we find something different in his approach. Unlike those earlier works in which the objections argue against the multiplicity of divine ideas, here they argue in *favor* of it. Thomas's replies are therefore dedicated to defending the unity of the divine essence rather than the plurality of the divine ideas.

The first objector cites Augustine's position that God has a different idea for a horse than for a man. Thomas responds that Augustine understands there to be this difference between the ideas based upon the diversity of relationships, as noted in the corpus of the article.[52] The second objector argues that created things are distinct precisely because God knows their distinction. Since he knows their distinction in himself, the ideas existing in him must also be many and distinct. Thomas replies that the ideas are indeed many and distinct on the part of the thing known since things are distinct just as God knows them to be distinct. The things that he knows, however, do not exist in his intellect according to the same mode of distinction they have in themselves: in themselves, things exist separately in an essential way but not so in the divine intellect, just as things also exist materially in themselves but immaterially in the divine intellect.[53]

It is in the *sed contra* rather than in the objections that we find an argument offered against the plurality of divine ideas. There, it is argued that nothing essential is multiplied in God; since the term "idea" is an essential name that is spoken of God, there cannot be many ideas. In reply, Thomas grants that a real plurality

51. *Quod.* 4, q. 1, a. 1 (Leonine ed., vol. 25.2.319:30–48). Wippel, *Divine Ideas*, 37.
52. *Quod.* 4, q. 1, a. 1, obj. 1 and ad 1 (Leonine ed., vol. 25.5.319:11–16 and 62–64).
53. *Quod.* 4, q. 1, a. 1, obj. 2 and ad 2 (Leonine ed., vol. 25.2.319:17–21; 320:64–81).

is not found in the essential names of God; a plurality does exist, however, according to the order of understanding *(ratio intelligentiae).*[54]

꩜

In *Quodlibet* 4, then, we find arguments that are by now quite familiar. Nevertheless, this passage does differ from Thomas's earlier works in its structure. It has been noted by some scholars that Thomas's approach here suggests that he really gives a negative answer to the question of whether there are many ideas. Authorities whom he had once cited in support of his opinion now appear in the arguments of his objectors.[55] Mark Jordan interprets this reversal in Thomas's approach as evidence that he is moving away from the language of ideas toward an emphasis on the imitability of the one divine essence. Jordan argues that given the Thomistic model, ideas are "otiose." As evidence, he quotes Aquinas's statement that "the divine essence, in so far as it is imitable in *this* way by *this* creature, is the proper reason or idea of this creature." Jordan thus concludes that there is no need for what he calls a "middle step."[56]

In response to Jordan, I would note that even though the structure of Thomas's argument in *Quodlibet* 4, q. 1 is reversed from that of his earlier works, as regards the argument's substance, there is nothing new. If we read Thomas's own words, there is no indication that he views the ideas as an unnecessary middle step. Indeed, in the sentence that immediately follows the one quoted by Jordan, Thomas observes that "Hence, there are in this way many ideas since the divine essence is understood according to the diverse re-

54. *Quod.* 4, q. 1, a. 1, *sed contra* and reply (Leonine ed., vol. 25.2.319:22–29; 320:82–85). Thomas is alluding here to the distinction between the divine attributes and the divine ideas.

55. Jordan, "Intelligibility of the World," 28. Cf. Branick, "Unity of the Divine Ideas," 172–73.

56. Jordan, "Intelligibility of the World," 28–29 (translation is Jordan's). *Quod.* 4, q. 1, a. 1 (Leonine ed., vol. 25.2.319:41–44): "Sic igitur divina essentia, secundum quod est imitabilis hoc modo ab hac creatura est propria ratio et idea huius creaturae, et similiter de aliis."

lations that things have to it, imitating it in different ways."[57] It is with *this* sentence, and not the prior one, that he concludes his argument. And with this sentence, we see him affirm the need for what Jordan terms a "middle step"—we see him affirm the multiplicity of ideas.

Thomas preserves such a step because, as we have seen, an idea for him is not simply the relationship that a creature has to God's essence; rather, it is God's *knowledge* of that relationship. Why then, one might ask, does the structure of this article suggest that Thomas is giving a negative answer to the question? One possible explanation is that within the public setting of the quodlibetal dispute, the opening arguments were in fact offered by someone in support of plurality. Consequently, Thomas would have seen a need to respond by defending the unity of the divine essence. Another possible explanation is suggested by Vincent Branick: the different approach that we find here indicates simply that "Thomas has reconciled for himself the unity of the multitude of divine ideas so well that either a yes or a no is a correct reply to this *quaestio*."[58]

Summary

From his earliest works, Thomas affirms the multiplicity of the divine ideas by enunciating the distinction between the divine essence as it is in itself and the divine essence as it is known by God as imitable. Beginning with the *De veritate,* we find Thomas drawing the further distinction between form as the actualizing principle of knowledge and form as the terminus of knowledge, the latter constituting an idea. This distinction, which is developed in the *Summa Contra Gentiles* and is embraced in all of his future writings, provides the foundation for his position regarding the multiplicity

---

57. *Quod.* 4, q. 1, a. 1 (Leonine ed., vol. 25.2.319:44–48): "Unde secundum hoc sunt plures ideae secundum quod intelligitur divina essentia secundum diversos respectus quos res habent ad ipsam, eam diversimode imitantes."

58. Branick, "Unity of the Divine Ideas," 172–73.

of divine ideas: the divine essence as the actualizing form of God's intellect is not an idea; rather that essence as the *terminus* of his knowledge is, inasmuch as God knows his essence according to its imitability. Since the divine essence can be imitated in a diversity of ways, God must have a knowledge of all of these ways. Thus, his intellect can have many ideas as the objects of his knowledge without compromising the simplicity of his essence.[59]

Throughout Thomas's various considerations of the multiplicity of divine ideas, we find the names of Augustine and Dionysius repeated as *auctoritates*. In the writings of Augustine, Thomas finds the most emphatic affirmation of the multiplicity of ideas. From Augustine's writings, he is provided not only with an account of the historical origins of the doctrine of ideas, but also with the position that the ideas are the proper notions of created things.[60]

59. Geiger, "Les idées divines," 179, 202.

60. Jordan, "Intelligibility of the World," 21–22. Augustine's *De Ideis* appears in his *De diversis quaestionibus LXXXIII* (on this work, see n. 8 above). In the *De Ideis*, Augustine presents the ideas as the principal forms *(principales formae)* of things, fixed and unchangeable *(stabiles atque incommutabiles)*, eternally forming all that comes into being and all that passes away, but remaining in themselves unformed. In short, they are transcendent principles or patterns of everything created. They do not, however, exist as separately subsisting entities as Plato taught; instead, they exist in the mind of God. As we have seen above, Augustine posits a multiplicity of ideas, noting that a man is clearly not created according to the same pattern as a horse (*De div. qq. 83*, 46 [CCSL, vol. 50.1.71–72]).

Regarding the multiplicity of the divine knowledge, Augustine observes that God's understanding is "simple in its multiplicity and uniform in its 'multiformity'" (*De civ. dei*, XII, 19 [Corpus Scriptorum Ecclesiastorum Latinorum (hereafter CSEL)] vol. 40.600:3–4]: *cuius sapientia simpliciter multiplex et uniformiter multiformis*). Nevertheless, he never offers a philosophical account of how the multiplicity of divine ideas can be reconciled with the simplicity of the divine essence. He does, however, offer something of a theological solution. According to Augustine, the divine ideas are not simply in the mind of God but are in the *Word* of God since the Word is God's wisdom (see *De Gen. ad litt.*, II, 8 [CSEL, vol. 28.45:8–15]; *De civ. dei*, XI, 10 [CSEL, vol. 40.528:4–10]; *Tr. in Ioann.*, II, 10 [CCSL, vol. 36.16:1–15]; ibid., I, 17 [CCSL, vol. 36.10:1–27]).

On the topic of the divine ideas in Augustine, see Boland, *Ideas in God*, 37 ff.; Mary T. Clark, *Augustine* (Washington: Georgetown University Press, 1994), 37 ff.; Étienne Gilson, *The Christian Philosophy of Saint Augustine*, trans. L. E. M. Lynch (New York: Random House, 1960), 106 ff., 207 ff.; Lawrence F. Jansen, "The Divine Ideas in the Writings of St. Augustine," *The Modern Schoolman* 22 (1945): 117–31; Theodore J. Kon-

In the writings of Dionysius, he finds a resolution to the problem posed by this multiplicity of ideas. Commenting on the *Divine Names,* Thomas explains that for Dionysius the exemplars are the understood notions *(rationes intellectas)* that preexist in God in a singular way. Indeed, it is this Dionysian model of exemplarism that Thomas adopts, allowing him to unify the ideas in the infinite act of being *(esse)* that is the divine essence.[61]

We have seen Thomas's observation that an idea consists in God's knowing his essence as imitable in different ways by created beings. Insofar as they do imitate the divine essence, created beings must resemble in some respect the infinite act of being *(esse).* This conclusion provides a further refinement in Thomas's doctrine of divine ideas since the ideas—which are *themselves* imitations of God—must represent in some way the infinite act of be-

---

doleon, "Divine Exemplarism in Augustine," *Augustinian Studies* 1 (1970): 181–95; Hans Meyerhoff, "On the Platonism of St. Augustine's *Quaestio De Ideis,*" *The New Scholasticism* 16 (1942): 16–45; John J. O'Meara, "The Neoplatonism of Saint Augustine," in *Neoplatonism and Christian Thought,* ed. Dominic J. O'Meara (Albany: State University of New York Press, 1982), 34–41; Eugene TeSelle, *Augustine the Theologian* (New York: Herder and Herder, 1970), 214 ff.

61. *In V De div. nom.,* lect. 3, nn. 666 and 669 (Marietti ed., 249 and 250). Dionysius discusses the divine ideas in chapter 5 of *The Divine Names,* where he considers how God, as the complete transcendence of Being, both precontains and causes all things. Dionysius calls the ideas paradigms (Gr. παραδείγματα, Lat. *exemplaria*), rational accounts (Gr. λόγοι, Lat. *rationes*), predefinitions (Gr. προορισμοί, Lat. *praediffinitiones*), and willings (Gr. θελήματα, Lat. *voluntates*). Unlike Augustine, he offers a philosophical solution to the problem of the multiplicity of ideas by explicitly identifying them with the divine essence, itself the paradigm by which all things are created *(Divine Names,* V, 8–9 [*Dionysiaca,* vol. 1.22.357–64]).

Regarding Dionysius's influence on Thomas's thought, see Boland, *Ideas in God,* 110 ff., 320 ff.; Henle, *Thomas and Platonism,* 383, 423–24; Jean Leclercq, "Influence and Noninfluence of Dionysius in the Western Middle Ages," in *Pseudo-Dionysius: The Complete Works,* 26–27; O'Rourke, *Pseudo-Dionysius,* esp. 124 ff., 255 ff.; Julien Péghaire, "L'axiome *bonum est diffusivum sui* dans le néoplatonisme et le thomisme," *Revue de l'Université d'Ottawa* 1 (1932): 5–30; Gregory P. Rocca, *Speaking the Incomprehensible God* (Washington: The Catholic University of America Press, 2004), esp. 49–76.

There are of course other authorities not mentioned by Thomas who influenced his doctrine, one of whom is his teacher Albert Magnus (Jordan, "Intelligibility of the World," 22). See James A. Weisheipl, O.P., *Thomas d'Aquino and Albert His teacher,* Etienne Gilson Series, no. 2 (Toronto: Pontifical Institute of Mediaeval Studies, 1980), 5, 7.

ing.[62] It is thus necessary to consider the issue of the multiplicity of ideas, not simply within the context of the simplicity of the divine essence, but also within the context of the unity of the infinite act of being that *is* that essence.

In his commentary on Boethius's *De Trinitate,* Thomas observes that "the first reason or principle of plurality or division is from negation and affirmation, so that the order of the origin of plurality is understood in this way: what must be understood first are being *(ens)* and non-being *(non ens),* from which the first divided things are themselves constituted and, consequently, the many."[63] Following this passage, Branick observes that to explain the multiplicity of ideas within the context of the infinite act of being is to do so in terms of that act *(esse)* and its negation *(non esse).*[64] We see intimation of this fact in the *De veritate* where Thomas observes that each thing imitates the divine essence in different ways according to its act of being *(esse)* which is distinct from every other: "Created things, however, do not perfectly imitate the divine essence; hence the essence is not understood unqualifiedly as the idea of things by the divine intellect but according to the proportion the creature that is to be made has to the divine essence *inasmuch as it falls short of it* or imitates it."[65]

Just as creatures fall short of the infinite perfection of the divine essence, so too do the divine ideas. One idea is distinguished from another according to the degree of perfection that it repre-

62. Branick, "Unity of the Divine Ideas," 189–90.

63. *In De Trin.,* q. 4, a. 1 (Leonine ed., vol. 50.121:118–23): "Sic ergo patet quod prima pluralitatis vel divisionis ratio sive principium est ex negatione et affirmatione, ut talis ordo originis pluralitatis intelligatur, quod primo sint intelligenda ens et non ens, ex quibus ipsa prima divisa constituuntur, ac per hoc plura."

64. Branick, "Unity of the Divine Ideas," 195.

65. *De ver.,* q. 3, a. 2 (Leonine ed., vol. 22.1.104–5:204–12): "Res autem creatae non perfecte imitantur divinam essentiam, unde essentia non accipitur absolute ab intellectu divino ut idea rerum sed cum proportione creaturae fiendae ad ipsam divinam essentiam *secundum quod deficit ab ea* vel imitatur ipsam; diversae autem res diversimode ipsam imitantur et unaquaeque secundum proprium modum suum cum unicuique sit esse distinctum ab altera." Emphasis added in translation.

sents, each one falling short of the complete perfection of the act of being that is the divine essence. In this respect, non-being in a relative sense must in some way enter even into the mind of God as a negating principle; for, in knowing things other than himself, God knows how they are *not* himself.[66] In short, it would seem that God can only consider himself as imitable inasmuch as he combines in his act of understanding both being *(esse)* and non-being *(non-esse)*.[67] As Wippel explains, "The very possibility of the creation of creatures presupposes that they are known by God. And this in turn rests on God's awareness of them (and their essences) as being—insofar as they do or can imitate him—and as nonbeing—insofar as they fall short of perfectly and fully imitating his unlimited perfections."[68]

Indeed, this positing of non-being that allows for the production of a multiplicity of creatures can *only* occur by intellection. Since God is being itself *(Ipsum Esse)*, non-being cannot enter into his essence except through intellection, since the only ontological status non-being has is as an *ens rationis.* It is for this reason that the ideas exist simply as known beings rather than as real ones and, moreover, that there can be many of them.[69] Thus it is ultimately Thomas's unique metaphysics of *esse* that provides the solution to the problems posed by a multiplicity of divine ideas.[70]

66. Branick, "Unity of the Divine Ideas," 197–99. Wippel notes that the relative non-being of the divine ideas is not the same as that of created essences: "The frame of reference is different in the two cases, since this time what is negated—the absolute fullness of divine perfection—is not and cannot be an intrinsic constituent of the existing entity, if and when this particular essence should be brought into being by God's causal activity" (John F. Wippel, "Thomas Aquinas on the Distinction and Derivation of the Many from the One: A Dialectic between Being and Nonbeing," *Review of Metaphysics* 38 [1985]: 589).

67. Wippel, "The Many from the One," *Review of Metaphysics* 38 (1985): 583–84. On this point, Wippel grants that he may be going beyond Thomas's *ipsissima verba.* However, in support of this interpretation, he cites the passage from the *De veritate* quoted above (ibid., 584n42). On relative nonbeing, see Wippel, *Metaphysical Thought,* 177–94.

68. Wippel, "The Many from the One," 585.

69. Branick, "Unity of the Divine Ideas," 199–200.

70. Branick explains, "The unity of the divine ideas, then, is achieved by transcend-

IS THOMAS'S DOCTRINE OF
IDEAS THOMISTIC?

The Divine Ideas in *SCG*

In considering the *Summa Contra Gentiles,* we found that the divine ideas are conspicuously absent from its account of God's knowledge. As I noted above, some scholars point to this absence as evidence that the ideas are not an integral part of Thomas's thought. R. J. Henle is but one example. He argues, moreover, that the presence of divine ideas in Thomas's other works is only due to his respect for *auctoritates* such as Augustine and Dionysius. According to Henle, each of the *ex professo* treatments of the divine ideas is preceded by a doctrine of divine cognition that is entire in itself. He thus maintains that when Thomas does address the ideas, "No new development in the substance of the doctrine appears within these questions." Despite Thomas's best efforts, Henle insists, his consideration of the divine ideas remains "somewhat strained."[71]

Étienne Gilson comes to a similar conclusion. In one of his later works, he notes that "it is hardly an exaggeration to say that at bottom everything St. Thomas said about the Ideas was in his view one more concession made to the language of a philosophy that

---

ing the level of heterogeneity or the level of essence as such and attaining the level of simplicity or the level of the act of *to be* as such. Without a metaphysics of *to be,* this level could not be reached. God could be considered only as a nature or a form among other forms. The ideas would be primarily forms. The two would meet on the same level with all their heterogeneity. Because there would be nothing beyond this essential level, its characteristic heterogeneity would become absolute. There would be no possibility of unifying the ideas in God. Heterogeneity of essence is not an absolute because of the more fundamental opposition between the act of *to be* and non-being. The reality of God present to himself explains the act of *to be* as exemplar. The same reality knowing himself and what he is not explains non-being as exemplar. Furthermore, God knowing himself as perfect presence to self is the result and expression of his very unity. Therefore, not only is heterogeneity compatible with but is explained only by the absolute unity of God. There is no conflict between truth and unity, because both flow from the one perfect act of *to be*" ("Unity of the Divine Ideas," 201).

71. Henle, *Thomas and Platonism,* 359.

was not really his own. No doubt it was also the recognition of St. Augustine's authority in theology." Like Henle, Gilson cites the absence of divine ideas in the *Summa Contra Gentiles* as evidence that Thomas did not consider them to be a necessary element of his philosophy.[72]

Why then, we might ask, do the divine ideas reappear in the *Summa theologiae?* According to Gilson, it is not because Thomas is "adding one more piece to a sort of philosophical mosaic." Indeed, Gilson does not even consider Thomas's doctrine of divine ideas to be philosophical at all; rather, he concludes, it represents a theological effort to reconcile an otherwise Augustinian doctrine with "the strictest philosophical truth." To speak of a multiplicity of ideas, he insists, is to employ a Platonic language foreign to the Aristotelianism of Thomas's theology. If we must use the language of ideas, Gilson thinks we should say instead that there is only *one* idea and that that idea is nothing other than God himself. As absolute existence, God is the exemplar of all created things, whereas those things are, in turn, but "finite and deficient approximations of the pure act of *esse*."[73]

More recently, James Ross has argued against what he terms a "photo-exemplarist" reading of Aquinas's divine ideas. According to Ross, photo-exemplarism holds that God has a multiplicity of ideas, each acting like a photograph or blueprint for both actual and possible things. He insists that this account is not only philosophically problematic but that it is also a misreading of Thomas, "For there is only *one* divine idea, the *same* no matter what God does."[74] In denying the multiplicity of divine ideas, therefore, he

72. Gilson, *Christian Philosophy*, 103–4.

73. Gilson, *Christian Philosophy*, 106–8.

74. Ross, "Aquinas' Exemplarism; Aquinas' Voluntarism," 173–74. Ross attributes this "photo-exemplarist" reading to Étienne Gilson, Armand Maurer, and John F. Wippel. As Maurer has shown, however, Ross in fact has much in common with Gilson on this topic (see Maurer, "Divine Ideas: A Reply," 213 ff.). This is a point that Ross comes to acknowledge in a future article (see Ross, "Response to Maurer and Dewan," 235).

is also denying that such a doctrine is truly Thomistic. As Ross asserts, "I say Aquinas explains the plurality of ideas as a multiplicity from the vantage of things made, but says, strictly speaking, there is only one divine idea; therefore, there is little left of Augustine's doctrine, except for the words."[75] Is the reading offered by these scholars correct, though? Does Thomas himself view the doctrine of divine ideas as foreign to his philosophical system? To begin to answer these questions, we should first consider in more detail why a treatment of the divine ideas is absent from the *Summa Contra Gentiles.*

In that work, as in his other systematic works, Thomas examines God's knowledge and seeks to reconcile the multiplicity of what God knows with the divine simplicity. It is true that Aquinas does not dedicate a distinct chapter to the divine ideas, but he does defend the existence of a plurality of "notions" *(rationes)* in the mind of God. As we have seen, from his earliest works Thomas uses the terms "idea" and "notion" interchangeably, or at least he treats ideas as types of notions. For this reason, I would contend that his defense of a multiplicity of notions in the mind of God is nothing other than a defense of a multiplicity of divine *ideas* by another name.

In support of this reading is Thomas's reference in c. 54 to Augustine's *De Ideis:* God produces a man by one notion and a horse by another. In the referenced text, Augustine does nothing less than defend both the existence and the multiplicity of divine ideas. As Thomas's other works reveal, he is well aware of this fact. That Thomas would cite this work in c. 54 indicates that the absence of divine ideas in the *Summa Contra Gentiles* is not doctrinally significant, as Henle and Gilson contend, but semantically so.[76] Indeed, Aquinas reveals as much at the end of the chapter when he tells us that Plato's theory of Ideas can, in a certain respect, be saved.

75. Ross, "Response to Maurer and Dewan," 235.
76. On Thomas's reference to Augustine there, see Wippel, *Divine Ideas,* 28.

Of course, we are still left with the question of why in this text Thomas only uses the term "idea" in passing. Here, we need to remember the dual role that he ascribes to ideas throughout his writings: as cognitive and as ontological principles. He consistently places a greater emphasis on their latter role. In texts explicitly addressing the divine ideas, therefore, his emphasis is always on the theme of exemplar causality. As Wippel has observed, Thomas's concern in those texts is to show how a perfectly simple God can produce a diversity of creatures; by contrast, his concern in the *Summa Contra Gentiles* is to show how such a God can *know* a diversity of creatures. Without an emphasis on the ontological issue in this text, there is less need for the language of ideas.[77]

Following this reading, we can see why in the *Summa theologiae,* Thomas would return to speaking of ideas. Gilson's contention is that the presence of ideas in that work is merely as a useless appendage. But, as Boland rightly asks, "Is it likely that so soon into a work whose aim was to avoid useless questions, Saint Thomas would include just such a useless question?"[78] Indeed, q. 15 on the divine ideas is not merely a reiteration of the issues examined in q. 14 on God's knowledge.[79] Thomas himself clearly sees a use in presenting this new *quaestio,* explicitly noting to the reader that he includes it because everything that is known is in the knower, and in God we call these notions *(rationes)* "ideas."[80]

Still, the critics of the divine ideas do more than simply call attention to their supposed absence from the *Summa Contra Gentiles.* As we have seen, it is the position of these critics that the language of divine ideas in Thomas's other works is not truly his own but

77. Wippel, *Divine Ideas,* 28, 38–39. Cf. Farthing, "Divine Exemplarity," 214. As we saw in chap. 1, Thomas presents the term "idea" as referring principally to practical knowledge.

78. Boland, *Ideas in God,* 213–14.

79. On this point, see Geiger, "Les idées divines," 204.

80. *ST* I, q. 14, *prologus* (Leonine ed., vol. 4.166): "Quia omne cognitum in cognoscente est, rationes autem rerum secundum quod sunt in Deo cognoscente, ideae vocantur, cum consideratione scientiae erit etiam adiungenda consideratio de ideis."

merely a respectful acknowledgement of Augustine's and Dionysius's authority. According to these critics, Thomas's true doctrine is that there is but one "idea," namely, God himself.

The critics' reading of Thomas's doctrine seems to follow when we consider the sort of multiplicity that he attributes to the divine ideas. From his earliest writings, Thomas holds that their multiplicity is not according to reality but according to reason. In other words, it is a *logical* multiplicity. For that reason, it might be tempting to dismiss this multiplicity as *merely* logical and, hence, of no philosophical significance. Nevertheless, Thomas's writings indicate that his doctrine of ideas consists of more than just empty words.

The multiplicity that Thomas attributes to the ideas, although logical, is ultimately rooted in an ontological reality. This fact becomes clear when we consider a distinction that he draws between two types of logical diversities. In examining the divine ideas in the *De veritate*, Thomas explains that in one way a logical multiplicity is reduced to some diversity of the thing. For example, there is a logical difference between *Socrates* and *Socrates sitting*, which is reduced to the difference between a substance and an accident. Similarly, there is a logical difference between *man* and *animal*, which is reduced to the difference between form and matter since a genus is taken from the matter and the *differentia* from the form. Thomas explains that the multiplicity resulting from this sort of logical difference is repugnant to the highest unity and simplicity found in God. In another way, however, logical difference is reduced, not to a diversity in the thing, but, rather, to the *truth* of the thing, which is intelligible in diverse ways. In this sense, a logical multiplicity is not repugnant to God's simplicity. It is in this sense, Thomas concludes, that there can be a multiplicity of notions (i.e., ideas) in God.[81]

What this passage reveals is that the multiplicity of divine ideas,

81. *De ver.*, q. 3, a. 2, ad 3 (Leonine ed., vol. 22.1.105:244–59).

although logical, is nevertheless reduced to the truth of the divine essence, an essence that is itself ontologically open to being imitated in a multiplicity of ways. We do not arbitrarily posit the ideas as a sort of handy way to talk about God's knowledge. As Branick notes, "It is not up to us to choose the multiplicity or not. There is a structure of reality which precedes our intellection and which forces us to consider God in a multiplicity of ideas, as long as we are working with ideas."[82] Indeed, Thomas himself is insistent that "although the relationships of God to creature are really founded in the creature, nevertheless according to reason and intellect they also exist in God; and, I say, not only according to the human intellect, but also according to the angelic and the divine."[83]

Henle, Gilson, and Ross are quite right that ontologically, there is but one exemplar of all things, which is God. As the fullness of being *(esse)*, the divine essence is imitable in diverse ways. Still, when Thomas addresses the subject of divine ideas, it is not simply to this imitability that he is referring. Rather, for him a divine idea consists in God's *knowing* his essence as imitable in these diverse ways. It is this knowledge that constitutes an idea. Since these ways are themselves diverse, so too is God's knowledge and, hence, his ideas. From the texts that we have considered in this chapter, it is clear that Thomas's doctrine of divine ideas is in no sense a mere concession to authority.

Indeed, Thomas's doctrine of divine ideas has the benefit of drawing the reader's attention to the complex philosophical issues concerning the divine understanding. As Geiger has observed, Thomas preserves this Augustinian doctrine precisely to show the

---

82. Branick, "Unity of the Divine Ideas," 171n1. Branick is here commenting on a passage concerning the divine attributes: *In I Sent.,* d. 2, q. 1, a. 3 (Mandonnet ed., vol. 1.70–71).

83. *In I Sent.,* d. 36, q. 2, a. 2, ad 2 (Mandonnet ed., vol. 1.842): "Quamvis relationes quae sunt Dei ad creaturam, realiter in creatura fundentur, tamen secundum rationem et intellectum in Deo etiam sunt; intellectum autem dico non tantum humanum, sed etiam angelicum et divinum." Cf. *De pot.,* q. 3, a. 16, ad 14 (Marietti ed., vol. 2.90); *De ver.,* q. 3, a. 2, ad 8 (Leonine ed., vol. 22.1.107:58–64).

apparent contradiction between the divine simplicity and the need to affirm God's knowledge of a multiplicity of objects.[84] What is more important, the doctrine enables Thomas to resolve this apparent contradiction—a problem that was neither posed nor resolved by Aristotle.[85] This apparent contradiction is further emphasized by Thomas's tendency over time to place a greater emphasis on the nature of mind as analytic in order to account for God's understanding of a multiplicity of things. As Lawrence Dewan observes, "Thomas is doing all he can do to introduce actual consideration of distinction into the content of divine knowledge."[86] He is able to account for this distinction precisely because he posits (logically) distinct divine ideas as present in the divine mind. Whereas Gilson claims that "the plurality of ideas known by God is only a plurality of natures in things," Thomas is insistent that it is the other way around—there is a plurality of natures in things only inasmuch as there is first a plurality of ideas *in* God.[87]

PHILOSOPHY, THEOLOGY, AND THE DIVINE IDEAS

Given that Thomas does embrace a doctrine of divine ideas, the question remains whether this doctrine is more of a theological than a philosophical one. As I have noted, Gilson does not consider it to be philosophical at all (to the extent that he even accepts it), arguing that Thomas's presentation of the divine ideas is really a theological effort to reconcile an otherwise Augustinian doctrine with the "strictest philosophical truth."[88]

84. Geiger, "Les idées divines," 179.
85. Ibid., 182.
86. Dewan, "Exemplarism: A Reply," 226.
87. Gilson, *Christian Philosophy*, 109. An earlier version of this section of this chapter originally appeared in *Wisdom's Apprentice: Thomistic Essays in Honor of Lawrence Dewan, O.P.*, ed. Peter A. Kwasniewski (Washington, D.C.: The Catholic University of America Press, 2007), 153-69.
88. See n. 73 above. Taking a more positive view of the divine ideas than does

The theological significance of the divine ideas is apparent in *Summa Contra Gentiles* I, c. 53. As we saw, Thomas there emphasizes the role of the Word in God's understanding of things other than himself. In book IV of that work, he presents the Word as the *ratio perfecta* of all things, again clearly revealing the Augustinian influence to which Gilson refers.[89] Perhaps the most explicit connection that Thomas makes between the divine ideas and the Word occurs in one of his scriptural commentaries, where he identifies the Word as the locus of the ideas. There, once again, we find him citing the authority of Augustine.[90] Why does Thomas locate the ideas there? Because, it is fitting to attribute them to the Word of God.

He explains why this is the case in the course of examining the Trinity in the *Summa theologiae.* Although the Trinity of Persons cannot be proven by demonstration, it is nonetheless fitting that they be explained by things that are clearer to us. Now, the essen-

---

Gilson, Marie-Dominique Chenu argues that the theological intelligibility of the *Summa theologiae* necessarily requires a consideration of the divine ideas because the doctrine provides a religious account of the destiny of created things (Marie-Dominique Chenu, O.P., *Introduction a l'étude de Saint Thomas d'Aquin* [Montreal: Université de Montréal, 1954], 267–68). Thus, as we will see in chap. 4, Thomas notes that there must be ideas even of individuals because providence extends not only to species but to individuals as well (See the section "Ideas of Individuals, Species, and Genera." In Thomas, see, e.g., *ST* I, q. 15, a. 3, ad 4 [Leonine ed., vol. 4.204]; *ST* I-II, q. 93, a. 1 [Leonine ed., vol. 7.162–63]). Nevertheless, Chenu also observes that the doctrine provides not only a religious account but a rational one as well (*Introduction,* 267–68).

For a consideration of the theological implications of Thomas's doctrine of divine exemplarism, see Greenstock, "Exemplar Causality," esp. 18–31. For a consideration of the role that Thomas attributes to the divine ideas in God's providence, see Boland, *Ideas in God,* 262–70.

89. *SCG* IV, c. 13 (Leonine ed., vol. 15.49). Regarding the role of the Word in Augustine's doctrine of divine ideas, see n. 60 above.

90. See *In Hebr.* XI, 2 (Marietti ed., vol. 2.409–10): "Nos autem dicimus secundum modum praedictum, quod ex invisibilibus rationibus idealibus in verbo Dei, per quod omnia facta sunt, res visibiles sunt productae. Quae rationes, et si realiter idem sunt, tamen per diversos respectus connotatos respectu creaturae differunt secundum rationem. Unde alia ratione conditus est homo, et alia equus, ut dicit Augustinus. Sic ergo saecula aptata sunt verbo Dei, *ut ex invisibilibus* rationibus idealibus in verbo Dei *visibilia,* id est omnis creatura, *fierent."*

tial attributes of God are clearer to us according to reason than are the Personal properties because we can derive from creatures certain knowledge of God's essential attributes, whereas we cannot derive from creatures God's Personal properties. Given knowledge of the essential attributes, however, we can make use of them to "manifest" the divine Persons, for there is some similitude or dissimilitude between a Person and an attribute. This approach to manifesting the divine Persons is termed by Thomas "appropriation" *(appropriatio)*. For example, the Son of God proceeds by way of intellect as the Word; thus those things that pertain to intellect can be appropriated to him by similitude.[91] Now, since ideas pertain to intellect, they can be appropriated to the Son. Hence, Thomas explains, the Word can be identified as the locus of the divine ideas.[92]

Nevertheless, Thomas is careful to note that essential attributes are not appropriated in such a way that they are proper to a Person, as if those attributes were to belong exclusively to one Person. Rather, they are appropriated simply by similitude or dissimilitude.[93] Thus, as Thomas notes in the earlier *De veritate*, the ideas can only be called the Word metaphorically.[94] Whereas an idea

91. *ST* I, q. 39, a. 7 (Leonine ed., vol. 4.407).

92. *ST* I, q. 32, a. 1, ad 1 (Leonine ed., vol. 4.350): "Philosophi non cognoverunt mysterium Trinitatis divinarum Personarum per propria, quae sunt paternitas, filiatio et processio; secundum illud Apostoli, I *ad Cor.* II: *Loquimur Dei sapientiam, quam nemo principum huius saeculi cognovit,* idest *philosophorum,* secundum Glossam. Cognoverunt tamen quaedam essentialia attributa quae appropriantur personis, sicut potentia Patri, sapientia Filio, bonitas Spiritui Sancto, ut infra patebit. . . . In libris etiam Platonicorum invenitur *In principio erat verbum,* non secundum quod verbum significat personam genitam in divinis: sed secundum quod per verbum intelligitur ratio idealis, per quam Deus omnia condidit, quae Filio appropriatur."

93. *ST* I, q. 39, a. 7, ad 1 (Leonine ed., vol. 4.407).

94. *De ver.,* q. 4, a 1 (Leonine ed., vol. 22.1.120:208–23): "Verbum igitur vocis, quia corporaliter expletur, de Deo non potest dici nisi metaphorice, prout scilicet ipsae, creaturae, a Deo productae verbum eius dicuntur, aut motus ipsarum, in quantum designant intellectum divinum sicut effectus causam. Unde eadem ratione nec verbum quod habet imaginem vocis poterit dici de Deo proprie sed metaphorice tantum, ut sic dicantur verbum Dei ideae rerum faciendarum. Sed verbum cordis, quod nihil est aliud quam id quod actu consideratur per intellectum, proprie de Deo dicitur

simply means an exemplar form, the Word of a creature in God means an exemplar form that is drawn from another. For this reason, Thomas concludes that the Word in God pertains to a Person, but an *idea* in him pertains to the divine essence.[95] As he explains in the *Summa theologiae,* the name "Word" principally signifies relation to the speaker and only consequently a relation to creatures. Thus the name "Word" is said personally of God. By contrast, the name "idea" principally signifies relation to a creature, and for that reason, is not said personally of God.[96]

Given these distinctions between the ideas and the Word, is it correct to say, as Geiger does, that the Word is treated in the *Summa Contra Gentiles* as *identical* to the divine ideas?[97] In c. 53, Thomas does indeed present the Word in place of the ideas, and he also ascribes to it in later chapters an archetypal character similar to that of the ideas. Nevertheless, if Thomas *is* identifying the two in this work, it would mark a significant change in doctrine. To understand better why he discusses the Word in this context, we need to consider what his intention is in c. 53.

In that chapter, Thomas is particularly concerned with addressing how there can be a multitude of objects in the divine intellect without compromising the simplicity of that intellect. As in other works, he draws a distinction between form as principle of knowledge and form as object of knowledge. In regard to the divine in-

---

quia est omnino remotum a materialitate et corporeitate et omni defectu, et huiusmodi proprie dicuntur de Deo, sicut scientia et scitum, intelligere et intellectum."

95. *De ver.,* q. 4, a. 4, ad 4 (Leonine ed., vol. 22.1.129:163–69): "Verbum differt ab idea: idea enim nominat formam exemplarem absolute, sed verbum creaturae in Deo nominat formam exemplarem ab alio deductam, et ideo idea in Deo ad essentiam pertinet sed verbum ad personam."

96. *ST* I, q. 34, a. 3, ad 4 (Leonine ed., vol. 4.370): "Nomen ideae principaliter est impositum ad significandum respectum ad creaturam, et ideo pluraliter dicitur in divinis, neque est personale. Sed nomen verbi principaliter impositum est ad significandam relationem ad dicentem, et ex consequenti ad creaturas, inquantum Deus, intelligendo se, intelligit omnem creaturam. Et propter hoc in divinis est unicum tantum verbum, et personaliter dictum." Note Thomas's emphasis again regarding the multiplicity of ideas.

97. See n. 42 above.

tellect, this distinction allows him to conclude that there can be a multiplicity of understood objects (notions, or ideas) even though there is only one principle of knowledge (the divine essence). In the *Summa Contra Gentiles,* however, we see that Thomas describes a single understood object in the divine intellect, namely, the Word. He does go on to conclude that through this Word, God can understand many things, but the introduction of the Word as a single understood intention provides yet one more affirmation of the simplicity of the divine intellect.

In the following chapter, Thomas proceeds to reexamine the question from a different perspective. Whereas his concern in c. 53 is to affirm the simplicity of the divine intellect, his concern in c. 54 is to affirm the *multiplicity* of objects understood by that intellect. In this chapter, there is no mention of the Word as understood intention. Thomas instead speaks in terms of "notions" *(rationes),* what he elsewhere calls "ideas." Here, again, the intention of the chapter has framed the discussion, and so it is fitting that Thomas emphasize the multiplicity of understood notions. Nevertheless, as in c. 53, he reaches the same basic conclusion: the divine intellect can know many things without compromising its simplicity.

Thomas does not explicitly draw a distinction between the Word and the ideas in these two chapters, but he does so implicitly by his very division of this consideration in two. In c. 53, the Word is presented as an "intermediary" through *(per)* which God knows a multitude of things.[98] In c. 54, there is no such intermediary; rather, Thomas presents God's cognition simply in terms of the divine essence: that essence comprises within itself the perfections of all beings, and in knowing it, God can grasp what is proper to every single thing according to proper (and, hence, diverse) notions. Furthermore, Thomas does not describe these notions as either being the Word itself or as being *in* the Word but simply as being in the

---

98. *SCG* I, c. 53 (Leonine ed., vol. 13.151): "Sic ergo per unam speciem intelligibilem, quae est divina essentia, et per unam intentionem intellectam, quae est verbum divinum, multa possunt a Deo intelligi."

divine intellect.[99] In short, there is no sense in these passages that the notions, or divine ideas, pertain uniquely to one of the Divine Persons rather than to the divine essence.

Gilson's criticisms to the contrary, we now have a sense that for Thomas, the doctrine of divine ideas is no mere theological concession to Augustine. Indeed, it is not even principally a theological doctrine. Rather, it is a *philosophical* one that plays a key role in Thomas's metaphysical thought. What that role is will become clearer in the coming chapters, once we have identified the different types of ideas that exist within the mind of God and how those ideas are related to the things that they exemplify.

99. *SCG* I, c. 54 (Leonine ed., vol. 13.153–55).

FOUR

IDENTIFYING GOD'S
EXEMPLAR IDEAS

On more than one occasion, Thomas asks the question whether there are divine ideas for everything God knows, and he answers this question in the affirmative.[1] The very phrasing of the question, however, raises a further one: what precisely does God know? Only by answering this question will we be able identify the various types of divine ideas. Thomas himself examines a list of things for which God might have ideas—things such as genera, species, individuals, prime matter, accidents, evil, and even pure possibles. Not all of these things, he concludes, have an idea in the mind of God. Moreover, for those that do, not all can be said to have an exemplar. In what follows below, we will consider this list, paying special attention to which divine ideas can be said to be exemplar causes.

---

1. See, e.g., *In I Sent.,* d. 36, q. 2, a. 3 (Mandonnet ed., vol. 1.844); *ST* I, q. 15, a. 3 (Leonine ed., vol. 4.204). Although Thomas answers this question in the affirmative, it is clear from what he says elsewhere that he is speaking of God's knowledge of everything other than himself. As noted, God does not have an idea of himself (see chap. 3, n. 46).

THE DIFFERENT TYPES OF
DIVINE IDEAS

Ideas of Individuals, Species, and Genera

Thomas first addresses the question of whether there are ideas of individuals in his commentary on the *Sentences* (1252–56). There, in reply to an objection, he insists that particular things do have proper ideas in God. Just as there is a different divine idea of man than there is of horse, so too there is a different divine idea of Peter who is one individual human being than there is of Martin who is another individual. Nevertheless, the distinction between man and horse is according to form, which perfectly corresponds to an idea, whereas the distinction between individual things of a single species is according to matter, which does not correspond perfectly to an idea. Hence, Thomas concludes here that the distinction between ideas of different species is more perfect than that between ideas of different individuals.[2]

In the *De veritate* (1256–57) he dedicates the entirety of q. 3, a. 8 to the question of whether there are divine ideas of individuals. There, he notes that Plato posited ideas only of species for two reasons. The first was that for Plato, the ideas do not produce matter but only form. Since the principle of individuation is matter, Plato thought that ideas could only correspond to individuals according to their specific natures, not according to their individuality. The second reason Thomas attributes to Plato is more of a conjecture. As he notes, Plato may have denied the existence of ideas of individuals because the principal intention of nature is to preserve the species. Thus, we see that even though generation does terminate in the production of *this* man, what nature intends is simply that *man* be generated. For the same reason, Plato did not posit ideas of genera.[3]

---

2. *In I Sent.*, d. 36, q. 2, a. 3, ad 3 (Mandonnet ed., vol. 1.845).

3. *De ver.*, q. 3, a. 8 (Leonine ed., vol. 22.1.115–16:40–63). In other works, Thomas

In contrast to Plato, Thomas notes, we hold that God is the cause of individual things, regarding both their form and their matter. We also hold that all individual things are determined *(diffiniuntur)* through divine providence. Thus, we must hold that there are ideas of individual things.[4] Indeed, in his *sed contra* Thomas suggests that individual things have more of a need for distinct ideas than do universals. Ideas are ordered to the being *(esse)* of things, but individual things have being more truly than do universals, which subsist only in individuals. Therefore, individuals have a greater need for ideas.[5]

We get a clearer picture of the distinction between the divine ideas of individuals and those of kinds when we consider the relationship of God's ideas to his intellect. As we saw in chapter 1, Thomas identifies four modes of knowledge in the *De veritate:* (1) knowledge that is actually practical; (2) knowledge that is habitually or virtually practical; (3) knowledge that is speculative regarding what cannot be produced through the knower's knowledge; and (4) knowledge that is speculative regarding what *is* capable of being so produced but is nevertheless not considered in that respect.[6]

Thomas then applies these observations to God's knowledge. (1) Since his knowledge is the cause of things, God knows certain things by ordaining them to exist at some point in time. Of these things, he has actually practical knowledge. (2) He knows other things that he is capable of making but does not intend to make at any point in time. Of these things, God has virtually practical knowledge.[7] (3) God also has speculative knowledge regard-

does attribute to Plato a doctrine of ideas of genera (see, e.g., *De spir. creat.*, a. 5. [*Quaes. disp.*, Marietti ed.(Turin and Rome: 1949), vol. 2.389]; *In Lib. de caus.*, prop. 3 [Saffrey ed., 18:8–21]).

4. *De ver.*, q. 3, a. 8 (Leonine ed., vol. 22.1.116:63–68).

5. *De ver.*, q. 3, a. 8, *sed contra* 2 (Leonine ed., vol. 22.1.115:35–39).

6. *De ver.*, q. 3, a. 3 (Leonine ed., vol. 22.1.107:85–121).

7. Earlier, in *De ver.*, q. 2, a. 8, Thomas describes this mode of divine knowledge instead as quasi-speculative (Leonine ed., vol. 22.1.70:78–81). On this point, see Dewan "Exemplarism: A Reply," 228n14. Cf. Wippel, *Divine Ideas*, 23n49.

ing those things that he cannot produce at all, such as evil. (4) Finally, he has speculative knowledge of certain things by resolving them into their distinct notes, even though those notes cannot exist separately from each other in reality. Thus, Thomas concludes, in God there is truly both practical and speculative knowledge.[8]

In light of this basic schema, as we saw in chapter 1, Thomas concludes that according to the strict sense of the word, a (divine) idea includes only a knowledge of that which can be formed, and, hence, a divine idea is practical—either actually or virtually so. When taken in the broad sense of the word, however, an idea can also pertain to purely speculative knowledge insofar as it is the notion *(ratio)* or likeness *(similitudo)* of a thing. Still, Thomas explains, properly speaking, the term "idea" refers only to practical knowledge (either actual or virtual), whereas the terms "notion" and "likeness" can refer either to speculative or to practical knowledge.[9]

Let us now return to Thomas's discussion in q. 3, a. 8 of the *De veritate* regarding divine ideas of individuals, keeping in mind on the one hand, his distinction between speculative and practical knowledge and on the other, his distinction between the strict and broad sense of the term "idea." In reply to the second objection, he explains that when the term "idea" is taken in the strict sense, it corresponds to what is capable of being produced. Thus, only one idea corresponds to an individual, species, genus, and individuated characteristics *(individuatis)* because Socrates, man, and animal are not distinguished according to reality *(secundum esse)*. When the term "idea" is taken in the broad sense, however, then several ideas correspond to an individual; for Socrates can be considered as Socrates, as a man, and as an animal.[10]

---

8. *De ver.,* q. 3, a. 3 (Leonine ed., vol. 22.1.107:122–42). Regarding the presentation of these four modes of knowing as they pertain to God's knowledge, I have followed Wippel in reversing Thomas's ordering of the third and fourth modes to correspond to the order of the original presentation (Wippel, *Divine Ideas,* 22n48).

9. *De ver.,* q. 3, a. 3 (Leonine ed., vol. 22.1.108:163–74).

10. *De ver.,* q. 3, a. 8, ad 2 (Leonine ed., vol. 22.1.116:74–84).

Although Thomas does not explicitly use the language of speculative and practical knowledge in this passage from the *De veritate,* his reply corresponds perfectly with the distinctions that he had laid out earlier in a. 3. What we find is that, according to the proper sense of the term, ideas belong only to God's practical knowledge since these ideas are actually or virtually productive. Since ideas taken in the strict sense *do* belong to practical knowledge, there are properly speaking only ideas of individuals because only individual things can actually be produced. According to the broader sense of the term, however, there are ideas that belong to speculative knowledge as well: ideas that also correspond to individual things but that are not productive since the things they denote (genera and species) do not exist as separated in reality.

Thomas next considers the status of divine ideas for individuals in *Quodlibet* 8 (1257) in a somewhat different context. In q. 1, a. 2, he examines whether the divine ideas are first related to created things according to the individuality of those things or according to their specific nature.[11] Thomas begins to address the topic with an analogy that is by now familiar: just as the forms of art works exist in the mind of the artisan, similarly there exist in the divine mind the exemplar forms of all creatures, and these forms we call the ideas. Less familiar than this analogy, however, is his subsequent illustration of its shortcomings.

Although both the artisan and God act in light of a form in mind, the artisan acts upon a presupposed matter, whereas God does not. Consequently, the exemplar forms in the mind of the artisan are not productive of matter—which is the principle of individuation—but only of form, which gives the work of art its species. Thus, the exemplar forms of human art are not directly related to works regarding their individuality. By contrast, the exemplar forms in the divine mind are productive of the whole thing, with respect to both its form and its matter. Therefore, the divine

11. *Quod. 8*, q. 1, *prologue* (Leonine ed., vol. 25–1.51:12–15).

exemplars are related to individual creatures, not only as to their specific natures, but also as to their singularity.[12]

Nevertheless, Thomas notes, the divine ideas are first related to the specific natures of things. Since an exemplar is that in imitation of which something is made, the character *(ratio)* of an exemplar requires that the assimilation of a work to that exemplar be intended by an agent. Consequently, an exemplar is first related to what the agent first intends in his work, and every agent first intends what is more perfect. Now, the nature of a species, Thomas explains, is the most perfect thing in every individual because it perfects a two-fold imperfection. On the one hand, it perfects matter, which is the principle of singularity and which stands in potency to the specific form; on the other hand, it perfects a generic form, which is in potency to the specific difference as matter is to form.[13]

Hence, what is first in the intention of nature is the most specific species: nature does not principally intend to generate Socrates, but rather it intends *in* Socrates to generate "man." Similarly, nature does not principally intend to generate "animal," otherwise its action would stop when it had brought about the nature of "animal." Thus, Thomas concludes, an exemplar in the mind of God is related first to the specific nature in any creature.[14] In short, as he notes in the *sed contra,* (divine) ideas are first related to the specific nature in individuals because things corresponding to ideas are more assimilated to their exemplars according to their form than they are according to their matter.[15]

In the first objection, Augustine is cited in defense of the posi-

---

12. *Quod.* 8, q. 1, a. 2 (Leonine ed., vol. 25.1.54:23–41).

13. *Quod.* 8, q. 1, a. 2 (Leonine ed., vol. 25.1.54:42–59).

14. *Quod.* 8, q. 1, a. 2 (Leonine ed., vol. 25.1.54–5:59–73). Thomas's position regarding what nature principally intends to generate is influenced by the thought of Avicenna. See *Liber primus naturalium,* ed. Simone Van Riet (Louvain-La-Neuve: Peeters and Leiden: Brill, 1992), I, c. 1, 8–9.

15. *Quod.* 8, q. 1, a. 2, *sed contra* (Leonine ed., vol. 25.1.54:15–22). At the end of the article, Thomas responds to this *sed contra* argument in his replies to objections by conceding its point.

tion that the ideas are first related to singular things. Citing the *83 Diverse Questions,* the objector notes that the divine ideas are certain forms or enduring reasons *(rationes)* of things that are contained in the divine intelligence. Although these ideas themselves neither come to be nor perish, everything that can come to be or perish is said to be formed according to them. But everything that comes to be or perishes exists only in a singular way. Therefore, the objector concludes, the ideas are first related to singular things.[16]

In response to this objection, Thomas reminds us that what is first in the order of intention is last in the order of execution. Thus, even though nature first intends to generate "man," this *individual* man is generated first, for "man" is not generated except inasmuch as this individual man is generated. Borrowing Augustine's language, Thomas explains that everything that proceeds does so according to the ideas *(secundum eas oritur omne quod oritur)* regarding the order of execution, in which singulars are first.[17]

At first glance, this article seems to contradict Thomas's position enunciated in the *De veritate*—namely, that ideas in the strict or proper sense of the term are of individuals rather than of species. If we consider the question addressed in *Quodlibet* 8, however, it becomes clear that there is in fact no contradiction. Thomas does not ask whether ideas are properly of individuals but, rather, how the ideas are *related* to individuals. Indeed, the only ideas that he addresses at all in this article are ideas of individuals. Rather than contradicting his observations in the *De veritate,* then, this passage instead complements them. As we saw in the *De veritate,* Thomas explains that God's ideas of individuals correspond to creatures regarding their individual, specific, and generic nature. What this passage from *Quodlibet* 8 reveals is simply that even though a divine idea is related to an individual creature in each of these re-

---

16. *Quod. 8,* q. 1, a. 2, obj. 1 (Leonine ed., vol. 25.1.53–54:6–14). See Augustine, *De div. qq. 83* (CCSL, 44.71:26–32).

17. *Quod. 8,* q. 1, a. 2, ad 1 (Leonine ed., vol. 25.1.55:75–83).

spects, it is first related to the creature's specific nature. In the end, then, this article says more about the creature as it is related to its exemplar idea than it does about that idea itself.

In *Summa Contra Gentiles* I (1259–64), as we have seen, Thomas does not employ the language of ideas in his discussion of God's knowledge. Hence, he does not offer an explicit consideration regarding the kinds of ideas God has. In c. 54 of book I, however, Thomas does observe that since God knows his essence in different ways, there are different and distinct notions *(rationes)* in the divine mind: for as Augustine notes in his *83 Different Questions,* the notion of a horse differs from that of a man.[18] These notions appear to be of individual things. As Wippel notes, furthermore, in c. 65 where Thomas considers whether God knows individual things, he does observe that a likeness of a form in the divine intellect is the productive principle of both the matter and the form of an individual thing.[19]

In *Summa theologiae* I (1266–68), Thomas's consideration of the kind of divine ideas is again presented in the context of the distinction between practical and speculative knowledge. As we saw in chapter 1, however, his treatment here differs from that found in the *De veritate.* Here in q. 14, a. 16, he concludes that (1) knowledge that is speculative by reason of the thing known is purely speculative, (2) knowledge that is speculative according to either its *mode* or its *end* is partly speculative and partly practical, and (3) knowledge that is ordained to an operation as an end is purely practical. Mapping these three modes of cognition onto the divine intellect, Thomas observes that God's knowledge of himself is purely speculative since he is not himself producible. Regarding all other things, God has knowledge that is both speculative and practical.[20]

Thus, Thomas explains, (1) regarding those things that *we* know

18. *SCG* I, c. 54 (Leonine ed., vol. 13.155).
19. *SCG* I, c. 65 (Leonine ed., vol. 13.179–80). Wippel, *Divine Ideas,* 41–42.
20. *ST* I, q. 14, a. 16 (Leonine ed., vol. 4.196–97).

speculatively by defining and dividing, God also has a speculative knowledge according to the mode of knowing. (2) Regarding those things that God can make but never does, his knowledge is speculative because of its end. (3) Regarding those things that he does make at some point in time, God's knowledge is practical. (4) Finally, regarding those things that are evil, God's knowledge is also practical, not because they are operable by him (for they are not), but because he can permit, impede, or direct them—just as the physician has practical knowledge of sicknesses because he can cure them by means of his art.[21]

In light of these distinctions between God's practical and speculative knowledge, we can now turn to see their relevance for Thomas's discussion of the divine ideas. In q. 15, a. 3, Thomas asks whether there are ideas of all the things that God knows. Noting that Plato held the ideas to be principles of knowing and producing things, Thomas observes that the divine ideas also have this twofold role in the mind of God. In short, they serve both a cognitive and ontological function. As we saw in chapter 1, Thomas next explains that an idea is called an "exemplar" inasmuch as it is a principle for making things. Such an idea belongs to God's practical knowledge. By contrast, an idea that is a principle of knowing is properly called a "notion" (ratio). Such an idea can also belong to God's speculative knowledge. Taken as an exemplar, an idea pertains to all things that are made by God at any point in time. Taken as a notion, an idea pertains to things in two ways: in one way, it pertains to all things known by God even if those things are never made at any point in time; in another way, it pertains to all things that are known by him according to a purely speculative knowledge.[22]

Of what, then, does God have ideas? Thomas develops this point in his reply to the fourth objection. The objection argues that Pla-

21. *ST* I, q. 14, a. 16 (Leonine ed., vol. 4.197).
22. *ST* I, q. 15, a. 3 (Leonine ed., vol. 4.204).

to had posited ideas only of species and not of individuals, genera, or accidents. Thus, God does not have ideas of such things either. In response, Thomas notes that a genus cannot have an idea that is distinct from that of a species inasmuch as the term "idea" denotes an exemplar, for a genus does not come to be except in some species. Thus, although he does not explicitly make the point, Thomas implies that there *are* distinct ideas of genera inasmuch as the term denotes a notion. He goes on to suggest that there are also distinct ideas of individuals. As he explains, Plato rejected the existence of such ideas for two reasons: the first is that individual things are individuated by matter, which he held was not caused by the ideas but was rather a co-cause with them; the second is that the intention of nature concerns only the species and not individuals, except insofar as the species is preserved. In contrast to this view, Thomas notes, we hold that divine providence extends itself not merely to species but to individual things as well.[23]

As in the *De veritate,* then, Thomas here affirms the existence of distinct ideas in the divine mind for individuals, species, and genera. Where the two presentations differ is in their terminology. In the *De veritate,* Thomas concludes that when the term "idea" is taken in its strict or proper sense, it pertains only to God's practical knowledge, whether actual or virtual. Taken in this sense, the term "idea" is treated by him as synonymous with the term "exemplar." Thus, there would exist in the divine mind exemplars not only for things that God actually makes at some point in time but also for things that he could make but never does. Here in the *Summa theologiae,* Thomas now restricts the term "exemplar" to refer only to those ideas of things that actually exist at some point in time, which is to say that he restricts it to refer only to ideas taken as ontological principles. All other ideas (including the virtually practical ideas described in the *De veritate*) are cognitive principles that belong to God's speculative knowledge. As such, Thomas now

23. *ST* I, q. 15, a. 3, ad 4 (Leonine ed., vol. 4.204).

concludes, these other ideas should not be termed "exemplars" but, instead, "notions" (rationes).[24]

Ideas of Prime Matter

As we have seen, one of the points where Thomas's doctrine of exemplarism departs from Plato's concerns the relationship of the ideas to matter. Whereas Plato viewed matter as a co-cause with the ideas, Thomas considers it to be yet another feature of the individual creature that is expressed by that creature's proper exemplar. Thomas goes even further, however, to consider whether the divine intellect possesses a distinct idea of prime matter.

In reply to an objection in his commentary on the *Sentences*, Thomas argues that because prime matter is from God, there must be an idea of it in him in some way. Matter does not have perfect being in itself; it does so only in a composite. Indeed, in itself, matter has an imperfect being according to the lowest grade of being, namely, being in potency. Therefore, it does not have the perfect character (ratio) of an idea except when it is in a composite. Hence, in itself, matter has only the imperfect nature of an idea. This is because the divine essence is imitable by a composite thing according to perfect being, but by matter according to imperfect being, and by privation in no way at all. Thomas sums up these observations by noting that a composite thing has a perfect idea in God by reason of its form; matter has an idea only imperfectly; whereas privation has no idea at all.[25]

In the *De veritate*, Thomas dedicates q. 3, a. 5 to considering whether God has an idea of prime matter. As before, he notes that because matter is caused by God, an idea of it must exist in him in some way since everything that is caused by God possesses some likeness to him. But now Thomas employs his distinction between the strict and broad senses of the term "idea." When the term is taken strictly,

---

24. See Wippel, *Divine Ideas*, 36–37; id., *Metaphysical Thought*, 302 ff.
25. *In I Sent.*, d. 36, q. 2, a. 3, ad 2 (Mandonnet ed., vol. 1.845).

we cannot hold that prime matter of itself has in God an idea distinct from that of the form or of the composite. The reason is that an idea, taken strictly, is related to a thing insofar as that thing can be brought into being; prime matter, however, cannot come into being without a form—indeed, neither can a material form come into being without matter. Thus, Thomas concludes that an idea, taken strictly, does not correspond to either matter or form alone but, rather, to the composite. Nevertheless, if an idea is taken according to the broad sense of the term as signifying a likeness or notion, then both matter and form can have distinct ideas by which they can be *known* distinctly, even though they cannot exist separately in reality. In this sense, then, there is a divine idea for matter.[26]

In this text, we get a different presentation from that found in *In I Sent.,* yet one that is in line with the distinction laid out earlier in the *De veritate* between God's speculative and practical knowledge. This refinement allows Thomas to answer the question whether there is a divine idea of prime matter. Even though it cannot exist by itself, prime matter can be considered by itself.[27] Thus, in noting that there is no idea of prime matter that pertains either to God's actually or virtually practical knowledge, Thomas implies that there *is* one as regards God's speculative knowledge.[28]

The next text in which Thomas explicitly considers whether there is a divine idea of prime matter occurs in q. 3, a. 1 of the *De potentia* (1265–66), where he examines whether God can create a thing from nothing.[29] There, in reply to an objection, Thomas presents the same distinction found in the *De veritate:* properly speaking, God does not have an idea of matter but of the compos-

---

26. *De ver.,* q. 3, a. 5 (Leonine ed., vol. 22.1.111–21:28–55).

27. *De ver.,* q. 3, a. 5, ad 3 (Leonine ed., vol. 22.1.112:68–71).

28. *De ver.,* q. 3, a. 5, ad 4 (Leonine ed., vol. 22.1.112:72–75).

29. As noted before, Thomas does not consider the divine ideas by name in the *Summa Contra Gentiles* (1259-64). Nevertheless, as Wippel has observed, "In SCG I, c. 65, in defending divine knowledge of individuals, Thomas states that God knows all things in his essence as in their source if they enjoy being in any way. These include both matter and accidents. But here [i.e., in *SCG* I] he does not explicitly take up the issue of a distinct idea for prime matter" (Wippel, *Divine Ideas,* 44).

ite since an idea is a productive form. Nevertheless, there can be said to be some idea *(aliquam ideam)* of matter since it imitates the divine essence in some way.[30]

Finally, Thomas addresses this issue again in the *Prima Pars* of the *Summa theologiae*. In reply to an objection in q. 15, a. 3, he reminds us of the distinction between Plato's position and his own: matter is not a co-cause with God but is created by him, although not without form. Thus, matter has its idea in God but not apart from the idea of the composite since matter in itself neither exists nor is knowable *(neque cognoscibilis)*.[31] Here, Thomas has departed both from his qualified defense in *In I Sent.* of an imperfect idea of matter *and* from his account in the *De veritate* of an idea of it according to the broad sense of "idea." The conclusion now is that since matter is unknowable in itself, there cannot be a distinct idea of it either according to God's practical or speculative intellect.[32]

Ideas of Accidents

Closely related to the issue of whether there is a divine idea of matter is whether there are ideas of accidents. Accidents, like matter, are found only in a composite, existing through the substance in which they inhere. For this reason, an objector in *In I Sent.* argues that God does not have distinct ideas of accidents but knows them instead as modifying a substance. In response, Thomas makes the same observation regarding accidents that he had made in this work regarding prime matter: since they do not have perfect being, accidents fall short of having a perfect idea. Nevertheless, to the extent that they do imitate the divine essence, the divine essence is their idea.[33]

30. *De pot.*, q. 3, a 1, ad 13 (Marietti ed., vol. 2.41).

31. *ST* I, q. 15, a. 3, ad 3 (Leonine ed., vol. 4.204).

32. Concerning how prime matter can be known, see Wippel, *Metaphysical Thought*, 321–22.

33. *In I Sent.*, d. 36, q. 2, a. 3, ad 4 (Mandonnet ed., vol. 1.845). On this point, see Jordan, "Intelligibility of the World," 21.

In the *De veritate*, Thomas offers a stronger defense of ideas for accidents, just as he offers a stronger defense of an idea for prime matter. God, he explains, is the immediate cause of every single thing because he works in all secondary causes and because all secondary effects originate from his predefinition of them. For this reason, there must be ideas in him not only of first beings but of secondary ones as well. Therefore, there must be ideas both of substances and of accidents but of different accidents in different ways.[34]

Here, Thomas draws a distinction between proper and separable accidents.[35] The former are caused by the principles of their subject and are not separable from it. Hence, these accidents are brought into being *(in esse producuntur)* together with their subject. For this reason, he explains, if we take the term "idea" in the strict sense as a form of something that is operable, then there is not a distinct idea for each accident, but, rather, there is only one that corresponds to the subject together with all of its accidents. In contrast to proper accidents, however, those that are separable from their subject do not depend upon that subject's principles, for they are brought into being by an operation other than the one by which the subject was produced. Thus, for example, it does not follow from the fact that a man is made a man that he be made a grammarian; rather, this accident is produced in him by another operation. Thomas concludes that there are indeed distinct divine ideas for separate accidents according to the strict sense of "idea." Furthermore, if we take the term idea in the broad sense, then there are distinct ideas for both kinds of accidents.[36]

Thomas again presents this distinction between separable and inseparable accidents in *Summa theologiae* I. There, in reply to the fourth objection of q. 15, a. 3, he examines this topic in light of his new distinction between an idea taken as an exemplar and as a no-

---

34. *De ver.*, q. 3, a. 7 (Leonine ed., vol. 22.1.114:58–65).

35. For more on this distinction, see Wippel, *Metaphysical Thought*, 268–75.

36. *De ver.*, q. 3, a. 7 (Leonine ed., vol. 22.1.114:66–99). Jordan, "Intelligibility of the World," 25.

tion *(ratio)*—an exemplar being a practical idea of an individual created at some point in time. Just as a genus does not have an exemplar distinct from that of the species, he explains, so too inseparable accidents do not have an exemplar distinct from that of their subject. Accidents that are added to a subject, however, do. Thomas does not explicitly address in this text whether there are distinct *notions* for either kind of accident, but the implication is that there are. Thus, while there are not distinct ideas of inseparable accidents according to God's practical knowledge, there are according to his speculative knowledge.[37]

Ideas of Evil

In the course of considering whether there are ideas for everything that God knows, Thomas also raises the question whether God has ideas of evil. In *In I Sent.*, he notes that evil, inasmuch as it *is* evil, is nothing since it is a certain privation. For this reason, there is no idea of evil in itself but only as it is a thing. Thus, God knows evil by means of knowing the opposed good, from which the thing that is subject to privation falls short. In other words, the only idea of evil is the idea that God has of the thing in which the evil is found.[38]

In the *De veritate*, Thomas dedicates q. 3, a. 4 to this question. There, he notes that if the term "idea" is taken in the strict sense, there is no idea of evil since an idea signifies a form that is the principle of informing a thing. Since nothing in God can be the principle of evil, evil cannot have an idea taken in the strict sense. Moreover, neither can it have an idea taken in the broad sense because, as Augustine notes, evil is named from its lack of form. Since a likeness is founded upon a form in which it participates in some way, evil cannot have any similitude in God.[39] In reply to an ob-

37. *ST* I, q. 15, a. 3, ad 4 (Leonine ed., vol. 4.204).
38. *In I Sent.*, d. 36, q. 2, a. 3, ad 1 (Mandonnet ed., vol. 1.844).
39. *De ver.*, q. 3, a. 4 (Leonine ed., vol. 22.1.110:66–80).

jection, Thomas notes as he had in *In I Sent.* that God knows evil by means of the idea of the good opposed to it. Inasmuch as evil is related to his knowledge in this way, it is as if he had an idea of it. Nevertheless, Thomas cautions, it is not as though this privation (the absence of the good) corresponds to God's understanding in place of an idea; for there cannot be a privation in God. I take him to mean here that the privation is not in God's understanding as though something were absent from his knowledge, an absence that would somehow stand in place of an idea. As Thomas indicates, any privation in God's knowledge would involve a privation in God himself, and this is impossible. Rather, the privation here is one in the created thing (or possible thing). God's knowledge of evil, then, is his knowledge that the good is not present in such a thing where it ought to be present.[40]

In *Summa Contra Gentiles* I, Thomas does not explicitly discuss whether there is a divine idea of evil, but if we take his discussion of the divine notions *(rationes)* to refer to the divine ideas, then he can be read as offering just such a consideration. In c. 71, Thomas argues that God has a knowledge of evil things, and in one of his arguments, he notes that since contraries can exist in the mind, the notion whereby we know evil is not repugnant to the good but rather pertains to the notion of the good. Since all notions of the good are found in God in light of his absolute perfection, Thomas concludes that the notion whereby evil is known must exist in him as well. As Wippel observes, however, even if we are to take the term *ratio* here as equivalent to idea, Thomas is still not defending the existence of an idea of evil as such.[41]

In *Summa theologiae* I, he again considers whether there is an idea of evil. In an objection, it is argued that there is no such idea, for if there were, there would be evil in God. In reply, Thomas again notes that evil is not known through its proper notion *(ratio)*

40. *De ver.,* q. 3, a. 4, ad 7 (Leonine ed., vol. 22.1.111:124–30).
41. *SCG* I, c. 17 (Leonine ed., vol. 13.46–7). Wippel, *Divine Ideas,* 45–46.

but rather through that of a good. Thus, he concludes that there is no divine idea of evil, considered either as an exemplar or as a notion.[42]

Ideas of Possibles

Finally, we must consider Thomas's thoughts regarding the existence of divine ideas for pure possibles, that is, those things that God has the power to make but never does make at any point in time. In recent years, there has been some debate about whether it is consistent with Thomas's metaphysics for God to have ideas of pure possibles and even about whether Thomas holds that God does indeed have such ideas.[43] Since the former question has been considered in detail by several scholars, and since considering it here would take us too far from the issues at hand, we will turn our attention simply to the latter one, namely, whether Thomas affirms the existence of such ideas.[44]

---

42. *ST* I, q. 15, a. 3, ad 1 (Leonine ed., vol. 14.204). Wippel, *Divine Ideas,* 46.

43. See Wippel, "The Reality of Nonexisting Possibles," 729–58. In this work, Wippel argues that for Thomas the ultimate foundation for metaphysical possibility is the divine essence and not the divine power or the divine will; something is possible because God recognizes that his essence can be imitated in some respect (ibid., 735–38). Hence, Wippel concludes that from the ontological standpoint, a possible is identical with its respective divine idea, although from a psychological standpoint, there is a logical distinction between the two (ibid., 734). James Ross takes issue with this interpretation in his article "Aquinas' Exemplarism; Aquinas' Voluntarism." Ross wishes to argue against the reading of even a logical plurality of divine ideas in Thomas's writings. Since he holds that there is only one divine idea regardless of whether God creates or not, he argues that possibles have no status as divine ideas or otherwise prior to creation (ibid., 174). The only possibility prior to the creation of anything, Ross concludes, rests in the divine power and not in God's understanding of his essence as imitable (ibid., 179–80). Hence, Ross sees possibility as grounded in the divine will (ibid., 194–95). For responses to Ross's arguments, see Maurer, "Divine Ideas: A Reply," and Dewan, "Exemplarism: A Reply." For Ross's reply to these two articles, see Ross, "Response to Maurer and Dewan."

44. Regarding the metaphysical role of the possibles in Thomas's philosophical system, see W. Norris Clarke, "What Is Really Real?"; James I. Conway, "The Reality of the Possibles," *The New Scholasticism* 33 (1959): 139–61, 331–53; Beatrice Hope Zedler, "Why Are the Possibles Possible?"; Wippel, "Reality of Nonexisting Possibles," 730–40.

In *In I Sent.*, Thomas does not directly address the existence of divine ideas for pure possibles. As we have seen, he presents the divine ideas there as God's knowledge of his essence as it is imitable by creatures. In reply to an objection, Thomas notes that while creatures have not existed from eternity, there have nevertheless been ideas of them in the divine intellect from eternity since God has from eternity known himself as imitable. It is clear from this passage that there are ideas of things that have existed or will exist but do not currently. In light of Thomas's observations, one could posit by extension the divine ideas for pure possibles, but Thomas himself neither affirms nor denies them.[45]

In the *De veritate*, we find that Thomas explicitly addresses the question of such ideas. In q. 2, a. 8, he considers whether God knows non-beings and things that are not, have not been, and will not be. In reply to an objection, he notes that according to the common parlance, an "idea" is a form belonging to practical knowledge and as such, there are only ideas of things that have been, are, or will be. If, however, we take the term idea as belonging to speculative knowledge, then nothing prevents there from being ideas of things that have not, do not, or will not exist.[46]

Thomas presents a slightly different account in q. 3, however, where he directly addresses the divine ideas. As we have seen, he notes in a. 6 that according to the strict sense of the term, an idea belongs to practical knowledge, either actual or virtual. Thus, the ideas that belong to actually practical knowledge pertain to those things that God makes at some point in time, but those that be-

---

45. *In I Sent.*, d. 36, q. 2, a. 2 (Marietti ed., vol. 1.842). Regarding the possibles in *In I Sent.*, Wippel observes that "In Dist. 38, q. 1, a. 4 Thomas defends God's knowledge of nonbeings, including his science of vision for things which will exist or have existed at some point in time, and his science of simple intelligence for those that will never be realized in fact but which exist in the power of a cause. As he puts it, through the last-mentioned kind of knowledge the simple nature of a thing which could have existed is known by God though its unqualified existence is not known, but only its existence in a qualified sense. But he does not explicitly say that there are divine ideas for such pure possibles, even though he does not deny this."

46. *De ver.*, q. 2, a. 8, ad 3 (Leonine ed., vol. 22.1.70:106–12).

long to virtually practical knowledge pertain to those things that God can make but never does. The difference between the two types of ideas is that those things toward which the possibles are directed are not determined to exist by God's will. For this reason, Thomas concludes, the possibles are in a certain sense indeterminate ideas. Thus, we see that in the *De veritate,* Thomas allows for the divine ideas of possibles.[47]

In book I, c. 66, of the *Summa Contra Gentiles,* Thomas offers several arguments to prove that God knows non-beings. He concludes that those things that neither are, nor will be, nor have been are known by God as possible to his power. God, however, knows them not as existing in themselves in any way but rather as existing solely in his power. These possibles are said by some to be known by God according to the knowledge of simple intelligence. By contrast, those things that are present, past, or future to us are known by God not only as in his power but also as in their proper causes and as they are in themselves.

Regarding these things, God is said to have "knowledge of vision." God has this knowledge because he knows every single being through his own essence, for the being *(esse)* of every single thing is drawn from that essence according to the manner of exemplarity. Hence, God knows non-beings according to the mode of being *(esse)* that they have, whether it is in the divine power, or in their causes, or in themselves.[48] While Thomas makes no explicit mention of the ideas in the *Summa Contra Gentiles,* then, we see that he does offer an argument similar to that found in the *De veritate* in defense of the existence of the possibles in the mind of God.

---

47. *De ver.,* q. 3, a. 6 (Leonine ed., vol. 22.1.113:35–47). Although Thomas describes the possibles here as being indeterminate ideas because the things toward which they are directed are not determined, he notes in his reply to the first objection that "quamvis quod nec est nec fuit nec erit non habeat esse determinatum in se, est tamen determinate in Dei cognitione" (*De ver.,* q. 3, a. 6, ad 1 [Leonine ed., vol. 22.1.113:48–51]). Regarding the differences between Thomas's presentation here and in q. 2, a. 8, ad 3, see Dewan, "Exemplarism: A Reply," 228n14. See also Wippel, *Divine Ideas,* 23n49.

48. *SCG* I, c. 66 (Leonine ed., vol. 13.184–85).

Thomas addresses the issue again in the *De potentia,* where he considers whether God can make that which he does not make. In replying to an objection, Thomas notes that according to its complete character *(completam rationem),* an idea is a form of art that is not only thought out by the intellect but is also ordered by the will to a work. Taken in this complete sense, there are no divine ideas for pure possibles. If, however, the term "idea" is taken in the incomplete sense as simply a form that is thought out in the mind of an artisan, then there are divine ideas of pure possibles, for God knows the full extent of his power. Hence, for everything that he can produce, God has ideas that in a certain way he has thought out *(rationes quasi excogitatas).*[49]

In *Summa theologiae* I, Thomas again affirms the existence of the divine ideas of pure possibles. As we have seen, in q. 15, a. 3, Thomas notes that an idea taken as an exemplar belongs to God's practical knowledge and pertains to all things that are made by him at any point in time. Taken as a notion *(ratio)* or principle of knowing, however, it belongs to God's speculative knowledge and can pertain even to those things that are never made by God at any point in time.[50]

Finally, as we have seen, in *Quodlibet* 4 (1271), Thomas describes an idea in q. 1 as a certain form, understood by an agent, in the likeness of which the agent intends to produce an exterior work. Following this definition, he observes that God knows and has known from eternity the diverse ways that creatures are going to imitate his essence.[51] Unlike the prior *ex professo* treatments of the divine ideas that we have considered, this one makes no mention of the existence of pure possibles but focuses instead upon the role of the divine ideas as exemplars. Nevertheless, as Wippel has observed, even though Thomas does not explicitly allow for ideas of

---

49. *De pot.,* q. 1, a. 5, ad 11 (Marietti ed., vol. 2.20).
50. *ST* I, q. 15, a. 3 and ad 2 (Leonine ed., vol. 4.204).
51. *Quod.* 4, q. 1, a. 1 (Leon ed., vol. 25–2.319:30–48).

pure possibles in this his final consideration of the divine ideas, neither does he explicitly exclude them.[52]

What we discern from the foregoing passages is that Thomas affirms the existence of divine ideas of pure possibles, and he locates them in God's speculative intellect since they pertain to things that are never made at any point in time. As Norris Clarke observes, although these ideas do not pertain to anything that has been made, they nonetheless possess as part of their intelligibility a set of relations to the real. They do so because they represent an imitation of their model, which is the divine essence, and because they possess a potential exemplar ordination toward creatures.[53] Nevertheless, since these ideas do not actually pertain to any real creature, they cannot properly be called exemplars.[54]

WHICH OF THESE IDEAS ARE EXEMPLARS?

From the various passages considered above, we find that over time Thomas develops a distinction between a strict and a broad sense of what constitutes an idea. It is in light of this distinction that he comes to identify the different types of divine ideas. Taken in the strict sense, an idea belongs to God's practical knowledge and is viewed as the form of something that is operable. Such ideas are of individuals and separable accidents. Taken in the broad sense, an idea belongs to God's speculative knowledge and is understood as the notion (ratio) or likeness (similitudo) of a thing. Such ideas are of genera, species, accidents (both proper and separable), and pure possibles.[55] In his earlier works, Thomas

52. Wippel, *Divine Ideas,* 37.
53. Clarke, "What is Really Real?" 88.
54. Dewan, "Exemplarism: A Reply," 234.
55. As we have seen, although Thomas holds in the *De veritate* that there can be ideas of pure possibles according to the strict sense of "idea," he departs from this view in the later *De potentia* and *Summa theologiae.* In those works, he treats the pure possi-

also affirms that matter has a divine idea taken in this broad sense; however, he comes to reject this position by the time of the *Summa theologiae*. As regards evil, he holds that since God knows it by means of its opposed good, it does not itself have an idea either in the strict or in the broad sense of the term.

As we have seen, Thomas considers the divine ideas to function as both ontological and epistemological principles. He views both roles as important, but the distinction that he makes between the strict and the broad sense of "idea" illustrates the priority that he attributes to the ontological role of ideas. Taken in the strict sense, an idea is productive—it is a form that something imitates because of the intention of an agent who predetermines the end for himself.[56] Here, then, we see one of Thomas's significant departures from the Platonic tradition: according to the strict sense that he has outlined, divine ideas are not properly of universals but of individually existing things. As he explains in the *De veritate*, individual things have being *(esse)* more truly than do universals, for universals subsist only *in* individuals. As a result, individuals have a greater need for ideas.[57] As Boland observes, "No clearer statement of his acceptance of radical aristotelian ontology is possible. The *quid est* is the concrete and in following Aristotle in this way Saint Thomas' account of the divine ideas is characterised by what has been called 'the radical intelligibility of the singular.'"[58]

Thomas's insistence that the proper sense of "idea" pertains to

---

bles as having ideas only in the broad sense as notions since they belong to God's speculative knowledge.

56. *De ver.*, q. 3, a. 1 (vol. 22.1.100:220–23).

57. *De ver.*, q. 3, a. 8, *sed contra* 2 (Leonine ed., vol. 22.1.115:35–39). See Branick, "Unity of the Divine Ideas," 194–95.

58. Boland, *Ideas in God*, 226. Boland is here referring to an observation made by Mark Jordan. See Jordan's "Intelligibility of the World," 23–24: "[T]he Aristotelian paradigm for intelligibility, so far as it is an account of definition by class-inclusion, seems incompatible with the account of the divine Ideas. Thomas does concede that formal distinctions are more intelligible than material ones because the latter are less complete in being. But this concession is only a parenthesis in an argument which moves toward the radical intelligibility of the singular."

an individual is reflected in his very use of the term "exemplar." As we have seen, he notes in the *De veritate* that something can be called an exemplar simply from the fact that another thing *can* be made in imitation of it even though that other thing is never made. Thus, he concludes there that an exemplar can belong to a knowledge that is virtually as well as actually practical, pertaining both to created individuals and to individuals that are purely possible.[59] In the *Summa theologiae*, however, Thomas restricts the term. As we have seen, he notes there that the word "exemplar" applies only to those divine ideas of individual things that exist at some point in time, and he calls the divine ideas of pure possibles (and of all other things) "notions" *(rationes)* instead.

As Lawrence Dewan has noted, this change in Thomas's vocabulary reflects a new interpretation of Dionysius's doctrine of exemplarism.[60] We have seen that in the *Divine Names*, Dionysius refers to the exemplars as divine "willings" *(voluntates)*.[61] In the *De veritate*, Thomas interprets this reference to mean that exemplars can be of pure possibles. He explains there that even though God never wills to produce what such ideas would exemplify, he nevertheless wills that he be *able* to produce those things. Thus, Thomas concludes that for Dionysius, the nature of an exemplar does not necessitate a will that is predefining and productive but simply one that is capable of being such.[62]

It is in his commentary on the *Divine Names* (1261-65 or 1265-68) that we first find a change in Thomas's interpretation of this Dionysian passage. God knows all things, he explains, but only those that he wills to produce are able to proceed from him. Moreover, only those notions *(rationes)* in imitation of which he wills to produce things in being *(esse)* can be called "exemplars." It is according

---

59. *De ver.*, q. 3, a. 3, ad 3 (vol. 22.1.108:185–94).

60. Dewan, "Exemplarism: A Reply," 233–34.

61. See the section on the *De Veritate* in chap. 2. See also *Divine Names*, V, 8 *(Dionysiaca*, vol. 1.22.359–60:S).

62. *De ver.*, q. 3, a. 6, ad 3 (vol. 22.1.113:60–67). See chap. 1, n. 30.

to these pre-definitions and willings that God has predetermined and produced all things.[63] As Dewan observes, here Thomas makes no effort to soften the sense of "willing" as he had in the *De veritate*. Now, he restricts the term "exemplar" to refer only to those ideas that are actually productive—at least in his reading of Dionysius's position.[64]

We find this new account of exemplarism reflected in Thomas's own doctrine in the *Summa theologiae*. Here, Thomas himself strictly reserves the term "exemplar" to refer to ideas of individual things that are actually created at some point in time. That he has abandoned what Dewan refers to as his earlier "soft" interpretation of Dionysius's term "willing" is made clear in Thomas's reply to an objection that cites the "pre-definitions and willings" passage from Divine Names V, 8. With respect to those things that neither are, nor will be, nor have been, Aquinas insists that there is no idea in God insofar as an idea denotes an "exemplar" but only insofar as it denotes a "notion" *(ratio)*. Thus, we find that Thomas, in an apparent effort to conform to Dionysius's doctrine of exemplarism, refines his own doctrine in the *Summa theologiae*.[65] Divine exemplarism is clearly enunciated as the relationship that a divine idea has to an individual thing that exists at some point in time, whether that thing be a substance or a separable accident.[66]

It has been observed by Wippel that when we review the texts on the divine ideas, the theme of exemplarity is most prominent.[67] In-

63. *In V De div. nom.,* lect. 3, n. 665–66 (Marietti ed., 249).

64. Dewan, "Exemplarism: A Reply," 233. Cf. Wippel, *Divine Ideas,* 6–7n15.

65. Dewan, "Exemplarism: A Reply," 233–34. See *ST* I, q. 15, a. 3, obj. 2 and ad 2 (Leonine ed., vol. 4.204). Here, we find the strong interpretation of willing offered even in an objection: "Deus cognoscit ea quae nec sunt nec erunt nec fuerunt, ut supra dictum est. Sed horum non sunt ideae: quia dicit Dionysius, V cap. *de Div. Nom.,* quod *exemplaria sunt divinae voluntates, determinativae et effectivae rerum.* Ergo non omnium quae a Deo cognoscuntur, sunt ideae in ipso." Thomas replies as follows: "Eorum quae neque sunt neque erunt neque fuerunt, Deus non habet practicam cognitionem, nisi virtute tantum. Unde respectu eorum non est idea in Deo, secundum quod idea significat exemplar, sed solum secundum quod significat rationem." See chap. 2, n. 20.

66. *ST* I, q. 15, a. 3, ad 4 (Leonine ed., vol. 4.204).

67. Wippel, *Divine Ideas,* 37–38.

deed, even in those texts where Thomas employs the term "exemplar" in a broader sense to include ideas of pure possibles, there is nonetheless in his method of presentation an emphasis upon the role of an exemplar as taken in the stricter sense found in the *Summa*. Thus, in *In I Sent.*, where Thomas acknowledges that divine ideas pertain both to God's speculative and his practical knowledge, he notes that according to common usage the term "idea" is taken for a form that is a principle of practical knowledge inasmuch as we call exemplar ideas the forms of things. In the *De veritate*, although Thomas does admit of exemplars for pure possibles, the definition that he provides of an idea nonetheless emphasizes its character as actually practical; for he describes an idea, not as a form that *can* be imitated because of the intention of an agent, but as a form that things actually do imitate because of that intention.

In the *Summa theologiae*, the role of the divine ideas as exemplars is emphasized not only in q. 15 of the *Prima Pars* but in q. 44 as well where Thomas observes that all things receive determinate forms by reason of the ideas in the mind of God. And in his final consideration of the divine ideas offered in *Quodlibet* 4, he again presents his discussion from the perspective of their role as exemplars, emphasizing God's understanding of the diverse ways that creatures imitate the one divine essence. In short, although Thomas does consider the divine ideas to be both cognitive and ontological principles, he clearly places greater emphasis on their ontological role as exemplars. And, inasmuch as divine ideas taken in the strict sense *are* exemplars, they are the extrinsic formal causes of individual things.[68]

---

68. See *In I Sent.*, d. 36, q. 2, a. 1 (Mandonnet ed., vol. 1.839–40); *De ver.*, q. 3, a. 1 (Leonine ed., vol. 22.1.100:220–23); *ST* I, q. 44, a. 3 (Leonine ed., vol. 4.460); *Quod.* 4, q. 1, a. 1 (Leon ed., vol. 25.2.319:30–48). The one exception is his treatment of the divine *rationes* that appears in the *Summa Contra Gentiles*. As Wippel explains, "If this emphasis on divine ideas recedes into the background in SCG I, this is primarily because Thomas's purpose there is to defend God's knowledge of a multiplicity of creatures rather than his production of them" (Wippel, *Divine Ideas*, 38–39). Regarding the absence of the term "idea" from Thomas's discussion of God's knowledge in this text,

THE METAPHYSICAL NEED FOR DIVINE
IDEAS AS EXEMPLAR CAUSES

But why, we might ask, do we need to posit divine ideas as exemplars? As we saw in the last chapter, Gilson thinks the ideas are not an essential element in Thomas's philosophy. That is not to say that Gilson denies the role of divine exemplarism in Aquinas's thought. To the contrary, he goes so far as to note that "exemplarism is one of the essential elements of Thomism."[69] Gilson simply thinks that God himself as the pure act of *esse* is a sufficient exemplar for all created things. Created things, in turn, are but "finite and deficient approximations of the pure act of *esse.*" Following his reading, ideas are thus unnecessary to account for divine exemplarism: "If you wish you can call this essential exemplarity of God an idea; it will not remain less identical with the divine essence itself."[70]

No doubt Gilson is in a sense correct. As we have seen, the divine ideas are really distinct neither from each other nor from the divine essence itself. Thus, the ideas are ultimately reducible to God's essence. Nevertheless, we have also seen Thomas insist that they are logically distinct from both. Here is where Gilson departs from Aquinas (as do Henle and Ross as well), dismissing his explicit doctrine of ideas. In doing so, Gilson also ends up dismissing a key distinction that Aquinas makes regarding divine exemplarism.

As we found in chapter 2, Thomas makes a point of distinguishing between two different types of divine exemplarism. One type is the exemplarism of the divine nature and its attributes, which

---

see both the textual analysis of *SCG* I and the section "Is Thomas's Doctrine of Ideas Thomistic" in chap. 3.

69. Étienne Gilson, *Le Thomisme,* 86: "Sans doute, une telle recherche n'aboutirait pas si nous ne faisons intervenir l'idée platonicienne et augustinienne de participation; mais nous verrons que, pris en un sens nouveau, l'exemplarisme est un des éléments essentiels du thomisme."

70. Gilson, *Christian Philosophy,* 106–7, 109.

is a kind of natural exemplarism. The other type is the exemplarism of the divine ideas, which is a kind of intellectual exemplarism. Although both the divine attributes and the divine ideas are ultimately reduced to the one divine essence, their manners of exemplifying things nevertheless differ in some significant ways. The exemplarism of the divine nature does not concern univocal perfections such as "man" or "animal" but rather transcendental perfections possessed in analogical ways. For this reason, it involves degrees of imitation with a more and a less, as is outlined in the Fourth Way. Regarding this sort of divine exemplarism, the deficient approximations that creatures have to their exemplar are clear—no creature perfectly imitates it since no creature is goodness itself, truth itself, or being itself. Regarding the exemplarism of the divine ideas, however, we find a different type of assimilation. In his commentary on the *Sentences,* Thomas explains that

The likeness of a work can be said [to be] in the worker in two ways: either as that which he has in his own nature, as man generates man, *or* as that which he has in his own intellect, as a work of art proceeds from the artisan in likeness to his own art. In both ways does a creature proceed from God in his likeness: according to the first way because beings are from Being and living things from Life; according to the second way because they proceed from ideal notions *(rationibus idealibus)*. Since, therefore, every single thing attains a perfect imitation to that which is in the divine intellect (for any kind of thing is of the sort he has ordained it to be), then in this sense of "likeness" any creature whatsoever can be called the "image" of an idea existing in the divine mind. For this reason Boethius says that the forms that are in matter can be called "images" in that they have come from those forms that are *without* matter.[71]

71. *In II Sent.,* d. 16, q. 1, a. 2 ad 2 (Mandonnet ed., vol. 2.400). Having identified this sense in which all creatures can be said to be made in God's image, Thomas explains that in another sense, only intellectual creatures are created in that image: "Similitudo operis potest dici ad operantem dupliciter; aut quantum ad id quod habet in natura sua, sicut homo generat hominem; aut quantum ad id quod habet in intellectu suo, sicut artificiatum ab artifice in similitudinem artis suae procedit. Utroque modo procedit creatura a Deo in similitudinem ejus. Primo modo, quia ab ente sunt entia, et a vivo viventia. Secundo modo, quia procedunt a rationibus idealibus. Cum ergo unaquaeque res pertingat ad perfectam imitationem ejus quod est in intellectu divino,

Whereas Thomas considers the exemplarism of the divine nature to involve a deficient imitation by creatures, it is clear from this passage that he does not consider the exemplarism of the divine ideas to involve the same sort of imitation. Rather, as he notes, creatures perfectly imitate their ideas. This conclusion makes sense if we recall his position that only ideas of individuals can function as exemplars. Thus, the exemplar of Socrates that is in the mind of God is the idea of "Socrates." Socrates cannot be more or less similar to this divine idea of himself: either he is like it or he is not; being Socrates does not admit of degrees. Hence, the likeness that he has to his divine idea must be perfect.[72]

We might ask, however, how it is possible for a finite, material

---

quia talis est qualem eam esse disposuit; ideo quantum ad hunc modum similitudinis quaelibet creatura potest dici imago ideae in mente divina existentis; unde dicit Boetius quod formae quae sunt in materia, possunt dici imagines, eo quod ab his formis venerunt quae sine materia sunt: sed quantum ad alium modum sola intellectualis natura pertingit ad ultimum gradum imitationis, ut dictum est, et ideo ipsa sola dicitur imago Dei." Emphasis added in translation.

Thomas's reference to Boethius here is to his *De Trinitate,* II, lines 51–56 (Loeb ed., 12–13): "Ex his enim formis quae praeter materiam sunt, istae formae venerunt quae sunt in materia et corpus efficiunt. Nam ceteras quae in corporibus sunt abutimur formas vocantes, dum imagines sint. Adsimulantur enim formis his quae non sunt in materia constitutae." Thomas cites this text on a number of occasions to argue that the divine ideas do not exist as separate forms, but rather as forms in the mind of God. See, e.g., *In II Sent.,* d. 15, q. 1, a. 2 (Mandonnet ed., vol. 2.372); ibid., d. 16, q. 1, a. 2 (Mandonnet ed., vol. 2.400); *De ver.,* q. 10, a. 7, ad 11 (Leonine ed., vol. 22.2.315:110–17); *SCG* II, c. 99 (Leonine ed., vol. 13.594); *SCG* III, c. 24 (Leonine ed., vol. 14.62); *De pot.,* q. 3, a. 8, ad 18 (Marietti ed., vol. 2.63); *ST* I, q. 65, a. 4, ad 1 (Leonine ed., vol. 5.153); *De malo,* q. 4, a. 1, ad 10 (Leonine ed., vol. 23.107:351–57).

72. Thomas again cites Boethius on this point: "Boetius formas materiales ponit esse imagines non Dei, sed formarum immaterialium, idest rationum idealium in mente divina existentium a quibus secundum perfectam similitudinem oriuntur" (*De ver.,* q. 10, a. 7, ad 11 [Leonine ed., vol. 22.2.318:327–32]).

To say that a creature such as Socrates shares a perfect likeness to his divine idea is not to assert that the creature is itself perfect. As we have seen, those divine ideas that function as exemplars are ideas either of individual substances or of individual separable accidents. God's idea of "Socrates" is thus, as it were, neutral with regard to any perfective separable accidents that Socrates might possess or lack. As we will see in chap. 6, the exemplar idea of an individual substance corresponds simply to its essence (see the section "Conclusions Regarding Thomas's Doctrine of Participation"). Hence, it is that essence that perfectly corresponds to the idea.

being to imitate perfectly an immaterial idea that is in the mind of God. Thomas offers something of an answer to this question in the *De potentia* when he considers how a name can be predicated of both God and creatures. Alluding to the different types of divine exemplarism, he again notes that a creature shares a likeness to God in two ways: both according to the divine intellect and according to the divine essence. Regarding the first way, a creature shares a likeness to God because it is like the form understood by him—a form, Thomas tells us, that has one and the same formality *(unius ratio)* as the created thing. Nevertheless, because this form *is* in the mind of God, it does not have the same mode of being *(modus essendi)* as the creature does since the creature exists *in re,* whereas the form in the mind of God exists only *in intellectu.* Regarding the second type of likeness, Thomas explains that the one divine essence is the likeness of all things but in a super-excelling way *(similitudo superexcellens).* For this reason, it does not share the same formality with any created thing.[73]

Following this passage, we can conclude that even though it is impossible for creatures to imitate perfectly the exemplar that is the divine nature, it *is* possible for them to imitate perfectly those exemplars that are divine ideas, precisely because such exemplars share the same formality with the things they exemplify. Moreover, not only is this perfect imitation a metaphysical possibility, it is a necessity.[74] As Thomas explains in the text quoted above from the commentary on the *Sentences,* creatures attain a perfect likeness to their ideas because God has ordained all things to be as they are. In other words, they attain this likeness because of God's intention,

73. *De pot.,* q. 7, a. 7, ad 6 (Marietti ed., vol. 2.204–5): "Inter creaturam et Deum est duplex similitudo. Una creaturae ad intellectum divinum: et sic forma intellecta per Deum est unius rationis cum re intellecta, licet non habeat eumdem modum essendi; quia forma intellecta est tantum in intellectu, forma autem creaturae est etiam in re. Alio modo secundum quod ipsa divina essentia est omnium rerum similitudo superexcellens, et non unius rationis."

74. The necessity of this imitation is, of course, a conditional one based upon God's freely willing creatures to exist.

which never fails. But this intentionality is part of the very character of an exemplar idea, for as we have seen, Thomas defines such an idea as "a form that something imitates because of the intention of an agent who predetermines the end for himself."[75] Thus, even though creatures fall short of the infinite perfection of the divine nature, they do not fall short of what God intends them to be.

God's exemplar ideas include this aspect of intentionality because in their very character they refer beyond themselves to the things that God wills to create. By contrast, the divine nature does not as such refer beyond itself. Hence, its mode of exemplarism does not directly include the characteristic of intentionality. Rather, it only includes intentionality indirectly, namely, inasmuch as the exemplarism of the divine nature presumes the exemplarism of the divine ideas. As Thomas explains, "The assimilation of a creature to God [i.e., to the divine nature] is accounted for in this way: that the creature fulfills what is in the intellect and will of God regarding it." Indeed, if God had never intended through his ideas to make anything like his nature, that nature would never have functioned as an exemplar in the first place.[76]

In chapter 3, we saw that Gilson's rejection of the divine ideas is problematic because it undermines Thomas's account of divine cognition. Now we see that this rejection is also problematic because it undermines Thomas's account of divine exemplarism. According to Gilson's reading, the only sort of divine exemplarism is that of the divine nature. As a result, Gilson unwittingly ends up rejecting Thomas's account both of God's intentionality and of a creature's ontological dignity. As we have seen, Gilson notes that created beings are finite and deficient approximations of the divine

75. See chap. 1, n. 50.

76. *De pot.,* q. 3, a. 16, ad 5 (Marietti ed., vol. 2.89): "Assimilatio autem creaturae ad Deum attenditur secundum hoc quod creatura implet id quod de ipsa est in intellectu et voluntate Dei."

The relationship between these two types of divine exemplarism will be examined in more detail in the context of Thomas's doctrine of participation (see chap. 6).

essence. That is indeed Thomas's position. But it is not his position that they are mere deficiencies. Although a created being such as Socrates falls short of the infinite perfection of God's essence, he nevertheless perfectly fulfills the finite perfection of his own essence. Moreover, God's intention to create him in this way is in no way deficient simply because Socrates does not perfectly imitate the fullness of God's nature. Rather, Socrates is precisely as God intended since, as Thomas explains, "any kind of thing is of the sort he has ordained it to be."[77] And it is the exemplarism of the divine ideas that accounts for this ordination.

Contrary to Gilson's claim, then, Thomas's doctrine of divine ideas does indeed form another piece in his "philosophical mosaic" and an integral one at that.[78] Geiger has observed that if one were to consider how Thomas's doctrine differs in content or function from that of his predecessors, one could rightly conclude that it is unnecessary to preserve the word "idea." Nevertheless, he continues, one could *not* conclude that Thomas's doctrine of divine ideas is itself useless, or unnecessary, or only a faithfulness to the vocabulary of a certain tradition. Indeed, from what we have seen, Aquinas preserves this doctrine for positive and systematic reasons.[79]

SUMMARY

Having considered the nature and types of divine ideas that Thomas identifies, we are now in a better position to examine their role as causes in his metaphysical system. Before doing so, it would be useful to summarize what we have discerned so far. In chapter 1, we found that Thomas considers ideas, whether human or divine, to have a twofold function: as cognitive and as causal principles. In the latter respect, they act as exemplar causes. We saw, however, that Thomas employs the term "exemplar" in an analogous way to

77. See above, n. 71.
78. Gilson, *Christian Philosophy*, 106–8.
79. Geiger, "Les idées divines," 179–80.

refer not only to causal ideas but also to the models toward which the artisan looks in making his works. He even employs the term at times to refer to the forms of natural agents. Nevertheless, Thomas considers the primary and proper sense of the term "exemplar" to refer to an actually practical idea. He defines such an idea as "a form that something imitates because of the intention of an agent who predetermines the end for himself." Hence, the term "exemplarism" primarily refers to the causality of just such an idea. In light of Thomas's definition, furthermore, we found that even though exemplarism entails efficient and final causality, it is properly reduced to the order of formal causality. Since exemplar ideas exist within the mind of the artisan apart from the things they exemplify, Thomas notes that their causality is an *extrinsic* formal causality.

In chapter 2, we saw Thomas provide several arguments to prove that just as exemplar ideas exist in the mind of the human artisan, so too do they exist in the mind of God. In chapter 3, we developed a clearer picture of these divine ideas. We found that Thomas posits the existence of ideas for everything that God knows—everything, that is, except himself. As we saw, a divine idea is not simply God's essence, nor is it even that essence as it is known by him. Rather, a divine idea is God's essence inasmuch as it is known by him *as imitable.* By positing this distinction, Thomas is able to affirm the plurality of divine ideas without compromising the unity of the divine essence. These ideas, he explains, are not the principles of God's understanding but are rather the *termini* of it. Thus, even though there is no real multiplicity of ideas within the divine essence, there is still a logical multiplicity of ideas regarding things understood by God.

In the current chapter, we found that this multiplicity includes ideas of such things as genera, species, individuals, and pure possibles. As becomes clear by Thomas's later works, however, not all of these ideas merit the name "exemplar" because not all of them function as causal principles. According to the strictest meaning of the term "exemplar" as Thomas comes to employ it, only those divine ideas that are of individual things made by God at some point in time can truly be called exemplars, for only they in fact exemplify things. These ideas are either of individual substances or of their separable accidents. Through such exemplars, God freely causes all of creation by an act of his will.

In the coming chapters, it remains for us to consider in more detail this causal relationship between the divine ideas and created beings. In doing so, we will discover whether Thomas can truly square this Neoplatonic doctrine of exemplarism with his Aristotelian understanding of formal causality.

FIVE

THE CAUSALITY OF THE DIVINE EXEMPLARS

We have thus far determined the sense in which Thomas considers ideas to act as causes, namely, as exemplars. We have also determined which of the *divine* ideas he identifies as causal principles: those of individual things that God creates at some point in time. But simply determining all of this does not reveal to us precisely how Thomas considers these divine ideas to act as exemplar causes. Thus, to understand better his account of the nature of this divine exemplarism, it will be useful for us to examine in more detail his analogy between the human artisan and God.[1] In doing so, we will need to address not only the similarities between these two agents but also the differences.

---

1. Because Thomas considers the primary sense of the term "exemplar" to refer to intellectual exemplars, the reader should presume that unless otherwise noted, the terms "divine exemplar" and "divine exemplarism" refer to God's actually practical ideas. Any reference to the divine nature as an exemplar will be made explicit for the reader.

DIVINE EXEMPLARISM AND
THE DIVINE WILL

From what we have seen, God, like the human artisan, causes things by his intellect. This conclusion follows, Thomas argues, when we consider that God's being *(esse)* is his act of understanding and, moreover, that everything acts insofar as it is in act.[2] Thus, the likenesses that exist in the divine intellect are productive of things.[3] Thomas notes that an intelligible form is a principle of operation in the way that heat is the principle of heating.[4] But just as form is not an active cause simply as form, neither is knowledge an active cause simply as knowledge. Whereas form as such has being *(esse)* through perfecting the thing in which it is by resting *(quiescendo)* in that thing, action requires a procession *(exeundo)* of something from an agent. Thus, knowledge as such only signifies that something is in the knower, not that an effect proceeds from him.[5]

How then does knowledge act as a cause? Only through the mediation of the will, Thomas explains, for the will by its very nature signifies a certain influence on what is willed.[6] The will adds to the intelligible form the inclination to an effect—an inclination that the form does not have of itself. Thus, as with the artisan, God's knowledge is a cause of things only inasmuch as his will is joined to it. It is for this reason that Thomas calls God's knowledge taken as a cause "knowledge of approbation" *(scientia approbationis).*[7]

Thus, knowledge directs an effect, but it is by means of a com-

---

2. *ST* I, q. 14, a. 8 (Leonine ed., vol. 4.180); *SCG* I, c. 50 (Leonine ed., vol. 13.144).

3. *De ver.,* q. 2, a. 5 (Leonine ed., vol. 22.1.63:297–98).

4. *ST* I, q. 14, a. 8 (Leonine ed., vol. 4.179).

5. *De ver.,* q. 2, a. 14 (Leonine ed., vol. 22.1.92:92–113). For an analysis of this article, see Serge-Thomas Bonino's commentary in *Thomas d'Aquin: De la Vérité ou La science en Dieu* (Fribourg: Éditions Universitaires de Fribourg, 1996), 547–60. Cf. *ST* I, q. 14, a. 8 (Leonine ed., vol. 4.179).

6. *De ver.,* q. 2, a. 14 (Leonine ed., vol. 22.1.92:108–10).

7. *ST* I, q. 14, a. 8 (Leonine ed., vol. 4.179–80).

mand of the will that the effect is determined to exist or not to exist.[8] It is for this reason that not all of the divine ideas are exemplars but only those that are productive.[9] As we have seen, even though exemplarism is properly reduced to formal causality, it nonetheless entails efficient causality since an agent must determine the end of what is exemplified. Hence, Thomas describes a divine exemplar as an idea that is "determined by the divine will to act."[10]

It is important for us to recognize this role of God's will in determining the divine ideas to act because it reveals the contingency of their exemplarism: unlike the Platonists whom he criticizes, Thomas rejects the theory of a necessary emanation. Since the divine nature is not determined but rather contains in itself the perfection of all being, God does not act by a necessity of nature.[11] It is true that he *knows* all things by the necessity of his nature because the divine perfection requires that all things be in him as understood, but this necessity does not entail a necessary creation. As Thomas explains, when someone knows something, he is in a certain way related to what he knows; by contrast, when someone wills something, the thing willed is related to *him*. The divine goodness, however, does not require that things other than the divine essence that are related to it actually exist.[12] Indeed, Thomas insists that those who do maintain a doctrine of necessary emanation cannot truly admit of divine ideas, for things that act from a necessity of nature do not predetermine the end of their effects for themselves.[13] This observation suggests that even though philoso-

---

8. *ST* I, q. 19, a. 4 (Leonine ed., vol. 4.237).

9. *In V De div. nom.,* lect. 3, n. 666 (Marietti ed., 249); *ST* I, q. 15, a. 3 (Leonine ed., vol. 4.204).

10. *De ver.,* q. 2, a. 10, *ad sed contra* 1 (Leonine ed., vol. 22.1.76–7:150–63): "Idea enim secundum praedictam assignationem accipitur secundum practicam cognitionem quae est ex hoc quod determinatur a divina voluntate ad actum."

11. *ST* I, q. 19, a. 4 (Leonine ed., vol. 4.237).

12. *SCG* I, c. 81 (Leonine ed., vol. 13.225).

13. *De ver.,* q. 3, a. 1 (Leonine ed., vol. 22.1.100:230–35): "Similiter etiam secundum eos qui posuerunt quod a Deo procedunt omnia per necessitatem naturae et non per

phers such as Plotinus or Avicenna may speak of divine ideas, they do not have a proper doctrine of exemplarism.

Because the nature of an exemplar idea includes the characteristic of the agent's predetermining the end of his effect, divine exemplarism bears a similarity to divine providence. As we have seen in earlier chapters, Thomas in fact maintains that God has ideas even of individual things since such things are determined by his providence.[14] Nevertheless, providence and divine exemplarism are not the same. To make this point clear, he explains that a created thing can be considered in two respects: as regards its species taken absolutely or as regards its order to an end. Now, the form of each preexists in God: the exemplar form of the thing's species exists in him as an idea, but the form of the thing as it is ordered to an end exists in God as providence.[15]

This distinction between providence and divine exemplarism reconfirms for us that Thomas considers the causality of the divine exemplars to be properly reduced to the order of formal causality. But what does this causality involve? As we have seen, Aristotle dismisses outright any talk of exemplar causality as but "empty words and poetical metaphors." To see if Thomas falls prey to his critique, we need to examine precisely how Aquinas considers the divine ideas to act as formal causes.[16]

---

arbitrium voluntatis, non possunt ponere ideas quia ea quae ex necessitate naturae agunt non praedeterminant sibi finem."

14. *De ver.,* q. 3, a. 8 (Leonine ed., vol. 22.1.116:64–68); *ST* I, q. 15, a. 3, ad 4 (Leonine ed., vol. 4.204).

15. *De ver.,* q. 5, a. 1, ad 1 (Leonine ed., vol. 22.1.139–40:186–92).

16. See *Metaphysics,* 1.991a20–22 (Barnes ed., vol. 2.1566). It should be noted here that Thomas's *ex professo* treatments of the divine ideas focus less on the nature of their causality than on such issues as their existence and their multiplicity. However, he provides a number of observations elsewhere throughout his writings from which we can discern a clear doctrine on this matter. Due to this fact and also to the consistency of his doctrine over time, my approach in this chapter will depend less upon a chronological consideration of the texts than it has in previous chapters.

DIVINE IDEAS AS FORMAL CAUSES

To begin with, it is clear from what we have said that since an exemplar is an extrinsic formal cause, by definition it is not part of the thing that it exemplifies. This is most clear in the case of the divine ideas, for if they were part of creatures, God's essence would also be part of them since his ideas are ontologically the same as his essence. Thomas is quite emphatic, however, that even though God is the formal cause of creatures, he is so only in an extrinsic manner.[17]

Here, it is helpful for us to recall from chapter 1 the different senses of "form" that Thomas outlines in the *De veritate.* In one respect, a form is that "by which" *(a qua)* a thing is formed, as the formation of an effect proceeds from the form of an agent. In another respect, a form is that "according to which" *(secundum quam)* something is formed; this form is part of a composite and, as such, is truly said to be the form of the thing. In the third respect, a form is that "in regard to which" *(ad quam)* something is formed. And such a form is an exemplar in imitation of which something is made.[18] "Hence," Thomas explains in the *Summa theologiae,* "through ideas the forms of other things are understood, existing *apart* from the things themselves."[19]

Although God's exemplar ideas are themselves extrinsic forms, they are nonetheless the causes of intrinsic form in created things. As Thomas explains,

It is clear that those things that are naturally made receive determinate forms. But this determination of forms must be reduced to the divine wis-

---

17. *De ver.,* q. 3, a. 1, *sed contra* 3 (Leonine ed., vol. 22.1.98:101–5). Cf. *SCG* I, c. 27 (Leonine ed., vol. 13.85–86). Thomas attributes to the Almaricians the error of positing God as the intrinsic formal principle of things. See *ST* I, q. 3, a. 8 (Leonine ed., vol. 4.48).

18. *De ver.,* q. 3, a. 1 (Leonine ed., vol. 22–1.99:159–82).

19. *ST* I, q. 15, a. 1 (Leonine ed., vol. 4.199): "*Idea* enim graece, latine *forma* dicitur: unde per ideas intelliguntur formae aliarum rerum, praeter ipsas res existentes." Emphasis added in translation.

dom as to a first principle that has thought out *(excogitavit)* the order of the universe—[an order] that consists in the distinction of things. Therefore we must say that in the divine wisdom there are notions *(rationes)* of all things, which we have above called *ideas:* that is, exemplar forms existing in the divine mind.[20]

Thomas's conclusion that the determination of forms in natural things is reduced to the divine ideas raises two important questions for us to consider. (1) The first is whether the causality of these exemplars is limited to the production of form alone or whether it also extends to the production of other principles within a creature. (2) The second question is whether this causality, inasmuch as it *is* productive of intrinsic form, excludes the causality of natural agents.

THE DIVINE IDEAS AND THE
PRODUCTION OF FORM

Regarding the first question, we find that Thomas's language does at times give the impression that the divine ideas are the cause of form alone. Again noting that the distinction and order of things proceed from the divine intellect, Thomas explains in the *Summa Contra Gentiles* that "in things that are made by an intellect, the form that is produced in the things made originates from a similar form that is in the intellect."[21] When speaking in the *De veritate* of the

20. *ST* I, q. 44, a. 3 (Leonine ed., vol. 4.460): "Manifestum est autem quod ea quae naturaliter fiunt, determinatas formas consequuntur. Haec autem formarum determinatio oportet quod reducatur, sicut in primum principium, in divinam sapientiam, quae ordinem universi excogitavit, qui in rerum distinctione consistit. Et ideo oportet dicere quod in divina sapientia sunt rationes omnium rerum: quas supra diximus ideas, id est formas exemplares in mente divina existentes."

21. *SCG* II, c. 42 (Leonine ed., vol. 13.364–65): "Si distinctio partium universi et ordo earum est proprius effectus causae primae, quasi ultima forma et optimum in universo, oportet rerum distinctionem et ordinem esse in intellectu causae primae: in rebus enim quae per intellectum aguntur, forma quae in rebus factis producitur, provenit a forma simili quae est in intellectu; sicut domus quae est in materia, a domo quae est in intellectu. Forma autem distinctionis et ordinis non potest esse in intellectu agente nisi sint ibi formae distinctorum et ordinatorum. Sunt igitur in intellectu

difference between God's knowledge and our own, Thomas notes that "from his intellect, forms flow forth *(effluunt)* into all creatures; hence, just as knowledge in us is an impression *(sigillatio)* of things in our souls, so conversely the forms of things are nothing other than a certain impression of the divine knowledge in things."[22]

Still, even though Thomas at times presents the exemplarism of the divine ideas solely in terms of an emanation of forms, these passages should not be read as excluding the procession of matter as well from these exemplars. We must recall that since God is the cause of both the formal and material principles of things, his knowledge of those things must also include both principles. Hence, he knows things not only according to their universal natures but also according to their individuality through matter.[23] As Thomas explains, the intelligible species of the divine intellect is "the principle of all the principles that enter into the composition of a thing, whether they be the principles of the species or the principles of the individual."[24] This is possible, he notes, because there can exist in the divine intellect a likeness even of matter which leaves, as it were, an impression in matter.[25]

---

divino formae diversarum rerum distinctarum et ordinatarum: nec hoc simplicitati ipsius repugnat, ut supra ostensum est."

22. *De ver.,* q. 2, a. 1, ad 6 (Leonine ed., vol. 22.1.41:297–306): "Verbum illud Algazelis intelligendum est de scientia nostra, quae in nobis acquiritur per hoc quod res imprimunt similitudines suas in animas nostras; sed in cognitione Dei est e converso, quia ab eius intellectu effluunt formae in omnes creaturas: unde sicut scientia in nobis est sigillatio rerum in animabus nostris, ita e converso formae rerum non sunt nisi quaedam sigillatio divinae scientiae in rebus."

23. *In I Sent.,* d. 36, q. 1, a. 1 (Mandonnet ed., vol. 1.832); *De ver.,* q. 2, a. 5 (Leonine ed., vol. 22.1.63:297–313).

24. *ST* I, q. 14, a. 11, ad 1 (Leonine ed., vol. 4.183–84): "Intellectus noster speciem intelligibilem abstrahit a principiis individuantibus: unde species intelligibilis nostri intellectus non potest esse similitudo principiorum individualium. Et propter hoc, intellectus noster singularia non cognoscit. Sed species intelligibilis divini intellectus, quae est Dei essentia, non est immaterialis per abstractionem, sed per seipsam, principium existens omnium principiorum quae intrant rei compositionem, sive sint principia speciei, sive principia individui. Unde per eam Deus cognoscit non solum universalia, sed etiam singularia."

25. *De ver.,* q. 2, a. 5, ad 13 (Leonine ed., vol. 22.1.64:399–404): "In intellectu divino qui est causa materiae potest esse similitudo materiae quasi in ipsam imprimens; non

Here, then, we find one of the limits of the analogy between divine exemplarism and human art: God is the cause of all the principles that enter into his work, whereas the human artisan is *not* the cause of all the principles that enter into his. An artisan knows his work by means of its form alone, and he produces the work in regard to its form alone since its matter has been prepared for him by nature.[26] For this reason, Thomas notes, "a chest that is in the mind of the artisan is not the likeness of everything that belongs to the chest, and in this way the artisan's knowledge and divine knowledge are not alike."[27] Unlike the exemplar forms that exist in the mind of the artisan, then, the divine exemplars are productive of matter.[28]

We see, therefore, that Thomas considers the divine ideas to give creatures more than just their forms: since the ideas are related to composite things inasmuch as those things can be brought into existence, these exemplars correspond to the entire composition of composite things.[29] Thomas's observation that "through ideas the forms of other things are understood, existing *apart* from the things themselves"[30] should not be read as suggesting that the exemplars are productive of form alone. As he explains, the ideas in the divine mind are not reproduced in creatures in the same way that they exist in God but, rather, are reproduced according to the mode that the nature of creatures allows. Hence, even though the divine ideas are themselves immaterial, they nonetheless produce material things.[31]

A divine exemplar could thus be described as a sort of *forma to-*

autem in intellectu nostro potest esse similitudo quae sufficiat ad materiae cognitionem, ut ex dictis patet."

26. *De ver.,* q. 2, a. 5 (Leonine ed., vol. 22.1.62:246–76).

27. *De ver.,* q. 2, a. 7, ad 4 (Leonine ed., vol. 22.1.68:132–37): "Arca quae est in mente artificis non est similitudo omnium quae possunt arcae convenire, et ideo non est simile de cognitione artificis et de cognitione divina."

28. *Quod. 8,* q. 1, a. 2 (Leonine ed., vol. 25.1.54:23–41).

29. *De ver.,* q. 3, a. 5 (Leonine ed., vol. 22.1.112:40–50).

30. *ST* I, q. 15, a. 1 (Leonine ed., vol. 4.199).

31. *De ver.,* q. 2, a. 10, ad 1 (Leonine ed., vol. 22.1.76:119–24).

tius since it corresponds to all of the principles in a creature. Thomas himself never employs such terminology in regard to the divine ideas, but the distinction that he provides elsewhere between a *forma partis* and a *forma totius* nonetheless offers us further insight into the nature of the exemplar ideas. In his commentary on the *Metaphysics*, Thomas explains (following Avicenna) that a *forma totius* differs from a *forma partis* as a whole differs from a part. Whereas a *forma partis* is a form that is found together with matter (the *forma secundum quam* of the *De veritate*), a *forma totius* embraces both form and matter inasmuch as it is the very quiddity of a species and, as such, is composed of both principles—although not as individuated.[32] Thomas presents examples of both types of form in his *De ente et essentia*. There, he notes that the *forma partis* is an integral part of a thing, as the form of a house is in the house. By contrast, a *forma totius* signifies the nature of a thing "prescinding" from determinate matter (but not from common matter). Thus, "humanity" is a form, not as if it were a part added to the essential parts of an individual man, but as it signifies the entire essence of the species "man."[33]

We have seen that a divine exemplar cannot be a *forma partis* since God's ideas do not enter into the constitution of created things. Rather, since it corresponds to both the form and the

---

32. *In VII Meta.*, lect. 9, n. 1469 (Marietti ed., 432).

33. *De ente*, c. 2 (Leonine ed., vol. 43.373:274–91). Although Thomas is clearly referring to a *forma partis* in this text, he does not explicitly employ this term. See also *In De Trin.*, q. 5, a. 2 (Leonine ed., vol. 50.143:67–121), where he discusses the distinction between an abstraction of the whole versus an abstraction of the part. Commenting on this passage, Armand Maurer explains that "[H]umanity is the essence of Peter; consequently it is his form or *ratio.* Notice that form in this context does not mean substantial form, for instance, the soul of man. The difference between these two meanings of the word 'form' is expressed by the terms *forma totius* (form of the whole) and *forma partis* (form of the part). The former is the whole essence, including both form and matter in a material substance. The latter is a part of the essence and excludes matter" (*The Division and Methods of the Sciences*, 4th ed., trans. by Armand Maurer [Toronto: Pontifical Institute of Mediaeval Studies, 1986], 27n16). See also Maurer's "Form and Essence in the Philosophy of St. Thomas," *Mediaeval Studies* 13 (1951): 170 ff.; Wippel, *Metaphysical Thought*, 202n15 and 328–29.

matter of a creature, a divine exemplar can be compared to a *forma totius*. However, unlike a *forma totius* that exists in *our* intellects, which corresponds only to the essence of a species, these divine forms correspond to the essences of individuals; for, as Thomas explains, according to the strict sense of the word "idea," "one idea corresponds to the singular, the species, the genus, and what is individuated in an individual thing."[34]

We have thus answered the first question that we needed to consider regarding the causality of the divine ideas: though forms themselves, these exemplars are nonetheless productive of both form and matter in created things. Nevertheless, since the exemplars do produce form, we must still answer the second question that was raised, namely, whether the causality of the divine ideas obviates the causality of natural agents.

DOES DIVINE EXEMPLARISM COMPROMISE NATURAL AGENCY?

In his *De Trinitate*, the Neoplatonic philosopher Boethius observes that "From the forms that are beyond matter come those forms that are in matter and that make up the body." It is an observation that Thomas makes reference to on several occasions.[35] This

---

34. *De ver.*, q. 3, a. 8, ad 2 (Leonine ed., vol. 22.1.116:74–79): "Si loquamur de idea proprie secundum quod est rei eo modo quo est in esse producibilis, sic una idea respondet singulari, speciei et generi, individuatis in ipso singulari, eo quod Socrates, homo et animal non distinguuntur secundum esse." Considering Thomas's doctrine of essence and how it differs from Aristotle's, Maurer observes that "[I]t now becomes possible to see that matter enters into the essence even regarded from the viewpoint of intelligibility. The existence of each being is a gift from God, created out of nothing according to an intelligible pattern which is a divine idea. In the case of a material being, matter forms a part of that intelligible pattern, so that even though strictly speaking there is no divine idea of prime matter, for in itself it neither exists nor is knowable, still there is a divine idea of the composite, which includes prime matter. Although unintelligible in itself, prime matter is thus essential to the full intelligibility of the composite and enters in full right into the essence of a material being" (Maurer, "Form and Essence," 175).

35. Boethius, *De Trinitate*, c. 2 (Loeb ed., 12:51–56): "Ex his enim formis quae praeter materiam sunt, istae formae venerunt quae sunt in materia et corpus efficiunt. Nam

observation, however, could be read to suggest that creatures play no active part in causing natural effects if Boethius's words were taken to imply that natural agents are not the source of forms in material things. In fact, Thomas tells us that several philosophers had held just such a position. As he explains in the *Summa Contra Gentiles,* these thinkers maintained that all natural effects are produced by God alone. Neither substantial form nor accidental form, they argued, could be produced except through creation because such forms cannot be made out of matter, for matter is not a part of form.[36] Thomas then proceeds to offer a brief history of this position.

Plato, he tells us, held that anything that does not exist *per se* is derived from something that *does* exist *per se.* Since natural forms do not exist *per se* but in matter, Plato concluded that they must be produced by forms that are without matter.[37] Later, the philosopher Avicebron also denied activity to natural agents but for a different reason. He argued that God alone is active and that since corporeal substances are most distant from God, they could not have any active power. According to Avicebron, the actions produced by bodies in fact result from the powers of spiritual substances that work through them.[38]

---

ceteras quae in corporibus sunt abutimur formas vocantes, dum imagines sint. Adsimulantur enim formis his quae non sunt in materia constitutae."

For Thomas's references to Boethius's observation, see, e.g., *In II Sent.,* d. 15, q. 1, a. 2 (Mandonnet ed., vol. 2.372); *In II Sent.,* d. 16, q. 1, a. 2 (Mandonnet ed., vol., 2.400); *SCG* II, c. 99 (Leonine ed., vol. 13.594); *SCG* III, c. 24 (Leonine ed., vol. 14.62); *ST* I, q. 65, a. 4, ad 1 (Leonine ed., vol. 5.153); *De ver.,* q. 10, a. 7, ad 11 (Leonine ed., vol. 22.2.315:110-17); *De pot.,* q. 3, a. 8, ad 18 (Marietti ed., vol. 2.63); *De malo,* q. 4, a. 1, ad 10 (Leonine ed., vol. 23. 107:351-57).

36. *SCG* III, c. 69 (Leonine ed., vol. 14.199).

37. Ibid.; Cf. *ST* I, q. 65, a. 4 (Leonine ed., vol. 5.152); *ST* I, q. 115, a. 1 (Leonine ed., vol. 5.538).

38. *SCG* III, c. 69 (Leonine ed., vol. 14.199). Cf. *ST* I, q. 115, a. 1 (Leonine ed., vol. 5.538). See Avicebron, *Fons vitae,* trans. into Latin by John of Spain and Dominic Gundissalinus, in *Die dem Boethius fälschlich zugeschriebene abhandlung des Dominicus Gundisalvi De unitate,* ed. Paul Correns, vol. 1, bks. 1–4, *Beiträge zur Geschichte der Philosophie und Theologie des Mittelalters* (Münster: Aschendorff Buchhandlung, 1891), II, 9, 39:23–40:27; ibid., III, 44, 176:25–177:14.

A more moderate approach was taken by Avicenna, who held that all substantial forms emanate *(effluere)* from the agent intellect, the lowest of the separate substances.[39] But while he posited this *dator formarum* as the source of substantial forms, he held accidental forms to be dispositions of matter that originate from the action of inferior agents disposing the matter. Avicenna took this position, Thomas notes, because active powers in bodies are found only in accidental forms, such as active and passive qualities; hence, Avicenna held that such forms are sufficient to cause other accidental forms, but they are not able to cause substantial ones.[40] In his *De potentia,* Thomas notes that Avicenna and his followers held this *dator formarum* to be the lowest intelligence among the separate substances, but "certain contemporaries *(moderni)* following them say that this is God."[41] This observation brings us back to our second question, for we might very well ask whether Thomas's own doctrine of divine exemplarism places him among the contemporaries whom he mentions.

Thomas is quick to dispel any such notion. In the same article, he proceeds to dismiss the position that God is a *dator formarum* who obviates the causality of natural agents. Everything, Thomas explains, is designed by nature to produce something like itself.[42] However, if substantial form were not generated by a natural agent (but by God, as these contemporaries argue), then there would be no need for a likeness in substantial form between that agent and

39. *SCG* III, c. 69 (Leonine ed., vol. 14.199). See Avicenna, *Philosophia prima* IX, c. 5 (Van Riet ed., 489–93:12–93).

De pot., q. 3, a. 8 (Marietti ed., vol. 2.61): "Et hoc *Avicenna* dixit esse intelligentiam ultimam inter substantias separatas." See Avicenna, *Philosophia prima* IX, c. 4 (Van Riet ed., 487:76–85).

40. *SCG* III, c. 69 (Leonine ed., vol. 14.199). Cf. *ST* I, q. 110, a. 2 (Leonine ed., vol. 5.512); q. 115, a. 1 (Leonine ed., vol. 5.538); *In II Sent.,* d. 1, q. 1, a. 4, ad 4 (Mandonnet ed., vol. 2.27).

41. *De pot.,* q. 3, a. 8 (Marietti ed., vol. 2.61): "*Quidam vero moderni* eos sequentes, dicunt hoc esse Deum."

42. Regarding Thomas's use of the principle *omne agens agit sibi simile,* see chap. 2, nn. 15 and 28.

its effect. Since we do find such a likeness, Thomas concludes that the effect receives its form from the natural agent and that it is unreasonable for us to pass over this generator in search of another one that is extrinsic to the natural order.[43] Indeed, Thomas is insistent time and again throughout his writings that any such argument against the activity of natural agents is contrary to our very sense experience.[44]

Why, then, do these thinkers make this error? Because of a misguided application of the principle that nature cannot make something out of nothing (ex nihilo)—in short, the position that nature cannot create. If natural agents were able to generate new substances through their own activity, then they would be causing forms to exist where there were no forms before. These thinkers reasoned, however, that this is to do nothing less than to make something out of nothing. Hence, they concluded that natural agents cannot generate things through their own activity. As Thomas notes, this erroneous opinion seems to have arisen from an ignorance regarding the nature of form. .

Natural form, Thomas explains, is not said "to be" in the same way as is a generated thing. A natural, generated thing is said "to be" properly and per se since it has being (esse) and subsists in that being. Form, by contrast, is not said "to be" since it neither subsists nor has being per se. Rather, form is said to exist or be a being (ens) only inasmuch as something exists by it. Having drawn this distinction, Thomas proceeds to explain that whatever is made is made according to the manner by which it exists, since the existence of a thing is the end of its production. Properly speaking, then, what is made per se is a composite thing. Hence, form is not properly made; rather, it is that by which something is made, since what is made is made through acquiring form. Here, then, we find

43. De pot., q. 3, a. 8 (Marietti ed., vol. 2.61).

44. See, e.g., In II Sent., d. 1, q. 1, a. 4 (Mandonnet ed., vol. 2.24); SCG III, c. 69 (Leonine ed., vol. 14.199); De pot., q. 3, a. 7 (Marietti ed., vol. 2.56); ST I, q. 115, a. 1 (Leonine ed., vol. 5.538).

the error of these thinkers, for they took the forms of natural things to be themselves subsistent, whereas in fact it is the composite that is subsistent by means of its form.[45]

But how do such composite things acquire their substantial forms? Thomas proceeds to explain in the same article from the *De potentia* that although nature makes nothing out of nothing, we are not prevented from saying that substantial forms exist due to an operation of nature. As we have seen, what is made is not the form but the composite, and this composite thing is not made *ex nihilo;* rather, it is made out of matter since matter, through its potency to form, is potentially the composite. Hence, Thomas explains, it is improper for us to say that form is made *in* matter; rather, we should say that from the potency of matter, form is "drawn out" or educed *(educatur).*[46]

Thomas explains that from the fact that it is the composite that is made and not simply the thing's form, Aristotle proves that this form must be from a natural agent. Since what is made must be like its maker, and since natural things are composite, their makers must also be composite. Consequently, the agent that generates natural things is not simply a form; rather, form is that *by which* the agent generates. And this form is one that exists *in* designated matter.[47] Here, then, we begin to see an answer to our question regarding Thomas's position on the causality of natural agents in relation to that of the divine ideas. As he observes in the *Summa,*

45. *De pot.,* q. 3, a. 8 (Marietti ed., vol. 2.61–62). Cf. *ST* I, q. 45, a. 8 (Leonine ed., vol. 4.477); q. 110, a. 2 (Leonine ed., vol. 5.512). As Thomas notes in the *Summa,* "Formae incipiunt esse in actu, compositis factis, non quod ipsae fiant per se, sed per accidens tantum" (*ST* I; q. 45, a. 8, ad 1 [Leonine ed., vol. 4.477]).

46. *De pot.,* q. 3, a. 8 (Marietti ed., vol. 2.62): "Nihil ergo obstat per hoc quod dicitur quod per naturam ex nihilo nihil fit, quin formas substantiales, ex operatione naturae esse dicamus. Nam id quod fit, non est forma, sed compositum; quod ex materia fit, et non ex nihilo. Et fit quidem ex materia, in quantum materia est in potentia ad ipsum compositum, per hoc quod est in potentia ad formam. Et sic non proprie dicitur quod forma fiat in materia, sed magis quod de materiae potentia educatur."

47. *De pot.,* q. 3, a. 8 (Marietti ed., vol. 2.62). Cf. *SCG* III, c. 69 (Leonine ed., vol. 14.200).

"corporeal forms are caused, not as emanations *(influxae)* from some immaterial form, but as matter that is brought from potency to act by some composite agent."[48]

We thus see that Thomas is careful to affirm the efficacy of natural agents. The operations of nature are not mingled with *(admiscetur)* creation, he tells us, but rather presuppose it:[49] just as the operations of art are founded upon the operations of nature since nature prepares the matter for art, so too the operations of nature are founded upon creation since creation furnishes nature with *its* matter.[50] Hence, Thomas draws a distinction between the causality of the divine ideas and that of natural agents: "according to the strict sense of the word, the ideas existing in the divine mind are neither generated nor are they generators, but are creative or productive of things."[51] As creative principles, the divine exemplars concreate form *and* matter; by contrast, natural agents generate things by educing form from preexistent matter.[52] It is because nat-

---

48. *ST* I, q. 65, a. 4 (Leonine ed., vol. 5.152): "Formae corporales causantur, non quasi influxae ab aliqua immateriali forma, sed quasi materia reducta de potentia in actum ab aliquo agente composito." Thomas is careful to note, however, that not all corporeal forms are caused by motion or generation. In *In II Sent.,* he identifies three exceptions. First, Thomas notes that because of the simplicity of its essence, a rational soul is subsistent, and hence, like the essence of an angel, it cannot be generated but can only be created. Second, he notes that since everything that is generated is generated from contrariety, bodies that are without contraries such as the heavenly bodies cannot be generated either. Finally, he notes that as regards those things that are generated by a univocal cause that is similar in species, it was necessary that the first individuals that came to be in their species—such as the first man and the first lion—were created immediately by God (*In II Sent.,* d. 1, a. 1, a. 4 [Mandonnet ed., vol. 2.25–26]; cf. *ST* I, q. 65, a. 4 [Leonine ed., vol. 5.152–53]). As regards the production of the rational soul, Thomas explains that natural agents are not entirely superfluous: "Quaedam vero creantur, etsi non praesupposita materia ex qua sint, praesupposita tamen materia in qua sint, ut animae humanae. Ex parte ergo illa qua habent materiam in qua, natura potest dispositive operari; non tamen quod ad ipsam substantiam creati, naturae actio se extendat" (*De pot.,* q. 3, a. 4, ad 7 [Marietti ed., vol. 2.47]).

49. *ST* I, q. 45, a. 8 (Leonine ed., vol. 4.477).

50. *In II Sent.,* d. 1, q. 1, a. 3, ad 5 (Mandonnet ed., vol. 2.23).

51. *De ver.,* q. 3, a. 1, ad 5 (Leonine ed., vol. 22.1.101:310–13): "Ideae existentes in mente divina non sunt generatae nec sunt generantes si fiat vis in verbo, sed sunt creativae et productivae rerum."

52. *De pot.,* q. 3, a. 1, ad 12 (Marietti ed., vol. 2.40–1).

ural agents are able to educe form from the potency of matter that Thomas can state: "We do not deny to created things their proper actions, although we do attribute all the effects of created things to God because [he is] operating in all."[53]

In answer to our second question, then, we see that divine exemplarism does not obviate the causality of natural agents. Regarding Boethius's observation on the origin of natural forms, therefore, Thomas concludes that "Boethius means that forms that are in matter originate from forms that are without matter as from first exemplars, *not* as from proximate forms *(proximis)*."[54] But what is the relationship between these two lines of causality? As we have just seen, Thomas holds that God, operating in all, is in some way the cause of the very effects of which natural agents are also causes. We must next consider how this double causality is possible.

THE DOUBLE CAUSALITY OF GOD AND NATURE

We have seen Thomas argue that a natural agent is the cause of the form of its effect inasmuch as the agent reduces matter from potency to act, thereby drawing out or educing the form from matter. In this way, a natural agent acts as a univocal cause *(causa univoca),* that is, as the cause of an effect that is of the same species as itself.[55] Now, Thomas explains that as regards two things in the same species, one cannot be a *per se* cause of form in the other: that is to say, the agent cannot be the cause of form as such. If it were, the agent

---

53. *SCG* III, c. 69 (Leonine ed., vol. 14.202): "Non igitur auferimus proprias actiones rebus creatis, quamvis omnes effectus rerum creatarum Deo attribuamus quasi in omnibus operanti."

54. *De pot.,* q. 3, a. 8, ad 18 (Marietti ed., vol. 2.63): "Nam Boëtius, intelligit formas quae sunt in materia, provenire ex formis quae sunt sine materia, sicut a primis exemplaribus, non sicut a proximis." Emphasis added in translation.

55. Regarding the nature of univocal causality, see, e.g., *In I Sent.,* d. 35, q. 1, a. 4, ad 1 (Mandonnet ed., vol. 1.820); *De pot.,* q. 7, a. 5 (Marietti ed., vol. 2.198); *ST* I, q. 13, a. 5, ad 1 (Leonine ed., vol. 4.147); *In II Phys.,* c. 7, lect. 11 (Leonine ed., vol. 2.88). See also Fabro, *Participation et causalité,* 338 ff.

would be the cause of its own form since it shares the same nature as its effect. Thus, for example, an individual man cannot be the cause of human nature absolutely, for he would then be the cause of himself. Rather, a univocal cause can only cause the form of another individual in the same species inasmuch as that form exists in matter. In short, it causes *this* matter to acquire *this* form. Thus, even though one man cannot be the cause of human nature absolutely, he can be the cause of human nature as it exists in *this* man. It is this mode of causality that Thomas terms "generation," according to which an agent's action presupposes determinate matter.[56]

The reason that natural agents can only cause form in this way is that the form by which they act is itself particular. To get a better understanding of the significance of this mode of causality, it is worth considering at length a passage from *Summa theologiae* I. In q. 115, a. 1, Thomas asks whether a body can be active. In response to the position of Plato and Avicebron that bodies cannot act because their forms are only participated forms, he notes that

This argument does not prove that corporeal form is not an agent but that it is not a *universal* agent. For as something is participated, in that respect it is necessary that what is proper to it be participated—just as to the extent light is participated in, to that extent is the nature of the visible participated in. But to act, which is nothing other than to make something actual, is essentially *(per se)* proper to an act as it *is* act: hence, every agent makes something like itself. If, then, something is a form [that is] not determined by matter subject to quantity, it is an indeterminate and universal agent. If, however, it is determined by *this* matter, it is a contracted and particular agent. Hence, if fire were a separate form, as the Platonists have posited, it would be in some way the cause of all ignition. But [in fact] *this* form of fire that is in *this* corporeal matter is the cause of *this* ignition, which [passes] from this body into that body. Thus, such actions come to be through the contact of the two bodies.[57]

56. *ST* I, q. 104, a. 1 (Leonine ed., vol. 5.464). See also *ST* I, q. 45, a. 5, ad 1 (Leonine ed., vol. 4.469–70); *SCG* II, c. 21 (Leonine ed., vol. 13.313). Despite Thomas's position that the human soul is created immediately by God, he commonly uses this example of man's generating man to illustrate this point.

57. *ST* I, q. 115, a. 1 (Leonine ed., vol. 5.539–40): "Sed ista ratio non concludit quod

Because, then, the operations of natural agents proceed from a form determined by designated matter, such agents are only particular agents. It is for this reason that they cannot be the cause of a nature absolutely but, rather, only as that nature exists in *this* individual. Consequently, Thomas concludes that such agents are the cause of the coming-to-be *(causa fiendi)* of a thing, but they are not the cause of its being *(causa essendi).*[58]

Thomas tends to employ this distinction between the *causa fiendi* and the *causa essendi* whenever he wishes to emphasize that only God can be the cause of the act of being *(esse)* in an unqualified sense. The distinction itself is a simple one, but Thomas's use of it has prompted debate among scholars. Wishing to reserve the creative act to God, some authors have argued that God alone is the cause of *esse.*[59] More recently, Wippel has argued that although Thomas insists that

forma corporalis non sit agens, sed quod non sit agens universale. Secundum enim quod participatur aliquid, secundum hoc est necessarium quod participetur id quod est proprium ei: sicut quantum participatur de lumine, tantum participatur de ratione visibilis. Agere autem, quod nihil est aliud quam facere aliquid actu, est per se proprium actus, inquantum est actus: unde et omne agens agit sibi simile. Sic ergo ex hoc quod aliquid est forma non determinata per materiam quantitati subiectam, habet quod sit agens indeterminatum et universale: ex hoc vero quod est determinata ad hanc materiam, habet quod sit agens contractum et particulare. Unde si esset forma ignis separata, ut Platonici posuerunt, esset aliquo modo causa omnis ignitionis. Sed haec forma ignis quae est in hac materia corporali, est causa huius ignitionis quae est ab hoc corpore in hoc corpus. Unde et fit talis actio per contactum duorum corporum." Emphasis added in translation.

In this passage, Thomas justifies the principle *omne agens agit sibi simile* with a brief deductive argument. Regarding Thomas's deductive arguments as justification for this principle, see Wippel, "The Axiom that Every Agent Produces Something Like Itself," 16–21.

58. Thomas gets this distinction from Avicenna. See Avicenna, *Philosophia prima* IX, c. 4 (Van Riet ed. 481–84). For Thomas's use of this distinction, see *In I Sent.,* d. 7, q. 1, a. 1, ad 3 (Mandonnet ed., vol. 1.177–78); *De ver.,* q. 5, a. 8, ad 8 (Leonine ed., vol. 22.1.160:324–39); *De pot.,* q. 5, a. 1 (Marietti ed., vol. 2.131–32); *ST* I, q. 104, a. 1 (Leonine ed., vol. 5.463–64). On his use of this distinction, see Fabro, *Participation et causalité,* 340 ff.; John F. Wippel, "Thomas Aquinas on Creatures as Causes of *Esse,*" *International Philosophical Quarterly* 40 (2000): 202 ff.; Meehan, *Efficient Causality,* 317 ff.

59. See, e.g., Gilson, *Christian Philosophy,* 123; Henri Renard, *Philosophy of God* (Milwaukee: Bruce, 1949), 20; James Anderson, *The Cause of Being* (St. Louis: Herder, 1952), 20, 28–30.

creatures cannot create or produce the act of being *(esse)* from nothingness, he nonetheless holds that they can be the cause of *esse* since the form that they educe from matter itself gives being. In this way, a natural agent is the cause of *esse,* but only as that agent acts through God's power.[60] For our purposes, the distinction between the *causa fiendi* and *causa essendi* is significant because it bears upon the relationship between the natural agent and the divine ideas as causes of form. Hence, with an eye to this notion, we will consider one of Thomas's mature texts regarding this distinction.

In *Summa theologiae* I, q. 104, a. 1, Thomas asks whether creatures need to be kept in existence by God. In the course of answering this question, he explains that every effect depends upon its cause inasmuch as that cause *is* a cause. But, as we have noted, some things are only the cause of an effect's coming-to-be and not directly of its being *(esse).* We see this in art: a builder is the cause of a house's coming-to-be, Thomas notes, but the being of the house depends upon its form, which gives order to its constituent materials. And we find this same distinction present in natural things.[61]

Now, if an agent is not the cause of form as such, it will not be a *per se* cause of the being that follows from that form; rather, it will only be the cause of the effect's coming-to-be. It is in this way that man begets man and that fire begets fire. Thus, Thomas concludes, "whenever a natural effect is suited to receive the impression of an agent according to the same nature that is in the agent, then the coming-to-be *(fieri)* of the effect depends upon the agent, but not

60. Wippel, "Causes of *Esse,*" 212–13. Wippel explains that "Causation of the particular determination (this or that kind of form) is owing to the created efficient cause insofar as it operates by its own inherent power as a principal cause. Causation of the act of being itself *(esse)* is assigned to it as an instrumental cause acting with the power of God and to God himself as the principal cause of the same. From this it follows that one should not maintain that Thomas denies that created causes can efficiently cause the act of existing or the act of being, at least in the process of bringing new substances into being" (ibid., 213). I will discuss below this notion of natural agents as instrumental causes.

61. *ST* I, q. 104, a. 1 (Leonine ed., vol. 5.464).

the effect's being *(esse)*."[62] Departing momentarily from the text, we might add as evidence of this fact that when such an agent ceases to exist, its effect does not cease to exist.[63] Thus, just as a house will not cease to stand simply because the builder has passed away, so too a parent's offspring does not cease to exist simply because the parent has passed away.

Returning to the article from the *Summa*, we find Thomas next explaining that sometimes effects are not suited to receive the impression of an agent according to the same nature that is in the agent. Elsewhere, he terms the cause of such effects an "equivocal cause" *(causa aequivoca).*[64] Thus, following the physics of his day, Thomas notes that the heavenly bodies are causes of the generations of inferior bodies that differ from them in species.[65] Unlike univocal causes, these agents *can* be the cause of form as such and not only as it is acquired in this matter. Hence, he concludes that universal agents are not only the cause of the coming-to-be of things but are also the cause of their being *(esse)*.

Now, just as the coming-to-be of a thing cannot persist when the relevant agent ceases its action, so too the being of a thing cannot persist when the relevant agent ceases *its* action. As an example of this principle, Thomas notes that the air is lit as long as the sun illuminates it and that air ceases to be lit as soon as the sun ceases to act upon it. The sun is light through its own nature whereas air is illuminated only by participating in the light of the sun—but

---

62. *ST* I, q. 104, a. 1 (Leonine ed., vol. 5.464): "Quandocumque naturalis effectus est natus impressionem agentis recipere secundum eandem rationem secundum quam est in agente, tunc fieri effectus dependet ab agente, non autem esse ipsius."

63. *De ver.,* q. 2, a. 3, ad 20 (Leonine ed., vol. 22.1.55:537–40): "Quamvis agens naturale, ut Avicenna dicit non sit causa nisi fiendi,—cuius signum est quod eo destructo non cessat esse rei, sed fieri solum." See Avicenna, *Philosophia prima* VI, c. 2 (Van Riet ed., 300-306). Cf. *In I Sent.,* d. 37, q. 1, a. 1 (Mandonnet ed., vol. 1.857–58).

64. Regarding the nature of equivocal causality, see, e.g., *SCG* I, c. 29 (Leonine ed., vol. 13.89); *De ver.,* q. 10, a. 13, ad 3 (Leonine ed., vol. 22.2.345:158–70); *ST* I, q. 4, a. 2 (Leonine ed., vol. 4.51–52). See Fabro, *Participation et causalité,* 338 ff.; Wippel, *Metaphysical Thought,* 517–18; Meehan, *Efficient Causality,* 320.

65. We will examine the causality of the heavenly bodies more closely below.

without participating in the very nature of the sun. So too, God alone is a being *(ens)* through his essence because his essence is his act of being *(esse)*, whereas every creature is a being by participation, and so its essence is not its act of being. Hence, Thomas concludes (following Augustine) that if God were to cease his action in governing created things, all species would cease to be and every nature would perish *(concideret)*.[66]

Thomas's distinction between natural agency and creation provides us with a framework for considering the relationship between the causality of natural agents and the divine ideas. God is the universal cause of all particular effects; indeed, Thomas holds that God is able to be such a cause precisely because the proper notions *(rationes propriae)* of all things exist in him as ideas.[67] Now, as we have seen, these exemplars are not generative but creative. Hence, they are the cause of the very being *(esse)* of things.[68] This is not to say that they are not in some way also the cause of the coming-to-be of things. It is impossible for being to be the proper effect of a particular agent, but coming-to-be must ultimately be the effect of a universal agent; thus, God can be cause of both the being *and* the coming-to-be of all things.[69] Hence, Thomas concludes that even though forms are educed through the causality of natural agents, God nonetheless works in the very operations of nature. In short, natural effects *as* natural effects can be attributed both to natural agents and to God.[70]

66. *ST* I, q. 104, a. 1 (Leonine ed., vol. 5.464): "Sic autem se habet omnis creatura ad Deum, sicut aer ad solem illuminantem. Sicut enim sol est lucens per suam naturam, aer autem fit luminosus participando lumen a sole, non tamen participando naturam solis; ita solus Deus est ens per essentiam suam, quia eius essentia est suum esse; omnis autem creatura est ens participative, non quod sua essentia sit eius esse. Et ideo, ut Augustinus dicit IV *super Gen. ad litt.*, *virtus Dei ab eis quae creata sunt regendis si cessaret aliquando, simul et illorum cessaret species, omnisque natura concideret.*"

67. *De ver.*, q. 3, a. 1, *sed contra* 4 (Leonine ed., vol. 22.1.98:107–16).

68. *De ver.*, q. 3, a. 6, *sed contra* 2 (Leonine ed., vol. 22.1.113:30–34): "Causa non dependet ab effectu; sed idea est causa essendi rem; ergo non dependet ab esse rei aliquo modo: potest igitur esse etiam de his quae nec sunt nec erunt nec fuerunt."

69. *De ver.*, q. 5, a. 8, ad 8 (Leonine ed., vol. 22.1.160:324–39).

70. On this point, see Fabro, *Participation et causalité*, 398 ff.

As Thomas himself acknowledges, it seems difficult at first to understand how natural effects could be attributed to both causes, for it seems as though it is impossible that one effect should proceed from two agents. This difficulty, however, is resolved when we consider that in every agent we can consider two things: the thing itself and the power *(virtus)* by which it acts. Since the power of the lower agent depends upon the power of a higher one, it is possible for one and the same effect to be caused by two agents.[71]

In the *De potentia*, Thomas provides us with a detailed consideration of this point. There, in q. 3, a. 7, he explains that one thing can be the cause of another's actions in four ways: (1) by giving the thing its power to act; (2) by preserving its power to act; (3) by moving (or applying) its power to act; and (4) by employing the thing instrumentally.[72] Thomas concludes that God works in the operations of nature in each of these four ways. Given the significance of this fourfold distinction, it is worth considering this article in some detail.

The first way in which one agent can be the cause of another's action is by giving the other agent its power *(virtus)* to act. In this sense, Thomas notes, that which generates is said to move heavy and light bodies since it gives this power to the agent. In this respect, God is the cause of all natural actions since he has given natural things the powers by which they are able to act.

The second way in which one agent can be the cause of another's action is by *preserving* the other agent's power to act. In this respect, Thomas explains, medicine that preserves the power of sight can be said to cause someone to see. For example, medicine can be said to cause someone to see by preserving the power of sight. Similarly, God is said to be the cause of all natural actions, not only by

71. *SCG* III, c. 70 (Leonine ed., vol. 14.206).

72. Regarding this division, see Meehan, *Efficient Causality,* 203–301; Fabro, *Participation et causalité,* 400 ff.; Wippel, "Causes of *Esse,*" 205–9; Jan Aertsen, *Nature and Creature,* trans. Herbert Donald Morton (New York: E.J. Brill, 1987), 314 ff.; te Velde, *Participation and Substantiality,* 164–75.

giving things the power to act, but also by preserving that power in being *(esse).*[73]

It should be noted that although these first two ways by which God is the cause of natural actions do differ, they are not really distinct. As Meehan observes, "the operation of God whereby he is the cause of the conferring of a power of action is not other than the operation whereby he conserves that power in being."[74] Still, these operations do differ according to reason, and for both we can discern a role for the divine ideas as exemplar causes.

Following the first way, these divine exemplars give things their powers. According to Thomas, the powers by which natural things act follow from their forms, for as he explains elsewhere, a natural thing is perfected by its form, whereby it has an inclination to its proper operations and to its proper end.[75] As we have seen, however, natural agents have an intention to induce likenesses in the things they generate, and this intention must be reduced to exemplars within the divine mind by which God directs everything to its end.[76] Since an exemplar idea gives a created being its form, it gives that being its powers, and it is by means of these that a created being acts for the end that God has determined for it. Furthermore, following the second way in which God causes the actions of nature, the divine exemplars also preserve these powers, for the exemplars are creative principles and give things their being *(esse).*[77]

The third way that God works in the operations of nature is as the cause of the coming-to-be of natural effects. This third way is founded upon the principle that nothing moves or acts of its own accord *(per se)* unless it is an unmoved mover *(movens non motum).* As Thomas explains, sometimes a thing moves another to act—not

73. *De pot.,* q. 3, a. 7 (Marietti ed., vol. 2.57–58).

74. Meehan, *Efficient Causality,* 295. See *De pot.,* q. 5, a. 1, ad 2 (Marietti ed., vol. 2.132).

75. *SCG* IV, c. 19 (Leonine ed., vol. 15.74).

76. *In I Meta.,* lect. 15, n. 233 (Marietti ed., 81).

77. *De ver.,* q. 3, a. 6, *sed contra* 2 (Leonine ed., vol. 22.1.113:30–34). While this observation appears in a *sed contra,* it is nonetheless consonant with Thomas's own view.

in the sense that it causes or preserves the active power of the other, but in the sense that it applies that power to action. In this way, a man causes a knife to cut by moving it, thus applying its sharp point to an object. Similarly, we find among lower natural agents that they do not act unless they are themselves moved *(mota),* and thus they are able to be the cause of alteration only through being altered themselves. By contrast, Thomas notes, the heavens cause alteration without being altered; still, they do not move unless they are themselves moved.[78] This hierarchy of movers proceeds until we arrive at God as the source of all motion. Hence, Thomas concludes, God is the cause of the action of every natural thing by moving and applying its power to acting.[79]

The fourth and final way in which one agent can be the cause of another's action is the way in which a principal agent causes the action of its instrument. As Thomas explains, the order of effects follows the order of causes due to the likeness of effects to their causes. Thus, a secondary cause cannot by its own power be the cause of an effect that is proper to a first cause; however, it *can* be the cause of such an effect as the instrument of the first cause. Through being moved, then, the secondary cause participates to some degree in the power of the first cause. Thus, an axe is not by its own form or power the cause of an artificial thing, but, rather, it is so by the power of the artisan who moves it, thereby enabling the axe to participate his power.[80]

Thomas concludes that in this fourth way, God is the cause of every action of natural things, for the higher a cause is, the more

---

78. Regarding the heavenly body as a *primum alterans non alteratum,* see Thomas Litt, O.C.S.O., *Les corps célestes dans l'univers de Saint Thomas d'Aquin* (Louvain: Publications Universitaires and Paris: Béatrice-Nauwelaerts, 1963), 189–96.

79. *De pot.,* q. 3, a. 7 (Marietti ed., vol. 2.58). The notions that Thomas expresses in discussing this third way are central to his arguments for God's existence based on motion.

80. *De pot.,* q. 3, a. 7 (Marietti ed., vol. 2.58). Regarding primary, secondary, and instrumental causality, see David B. Burrell, C.S.C., *Freedom and Creation in Three Traditions* (Notre Dame: University of Notre Dame Press, 1993), 97–101.

universal and efficacious it is. And the more efficacious it is, the more deeply does it penetrate an effect. Hence, every natural agent is active only because it is ultimately an instrument of God's action. As evidence, Thomas observes that in any natural thing we find that it is (1) a being *(ens)*, (2) a natural thing, and (3) of such a nature. The first of these is common to all beings; the second to all natural things; the third to things within a species; and, if we consider accidents, a fourth is proper only to *this* individual.

Now, as we have already seen, an individual natural agent cannot be the cause of form taken absolutely but only as it comes to be in a particular individual. Hence, Thomas explains here that such an agent can only be the cause of another individual of the same species inasmuch as the agent is itself an instrument of a higher cause that embraces the whole species. It is for this reason that natural agents can only generate something of the same species through the power of the heavenly bodies. Furthermore, nothing is the cause of being *(esse)* except through the power of God, for being is the most common first effect and is more intimate to all things than is any other effect. Hence, this effect belongs to God's power alone. Thus, Thomas concludes, God is the cause of every action since every agent is the instrument of the divine power's operating.[81]

Thomas's presentation of these last two ways in which God operates in nature may at first glance appear to be the same. As we saw, in discussing the third way *(viz.,* how one thing can be said to move another by applying its power to act), Thomas gives the example of a man's causing a knife to cut by moving it. How, we might ask, does this example differ from that of the axe mentioned in the fourth way? Are not both examples instances of instrumental causality? Here we must consider what Thomas says elsewhere regarding the nature of an instrument's causality.

---

81. *De pot.,* q. 3, a. 7 (Marietti ed., vol. 2.58). Although the proper cause of *esse* is God's power alone, the implication here, as Wippel notes, is that some created agents can exercise such causality as the instruments of God's power (Wippel, "Causes of *Esse,*" 208–9).

In the *Summa theologiae,* Thomas explains that any instrument has two actions: one that is instrumental and the other not. The first type of action is performed through the power of a principal agent and not through the instrument's own power *(virtute propria).* By contrast, the second type of action *is* performed through a power that is the instrument's own because that power belongs to the instrument according to its proper form. Thus, an axe is unable to make a bed except as the instrument of art, but it is nevertheless able to cut on account of its sharpness. Thomas is careful, however, not to deny the dignity of the instrument's role in the former action. Although such an action is not proper to the instrument, it nevertheless occurs only because the instrument exercises its proper action—for the bed is made by means of the axe's cutting.[82] Still, it is important to realize that the bed as such is above the ability of the instrument's proper form, for the bed as bed (and not simply as cut wood), is properly the effect of the artisan and not of the axe.[83]

When any agent acts in an instrumental way, then, it causes its effects through the power of a principal cause; but, when it acts through its proper form, it causes its effect through its own power. Why, then, does Thomas give the example of the knife when discussing the third way in which the action of an agent is caused by another? Because even though an instrument has its own proper power by which it is a cause, it can only exercise this causality by being moved from potency to act—as is the case with all created agents since only God is an unmoved mover. Thus, even though cutting is indeed an action proper to the axe, the axe nevertheless performs this action only because it is moved by another agent— not instrumentally, but rather from potency to act. We find this same distinction as regards the actions of natural agents.[84]

---

82. *ST* III, q. 62, a. 1, ad 2 (Leonine ed., vol. 12.20).

83. *De ver.,* q. 27, a. 4 (Leonine ed., vol. 22.3.805:285–304). Meehan, *Efficient Causality,* 298–99.

84. Meehan, *Efficient Causality,* 302–3.

Thus, in the text from the *De potentia*, we saw Thomas observe (following the physics of his time) that natural agents generate something of the same species only through the power of the heavenly bodies. A natural agent such as a horse is the cause of form only as form comes to be in a particular thing; to identify the universal cause of the nature as such, we must look beyond that agent. The Platonists did this by positing forms that are separated from matter, but according to Aristotle, this universal cause is rather some heavenly body. Hence, he observes that man and the sun generate man.[85] Thomas follows Aristotle in positing the heavenly bodies as universal causes of specific natures in individuals,[86] but he notes that the heavenly bodies, as bodies, only have material power. Hence, they are only capable of acting upon bodies in a bodily way: namely, by moving elementary qualities such as hot and cold.[87] The spiritual power whereby the heavens cause specific natures must thus be reduced to another, higher cause. For this reason, Thomas combines elements of Plato's position with that of Aristotle. Thus, he explains in the *Summa Contra Gentiles* that

All forms that exist in lower bodies *(inferioribus)* and all movements are derived from intellectual forms that exist in the intellect of some substance or substances. Thus Boethius says that *the forms that exist in matter have originated from forms that exist without matter*. In this respect, the saying of Plato is shown to be true: that separate forms are the principles of forms that exist in matter—although Plato had posited them as *per se* subsistent, causing sensible forms immediately. We, however, posit them as existing in an intellect and causing lower forms through the motion of the heaven.[88]

85. *De sub. sep.*, c. 10 (Leonine ed., vol. 40.60:126–150): "Secundum Aristotilis autem sententiam hanc universalem causam oportet ponere in aliquo caelestium corporum, unde et ipse has duas causas distinguens dixit quod homo generat hominem et sol."

86. On this point, see Litt, *Les corps célestes*, 166–73; Meehan, *Efficient Causality*, 322–23.

87. *De ver.*, q. 5, a. 10, ad 4 (Leonine ed., vol. 22.1.171:214–28).

88. *SCG* III, c. 24 (Leonine ed., vol. 14.62): "Oportet autem quod species eorum quae causantur et intenduntur ab intellectuali agente, praeexistant in intellectu ipsius: sicut formae artificiatorum praeexistunt in intellectu artificis, et ex eis deriventur in effectus. Omnes igitur formae quae sunt in istis inferioribus, et omnes motus, deri-

According to Thomas, then, the motions of sublunary bodies can be traced back not only to the motions of the heavenly bodies but beyond these to intellectual forms, that is, to ideas. Furthermore, as his language here suggests, Thomas is not only speaking of the *divine* ideas but also of those ideas that exist in the intellect of other separate substances. Thus, he explains in the *Summa theologiae* that Boethius's observation regarding forms existing apart from matter can perhaps be understood to refer to the angels since "from them originate the forms that are in matter, not by emanation *(influxum)* but by motion."[89] The angels are the cause of natural movements in the sublunary world inasmuch as they cause local motion by causing the first motion, namely, the motion of the heavens.[90]

---

vantur a formis intellectualibus quae sunt in intellectu alicuius substantiae, vel aliquarum. Et propter hoc dicit Boetius, in libro *de Trin., quod formae quae sunt in materia, venerunt a formis quae sunt sine materia.* Et quantum ad hoc verificatur dictum Platonis, quod formae separatae sunt principia formarum quae sunt in materia: licet Plato posuerit eas per se subsistentes, et causantes immediate formas sensibilium; nos vero ponamus eas in intellectu existentes, et causantes formas inferiores per motum caeli." See Boethius, *De Trinitate,* II, lines 51-56 (Loeb ed., 12-13).

89. *ST* I, q. 65, a. 4, obj. 1 and ad 1 (Leonine ed., vol. 5.152–53). The quotation from Boethius (*De Trinitate,* II, lines 51-56 (Loeb ed., 12-13) is cited by Thomas's objector who notes that "Videtur quod formae corporum sint ab angelis. Dicit enim Boetius, in libro *de Trin., quod a formis quae sunt sine materia, veniunt formae quae sunt in materia.* Formae autem quae sunt sine materia, sunt substantiae spirituales: formae autem quae sunt in materia, sunt formae corporum. Ergo formae corporum sunt a spiritualibus substantiis." In response, Thomas replies, "Boetius intelligit per formas quae sunt sine materia, rationes rerum quae sunt in mente divina: sicut etiam Apostolus dicit, *Hebr.* XI: *Fide credimus aptata esse saecula verbo Dei, ut ex invisibilibus visibilia fierent.*—Si tamen per formas quae sunt sine materia, intelligit angelos, dicendum est quod ab eis veniunt formae quae sunt in materia, non per influxum, sed per motum."

Thomas is insistent that angels cannot inform matter but can only act upon corporeal substances through motion. See, e.g., *ST* I, a. 110, a. 2 (Leonine ed., vol. 5.512).

90. *ST* I, q. 110, a. 3, ad 2 (Leonine ed., vol. 5.513). Unlike Aristotle, Thomas holds that the spiritual substances are capable of causing motion in the lower bodies immediately as well (*ST* I, q. 110, a. 1, ad 2 [Leonine ed., vol. 5.510]). Regarding the angelic influence on corporeal creatures, see James Collins, *The Thomistic Philosophy of the Angels* (Washington, D.C.: The Catholic University of America Press, 1947), 305–21).

In the *De spiritualibus creaturis,* Thomas describes a twofold order of spiritual substances: some are movers of the heavenly bodies and are united to them as movers to the moveable (rather than as their souls), whereas other spiritual substances are the ends of these movements (*De spir. creat.,* a. 6 [Marietti ed., vol. 2.392]). Thomas's dis-

Thomas thus explains that the forms present in matter proceed from this motion of the heavenly bodies, a motion brought about through the agency of the angels—or, more precisely, through this motion, these forms proceed from the intelligible forms that are present in the intellects of the angels.[91] And, ultimately, this motion from the angelic ideas must be traced back to the *divine* ideas.[92] Thus, through his exemplar ideas, God as principal agent is the cause of natural effects by moving natural agents instrumentally. Indeed, it is in part because God does operate in natural agents in this way that Thomas posits a plurality of divine ideas. As he explains, "Since we hold that God is the immediate cause of every single thing inasmuch as he works in all secondary causes and inasmuch as all secondary effects originate from his predefinition, we thus posit in him ideas not only of first beings but of secondary ones as well."[93]

---

tinction between these two orders of angels is not meant to supplant the traditional celestial hierarchy that consists of nine orders; rather, he is simply considering here the orders of angels that preside over corporeal creatures. In the *Summa theologiae,* he observes that in the traditional celestial hierarchy, "ad ordinem Virtutum pertinere videntur omnes angeli qui habent praesidentiam super res pure corporeas; horum enim ministerio interdum etiam miracula fiunt" (*ST* I, q. 110, a. 1, ad 3 [Leonine ed., vol. 5.511]). It should be noted, furthermore, that Thomas departs from Aristotle's numbering of the separate substances, arguing that their number cannot be discerned simply from the heavenly movements since not all angels act as planetary movers (*De sub. sep.,* c. 2 [Leonine ed., vol. 40.46:188–212]).

91. *ST* I, q. 65, a. 4, ad 2 (Leonine ed., vol. 4.153): "Formae participatae in materia reducuntur, non ad formas aliquas per se subsistentes rationis eiusdem, ut Platonici posuerunt; sed ad formas intelligibiles vel intellectus angelici, a quibus per motum procedunt; vel ulterius ad rationes intellectus divini, a quibus etiam formarum semina sunt rebus creatis indita, ut per motum in actum educi possint."

92. *ST* I, q. 65, a. 4 (Leonine ed., vol. 4.152): "Sed quia agens compositum, quod est corpus, movetur a substantia spirituali creata, ut Augustinus dicit III *de Trin.;* sequitur ulterius quod etiam formae corporales a substantiis spiritualibus deriventur, non tanquam influentibus formas, sed tanquam moventibus ad formas. Ulterius autem reducuntur in Deum, sicut in primam causam, etiam species angelici intellectus, quae sunt quaedam seminales rationes corporalium formarum."

93. *De ver.,* q. 3, a. 7 (Leonine ed., vol. 22.1.114:58–65): "Quia nos ponimus Deum immediatam causam uniuscuiusque rei secundum quod in omnibus causis secundis operatur et quod omnes effectus secundi ex eius praediffinitione proveniant, ideo non solum primorum entium sed etiam secundorum in eo ideas ponimus et sic substantiarum et accidentium sed diversorum accidentium diversimode."

Returning to the text from the *De potentia,* we find Thomas concluding that if we consider a particular agent, each one is immediate to its effect. If, however, we consider the *power* by which that agent acts, then the power of the higher cause will be more immediate to the effect than will the power of the lower. This is so because a lower cause is not conjoined to its effect except through the power of a higher cause. In support of this position, Thomas refers to the first proposition from the *Liber de causis,* which states that the power of the first cause acts by priority in an effect and enters more powerfully into it.[94] Still, he is careful to note that the priority of the first cause should not be understood to obviate the causality of natural agents: after reviewing the four ways by which God works in the operations of nature, Thomas observes that "When we add to these that God is his power, and that he is within everything—not as part of its essence but as preserving the thing in being *(esse)*—it follows that he acts in every agent immediately *not excluding the operation of will and of nature.*"[95]

---

94. *De pot.,* q. 3, a. 7 (Marietti ed., vol. 2.58). Thomas then proceeds to compare and contrast God's causality with that of the heavenly bodies. Cf. *SCG* III, c. 70 (Leonine ed., vol. 14.206); *In I Sent.,* d. 37, q. 1, a. 1, ad 5 (Mandonnet ed., vol. 1.858–59).

95. *De pot.,* q. 3, a. 7 (Marietti ed., vol. 2.58): "*Et ideo potest dici* quod Deus in qualibet re operatur in quantum eius virtute quaelibet res indiget ad agendum: non autem potest proprie dici quod caelum semper agat in corpore elementari, licet eius virtute corpus elementare agat. Sic ergo Deus est causa actionis cuiuslibet in quantum dat virtutem agendi, et in quantum conservat eam, et in quantum applicat actioni, et in quantum eius virtute omnis alia virtus agit. Et cum coniunxerimus his, quod Deus sit sua virtus, et quod sit intra rem quamlibet non sicut pars essentiae, sed sicut tenens rem in esse, sequetur quod ipse in quolibet operante immediate operetur, non exclusa operatione voluntatis et naturae." Emphasis added in translation. Cf. *In I Sent.,* d. 37, q. 1, a. 1, ad 5 (Mandonnet ed., vol. 1.859); *ST* I, q. 105, a. 5, ad 1 (Leonine ed., vol. 5.476).

Regarding the role of God's causality in acts of the human will, see Brian Shanley, "Divine Causation and Human Freedom in Aquinas," *American Catholic Philosophical Quarterly* 72 (1998): 99–122. Shanley argues that for Aquinas, God's creative causality extends to human actions without compromising the freedom of man's will. This article complements an earlier paper by Shanley in which he had argued against Stump and Kretzmann's position that God's knowledge is all-pervasive because his creative act is so (Brian Shanley, "Eternal Knowledge of the Temporal in Aquinas," *American Catholic Philosophical Quarterly* 71 [1997]: 197–224). For Stump and Kretzmann's reply, see Eleonore Stump and Norman Kretzmann, "Eternity and God's Knowledge: A

Following Thomas's observations regarding these four ways, we can develop a clearer picture of the relationship between the exemplarism of the divine ideas and the causality of natural agents. Like the axe that Thomas describes, a natural agent is an instrument with two actions. As the instrument of universal agents, its action is to be the cause of form taken absolutely, an effect that is above the ability of the natural agent's own powers.[96] Thus considered, a natural agent is the cause of form only because it is the instrument of the heavens, of the angels, and, ultimately, of God himself. As we have seen, this instrumental causality is exercised through the ideas in the minds of the angels and of God. But also like the axe, the natural agent has an action proper to itself following from its form: it is the cause of *this* matter acquiring *this* form. As we have seen, Thomas holds that form comes to be in a particular effect, not as a result of a divine emanation, but rather through the generative act of eduction. Thus, even though God concreates form with matter through his ideas, this exemplarism does not exclude natural agency.

As Thomas explains in the *De potentia*, form as found in natural effects can be considered in two respects. In one respect, it can be considered as it is in potency, and it is in this respect that form is concreated by God with matter, that is, without any action of nature occurring to dispose the matter for form. In another respect, however, form can be considered as it is in act, and in this way it is not created but rather is educed from the prior state of potency.[97] Thus, Thomas notes in the *Summa theologiae* that "forms par-

Reply to Shanley," *American Catholic Philosophical Quarterly* 72 (1998): 439–45. For Shanley's response to this reply, see Brian Shanley, "Aquinas on God's Causal Knowledge: A Reply to Stump and Kretzmann," *American Catholic Philosophical Quarterly* 72 (1998): 447–57.

96. Furthermore, as Wippel argues, natural agents are also instrumentally the cause of their effect's being *(esse)* in the context of substantial change. See Wippel, "Causes of *Esse*," esp. 212–13.

97. *De pot.*, q. 3, a. 4, ad 7 (Marietti ed., vol. 2.47). "Forma potest considerari dupliciter: uno modo secundum quod est in potentia; et sic a Deo materia concreatur, nulla disponentis naturae actione interveniente. Alio modo secundum quod est in actu; et

ticipated in matter are reduced . . . to the ideas *(rationes)* in the divine intellect, from which also the seeds of forms are implanted in created things so that, through motion, they can be brought *(educi)* into act."[98] It is this act of eduction that is proper to the natural agent. But even so, we must remember that God is still operating in nature according to the third way discussed above: for the motion that Thomas describes here is ultimately dependent upon the Prime Mover's moving the natural agent from potency to act, thereby applying its power.[99]

Thus, both God and the natural agent are causes of the same effect in its entirety, just as a work of art is said to be the result of both the artisan and his instrument but in different ways.[100] Rath-

---

sic non creatur, sed de potentia materiae educitur per agens naturale; unde non oportet quod natura aliquid agat dispositive ad hoc quod aliquid creetur."

Thomas is careful to note, however, that God can prescind from the natural order to produce effects without their proximate causes. See, e.g., *SCG* III, c. 99 (Leonine ed., vol. 14.307); *De pot.,* q. 3, a. 7, ad 16 (Marietti ed., vol. 2.56); *ST* I, q. 105, a. 1, ad 3 (Leonine ed., vol. 5.471); *ST* I, q. 105, a. 6 (Leonine ed., vol. 5.477).

98. *ST* I, q. 65, a. 4, ad 2 (Leonine ed., vol. 4.153): *"Formae participatae in materia reducuntur,* non ad formas aliquas per se subsistentes rationis eiusdem, ut Platonici posuerunt; sed ad formas intelligibiles vel intellectus angelici, a quibus per motum procedunt; vel ulterius *ad rationes intellectus divini, a quibus etiam formarum semina sunt rebus creatis indita, ut per motum in actum educi possint."* Emphasis added.

Thomas's reference here to *formarum semina* brings to mind Augustine's doctrine of the *rationes seminales.* Augustine's doctrine, however, presents natural agents as bringing out effects that were implanted by God at the first moment of creation. By contrast, as we see here, Thomas's doctrine of natural causality is founded upon the Aristotelian notion of the passive potency of matter. Still, Thomas does attempt to integrate Augustine's doctrine of the *rationes seminales* into his system. See *ST* I, q. 115, a. 2 (Leonine ed., vol. 5.540–41). Regarding Augustine's doctrine of seminal reasons, see *De Gen ad litt.,* V, 23 (CSEL, vol. 28.168:21–25); ibid., VI, 10 (CSEL, vol. 28.182:18–25, 183:1–13); ibid., IX, 17 (CSEL, vol. 28.291:15–23). See also Clark, *Augustine,* 36–37; Gilson, *Christian Philosophy of Saint Augustine,* 207–8; TeSelle, *Augustine the Theologian,* 214–21.

99. As Meehan explains, "To the extent that this motion is an application, strictly speaking, of a permanent virtue within the inferior cause, God is simply the cause (in his order) of the effect which is proper to the secondary cause. In the measure, however, that this motion is a transitory participation in a superior virtue, God brings it about that the inferior agent attains an effect which is proper to himself. He perfects both formalities always by one and the same virtual motion" (Meehan, *Efficient Causality,* 300).

100. *SCG* III, c. 70 (Leonine ed., vol. 14.207).

er than excluding natural causality, God's power is like a mediator uniting the power of a natural agent with its effect.[101] It is true that God has more influence on a natural effect since he is the first cause, but as Thomas explains, the effect is more like the natural agent since that agent in a certain way determines God's action to this particular effect.[102] Moreover, the natural agent's ability to determine God's action is possible because it has been given the power to educe form from the potency of matter. Thus, Thomas concludes that "just as the divine power (viz., the first agent) does not exclude the action of a natural power, so neither does the first exemplar form (which is God) exclude the derivation of forms from other lower forms that bring about forms like themselves."[103]

SUMMARY

We now have a better picture of the causality exercised by the divine ideas. As with exemplars in general, these exemplars in the mind of God are extrinsic formal causes. In positing the existence of such forms, Thomas shares something in common with the Platonists whom he frequently criticizes; yet unlike those Platonists, he rejects the notion that the divine ideas cause things through a necessary emanation. Rather, the causality of these extrinsic forms proceeds from an act of God's will, not from the necessity of his

101. *In II Sent.,* d. 1, q. 1, a. 4 (Mandonnet ed., vol. 2.26): "Unde operatio creatoris magis pertingit ad intima rei quam operatio causarum secundarum: et ideo hoc quod creatum est causa alii creaturae, non excludit quin deus immediate in rebus omnibus operetur, inquantum virtus sua est sicut medium conjungens virtutem cujuslibet causae secundae cum suo effectu."

102. *De ver.,* q. 5, a. 9, ad 10 (Leonine ed., vol. 22.1.167:458–65): "Causa prima magis dicitur influere quam secunda in quantum eius effectus est intimior et permanentior in causato quam effectus causae secundae; effectus tamen magis similatur causae secundae quia per eam determinatur quodam modo actio primae causae ad hunc effectum."

103. *De pot.,* q. 3, a. 8, ad 17 (Marietti ed., vol. 2.630): "Sicut virtus divina, scilicet primum agens, non excludit actionem virtutis naturalis, ita nec prima exemplaris forma, quae est Deus, excludit derivationem formarum ab aliis inferioribus formis, quae ad sibi similes formas agunt."

nature. Thomas does hold that God necessarily has ideas of every possible thing, but ideas that actually exemplify created things do so only as a result of his free choice.

We saw, furthermore, that while the divine exemplars are themselves forms, they are nevertheless the cause of all the principles that enter into created things, including both form and matter. Thomas's God is not the *dator formarum* described by certain Avicennian *moderni* of his time. Properly speaking, God's exemplar ideas are not generative principles but creative ones, concreating form in the potency of matter. Still, even though these exemplars are not proximate causes of generation, they *are* principal ones as the universal causes of natural forms. This is so because form as such is not the proper effect of natural agents. Yet, inasmuch as natural agents are the instruments of universal agents, they do participate in the causality of form taken absolutely. Hence, Thomas holds that natural forms considered in this respect are derived from the motion of the heavens, which motion in turn is reduced to the intelligible species in the angelic intellect and, ultimately, to the ideas in the mind of God.

Natural agents, however, still possess their own proper actions—actions that follow from their proper forms. The effect of these actions is to cause *this* form to come to be in *this* matter. The exemplarism of the divine ideas, therefore, does not exclude natural agency but facilitates it, for it is through the combined agencies of God and the natural agent that a natural effect comes to be— "not so that the same effect is attributed to a natural cause and to the divine power as though part is made by God and part by the natural agent," Thomas explains, "but so that in a different way the whole effect is from each: just as the whole same effect is attributed to an instrument and also to the principal agent."[104]

---

104. *SCG* III, c. 70 (Leonine ed., vol. 14.207): "Patet etiam quod non sic idem effectus causae naturali et divinae virtuti attribuitur quasi partim a Deo, et partim a naturali agente fiat, sed totus ab utroque secundum alium modum: sicut idem effectus totus attribuitur instrumento, et principali agenti etiam totus."

Having considered in this chapter how the divine ideas are related to creatures as causes are related to their effects, it remains for us in the final chapter to examine this same relationship but from the perspective of the effect as participating in its cause. In other words, we must consider how Thomas's account of the divine ideas fits into the structure of his theory of participation.[105]

105. An earlier version of this chapter originally appeared as "The Causality of the Divine Ideas in Relation to Natural Agents in Thomas Aquinas," in *International Philosophical Quarterly* 44 (2004): 393–409.

SIX

PARTICIPATION
AND THE DIVINE
EXEMPLARS

⌁

The theory of exemplarism is one that is closely related to the theory of participation; to mention the former is
to call to mind the latter. Any discussion of exemplarism,
therefore, would be incomplete without a consideration of
participation. Beginning with Plato's theory of the ideas, a
doctrine of participation has been offered by philosophers
as an explanatory account of the dependence that things
have upon their exemplars. Thus, it is no surprise to find
that in treating of the divine ideas, Thomas too addresses
the notion of participation.

In this chapter, we will examine Thomas's doctrine of
participation in general as well as how it relates to his theory of divine exemplarism. But before doing this, it will
be useful for us first to consider his understanding of Plato's account of participation. Not only will such a consideration reveal to us Thomas's thoughts about Plato's
doctrine; it will give us some insight into Aquinas's own
theory of participation.

THOMAS'S RESPONSE TO PLATONIC
PARTICIPATION

It has already been noted that Thomas's knowledge of Plato's thought is almost entirely (or even entirely) derived from second-hand sources.[1] Following these sources, Thomas explains that Plato posited the existence of separately subsisting Ideas as the species of sensible things. Plato's Ideas are thus presented as the cause of the very being of these things since the latter would participate in the Ideas.[2] For example, following this account, Socrates is a man because he participates in the Idea of Man.[3]

According to Thomas's reading, Plato's participation involves an assimilation of a participant (a sensible thing) to a participated Idea whereby that participant receives an impression *(impressio)* from the Idea.[4] It receives this impression, he explains, because the Idea mingles *(permiscere)* with the sensible things.[5] Hence, the Idea of Man causes Socrates to exist *qua* man by mingling with him. Moreover, the Idea of Animal causes him to exist *qua* animal also through mingling with him. Plato posited a hierarchy of numerous Ideas in which any single sensible thing participates.[6] By means of this structure of participation, Aquinas explains, Plato accounted for the generation and existence of all sensible things.[7]

Given what we now know about Thomas's doctrine of divine exemplarism, we can immediately discern significant differences between this account of participation and any doctrine that Thomas himself would adopt. To begin with, Thomas takes issue with Plato's positing Ideas as the essences of sensible things. Following

1. See chap. 1, n. 73.

2. *SCG* III, c. 69 (Leonine ed., vol. 14.199).

3. *ST* I, q. 6, a. 4 (Leonine ed., vol. 4.70).

4. *ST* I, q. 65, a. 4 (Leonine ed., vol. 5.152).

5. *In I Meta.,* lect. 15, n. 229 (Marietti ed., 80).

6. *Quaes. disp. de an.,* q. 11 (Leonine ed., vol. 24–1.99.181–88).

7. *In VII Meta.,* lect. 6, n. 1381 (Marietti ed., 409); *In VII Phys.,* lect. 6, n. 926 (Leonine ed., vol. 2.345.8).

Aristotle, he notes that because these Ideas would exist apart from the things that participate in them, they could not possibly be the very substance of those things.[8] In fact, Thomas holds that this is no less true of the *divine* ideas: they are not and cannot be the very substance of created things.[9]

Thomas's doctrine of participation, furthermore, could not involve the sort of mingling between exemplar and exemplate that he sees in Plato's theory. As we found in chapter 5, although the divine ideas are the forms of things, they are not intrinsic to the things that they form.[10] If they were, then God himself would enter into the composition of creatures, which is impossible.[11] Thus, the divine ideas do not mingle with the things that they exemplify.

Regarding Plato's notion that sensible things are generated by participating in separately subsisting Ideas, Thomas follows Aristotle's critique. As he explains, these Ideas are supposedly eternal and unchanging principles. If individuals were to be generated by participating in them, these participants would share in their likeness and would also be eternal and unchanging. But clearly they are not.[12] Once more, Thomas holds that this conclusion about Plato's Ideas is no less true regarding his own doctrine of the *divine* ideas: as we have seen, Thomas does not consider them to be generative principles but, rather, creative ones.[13]

Again following Aristotle, Thomas criticizes Plato's theory of participation because it multiplies entities unnecessarily: Socrates would participate, not only in the Idea of Man, but in every other Idea that corresponds to him, whether it be the Idea of Animal or

8. *In I Meta.*, lect. 15, n. 236 (Marietti ed., 81–82). Cf. *Metaphysics*, 1.9.991a19–32 (Barnes ed., vol. 2.1566–67).

9. *De ver.*, q. 2, a. 4, ad 6 (Leonine ed., vol. 22.1.58:267–68).

10. See the section "Divine Ideas as Formal Causes." See also *De ver.*, q. 3, a. 1, *sed contra* 3 (Leonine ed., vol. 22.1.98:101–5).

11. *ST* I, q. 3, a. 8 (Leonine ed., vol. 4.48); *SCG* I, c. 27 (Leonine ed., vol. 13.85–86).

12. *In I Meta.*, lect. 15, n. 237 (Marietti ed., 82). *Metaphysics*, 1.9.991b3–7 (Barnes ed., vol. 2.1567).

13. See the section "Does Divine Exemplarism Compromise Natural Agency" in chap. 5. See also *De ver.*, q. 3, a. 1, ad 5 (Leonine ed., vol. 22.1.101:310–13).

even of Two-Footed. That there should be such a multiplicity of exemplars is unfitting, Thomas argues.[14] If Animal were one thing and Two-Footed another, there would not be a single two-footed animal.[15] Thomas also rejects this sort of multiplicity of exemplars among the *divine* ideas; although there is a diversity of notions for genera and species in the mind of God, these notions are merely speculative ideas. Regarding those ideas that are actually practical (namely, exemplars), each created thing has only one that exemplifies it: an idea that corresponds to its individuated characteristics, its species, and its genera. This is so because in a being such as Socrates, the characteristics of Socrates, man, and animal are not distinguished according to reality.[16] Thomas's position implies that a created being would participate in but one idea: its own individual exemplar.

Finally, Thomas tells us that Plato's model of participation involves neither efficient nor final causality, for the Ideas that he describes are merely formal causes.[17] As we have seen, however, although exemplarism for Thomas is properly reduced to the order of formal causality, it entails both efficient and final causality as well. This fact suggests that participation for him also involves all three modes of causality.

By looking at Thomas's critique of Platonic participation, then, we begin to get a picture of what his own theory of participation involves as well as how it would relate to his account of the divine ideas. In summary, we know that for Thomas, (1) participation does not entail the divine ideas entering into composition with created beings, nor does it entail their acting as the essences of created be-

---

14. *In I Meta.*, lect. 15, n. 234 (Marietti ed., 81). *Metaphysics*, 1.9.991a23–b1 (Barnes ed., vol. 2.1566–67).

15. *De sub. sep.*, c. 11 (Leonine ed., vol. 40.61–62:48–56). Following Aristotle, Thomas is also critical of Plato's position that the more specific Ideas participate in more general ones since exemplars would thus be both exemplars and copies (*In I Meta.*, lect. 15, n. 235 [Marietti ed., 81]. *Metaphysics*, 1.9.991a23–b1 [Barnes ed., vol. 2.1566–67]).

16. *De ver.*, q. 3, a. 8, ad 2 (vol. 22.1.116:74–84).

17. *In I Meta.*, lect. 15, n. 237 (Marietti ed., 82); lect. 17, n. 259 (Marietti ed., 90); lect. 11, nn. 178–79 (Marietti ed., 61).

ings. (2) Furthermore, participation for him does not involve the divine ideas generating sensible things, but rather acting as creative principles. (3) If he holds that creatures do indeed participate in the divine ideas, this participation would not involve any creature really participating in a multiplicity of ideas.[18] (4) Finally, there is reason to believe that for Thomas, participation would involve not only formal causality but efficient and final causality as well. These conclusions, however, tell us more about what his doctrine does *not* involve than about what it does. If we wish to discern how this doctrine is related to his account of the divine ideas, therefore, we will need to consider precisely what in fact Thomas thinks participation entails.

WHAT THOMAS MEANS BY "PARTICIPATION"

Thomas makes reference to participation in numerous places throughout his writings, but his most explicit and detailed consideration of the matter occurs in his commentary on Boethius's *De Hebdomadibus* (1257–59).[19] In the commented work, Boethius considers the way in which substances are said to be good, asking how they can be good insofar as they exist even though they are not substantially good. In the course of this consideration, he addresses the meaning of participation. Commenting on Boethius's question, Thomas concisely presents the issues raised in this treatise: "Something is said of something in two ways: in one way substantially, in the other way by participation. The question, therefore, is whether beings are good essentially *(per essentiam)* or by participation. Now to understand this question we must consider that in the question it is presupposed that [for] something 'to be essentially' and 'to be by participation' are opposites."[20]

---

18. At least substantially. I will address participation in accidents below.

19. Torrell observes that "the current state of research does not allow us to specify the date further, nor its circumstances" (Torrell, 345–46). See Leonine ed., vol. 50.263–64.

20. *In De hebd.,* c. 3 (Leonine ed., vol. 50.275–76:40–49): "Dicit ergo primo quod

Earlier in his commentary, Thomas explains that a being *(ens)* or "that-which-is" *(id quod est) is* because it participates in *esse.* He proceeds to consider Boethius's observation that "what is" *(quod est)* can participate something, and in the course of this consideration Thomas offers an analysis of the meaning of participation. "'To participate' *(participare),"* he explains, "is, as it were, 'to take a part' *(partem capere)."* Thus, when something receives in a particular way what another has in a universal way, it is said to participate in what the other has.[21] Thomas then proceeds to describe three different ways in which such participation can occur.

Regarding the first mode of participation, he simply gives us two examples: according to this mode, man is said to participate in animal and Socrates to participate in man.[22] Although these are only examples, we can infer from them that any species can be said to participate in its genus and any individual to participate in its species, and this is precisely because neither participant has the intelligible content *(ratio)* of its respective perfection according to the complete universality of that perfection. This first mode has traditionally been interpreted by scholars as a logical participation rather than a real one, although Thomas does not explicitly call it such.[23] This reading follows from the need to reconcile some seemingly contradictory observations on participation by Thomas in other texts. As we have just noted, here in the commentary on

supposito omnia esse bona *inquirendum est* de modo, quomodo scilicet bona sunt. Dupliciter autem aliquid de aliquo dicitur, uno modo substantialiter, alio modo per participationem. Est ergo quaestio utrum entia sint bona per essentiam vel per participationem. Ad intellectum autem huius quaestionis considerandum est quod in ista quaestione supponitur quod aliquid esse per essentiam et per participationem sunt opposita."

21. *In De hebd.,* c. 2 (Leonine ed., vol. 50.271:68–71): "Secundam differentiam ponit ibi: *Quod est participare* etc. Quae quidem differentia sumitur secundum rationem participationis. Est autem participare quasi partem capere. Et ideo quando aliquid particulariter recipit id quod ad alterum pertinet universaliter, dicitur participare illud . . . ."

22. *In De hebd.,* c. 2 (Leonine ed., vol. 50.271:74–77).

23. See Fabro, *La nozione,* 27–28, 145–46, 149–50; Geiger, *La participation,* 48–49; te Velde, *Participation and Substantiality,* 76–82; Wippel, *Metaphysical Thought,* 96–97.

the *De Hebdomadibus,* he describes a species as participating in its genus and an individual as participating in its species. Yet in his commentary on the *Metaphysics,* Thomas observes to the contrary that "A genus is not predicated of a species by participation but by essence. Man is an animal essentially, not only participating in something of animal."[24]

As we saw above, Thomas observes in his commentary on the *De Hebdomadibus* that for something to be essentially *(substantialiter)* stands in opposition for it to be by participation. Nevertheless, after noting this, he then proceeds to explain there that even though this opposition would be true for Plato who posited that the Idea of Animal is other than that of Man, it is not true for Aristotle. Indeed, Thomas notes that the essence of animal does not exist apart from man's specific difference; hence, he concludes that according to Aristotle's opinion, nothing prohibits what is predicated of a thing through participation also to be predicated of it essentially.[25]

But how can something be predicated of another both by participation and essentially? Is Thomas contradicting himself? Not if each predication is made in a different way. As Fabro has noted, if we follow the Aristotelian doctrine of immanence, it is according to their ontological contents that genera and species are predicated essentially of their respective subjects.[26] Nevertheless, the receptive subjects possess the intelligible content of these perfections

24. *In VII Meta.,* lect. 3, n. 1328 (Marietti ed., 329): "Genus autem non praedicatur de speciebus per participationem, sed per essentiam. Homo enim est animal essentialiter, non solum aliquid animalis participans. Homo enim est quod verum est animal."

25. *In De hebd.,* c. 3 (Leonine ed., vol. 50.276:55–63): "Sed in alio participationis modo, quo scilicet species participat genus, hoc etiam verum est secundum sententiam Platonis qui posuit aliam esse ideam animalis et bipedis hominis; sed secundum Aristotelis sententiam qui posuit quod homo vere est id quod est animal, quasi essentia animalis non existente praeter differentiam hominis, nihil prohibet id quod per participationem dicitur etiam substantialiter praedicari." Cf. *Quod.* 2, q. 2, a. 1 (Leonine ed., vol. 25–2.214–15:51–72).

26. Cornelio Fabro, "The Intensive Hermeneutics of Thomistic Philosophy: The Notion of Participation," *Review of Metaphysics* 27, Commemorative Issue Thomas Aquinas 1224–1274 (1974): 471.

in a partial fashion, and so genera and species are also predicated of these subjects by participation—but it is a participation only according to reason since it concerns a less extended intelligibility sharing in a more extended one. It is for this reason that this first mode of participation can be referred to as a logical participation.[27]

Regarding the second mode of participation, Thomas again provides us simply with examples: according to this mode, a subject participates in an accident and matter participates in form. As with the first mode of participation, we again have something receiving in a particular way what another has in a universal way, for as Thomas notes, both substantial and accidental forms are common according to their intelligible structure and are determined by their subject.[28] Unlike the first mode of participation, however, this one is not logical but *ontological* or real. Here, the subject really participates in the form that it receives; the result is a composition between the receiver and the received perfection.[29]

Finally, regarding the third mode of participation, Thomas yet again provides us simply with an example: according to this mode, an effect is said to participate in its cause, especially, he notes, when the effect is not equal to the power of its cause. Thus, for example, we can say that air participates in the light of the sun since it does not receive that light with the same brightness that is in the sun.[30] This mode of participation appears to involve what Thomas elsewhere terms equivocal causality, which we considered in chapter 5. As with the second mode of participation, this kind is ontological or real.

Having laid out these three modes of participation, Thomas proceeds to consider the ways in which the act of being *(esse)* can and cannot be said to participate something. Since *esse* itself is most

27. Wippel, *Metaphysical Thought*, 97.
28. *In De hebd.*, c. 2 (Leonine ed., vol. 50.271:77–80).
29. Wippel, *Metaphysical Thought*, 98.
30. *In De hebd.*, c. 2 (Leonine ed., vol. 50.271:80–85).

common, he concludes that it does not participate in anything else. That-which-is or being *(ens)* is also most common, but it can nonetheless be said to participate in *esse*—not in the way that the less common participates in the more common, Thomas explains, but in the way that the concrete participates in the abstract.[31] For our purposes, it is sufficient here simply to have noted the three modes that he outlines. Having looked at them, we now have a general understanding of the meaning that he ascribes to participation. To get a better understanding of this meaning, we will turn next to consider what scholars have made of it, focusing in particular on the interpretations of Fabro, Geiger, and Wippel.[32]

DIFFERENT INTERPRETATIONS OF
PARTICIPATION IN AQUINAS

Since around the time of the Second World War, there has been a growing recognition among scholars of the significance of Thomas's theory of participation. This development has been due in large measure to the efforts of both Cornelio Fabro and Louis Geiger. Yet while both scholars share a common recognition of the importance of this theory in Thomas's system, they nonetheless differ regarding how they think that theory should be understood.

In his formative work *La nozione metafisica di partecipazione,* Fabro identifies what he sees in Thomas's writings as two fundamental modes of participation: what he terms "predicamental-univocal participation" and "transcendental-analogical participation." Accord-

31. *In De hebd.,* c. 2 (Leonine ed., vol. 50. 271:85–113). For an analysis of this consideration, see Wippel, *Metaphysical Thought,* 98 ff.

32. The authors on this list by no means exhaust the scholarship on this topic, but they most effectively bring to light those issues that are relevant for our consideration. For other work on this topic, see Little, *Platonic Heritage;* Henle, *Thomas and Platonism;* W. Norris Clarke, "The Limitation of Act by Potency in St. Thomas: Aristotelianism or Neoplatonism?" *The New Scholasticism* 26 (1952): 167–94; id., "The Meaning of Participation in St. Thomas," *Proceedings of the American Catholic Philosophical Association* 26 (1952): 147–57; te Velde, *Participation and Substantiality.*

ing to the first mode, Fabro explains, all the individual participants share the same formality that they have through their essential content. These participants really exist in themselves, but what they participate in does not; rather, it exists only *in* the participants.[33] Furthermore, both the participated and the participant belong to the realm of finite substance outlined in Aristotle's *Categories*. It is for this reason that Fabro terms this "*predicamental* participation." And he identifies such participation with the first two modes outlined by Thomas in his commentary on the *De Hebdomadibus*. Thus, Fabro"s predicamental participation includes both logical participation *and* a mode of real participation, namely, that whereby matter participates in form or a subject in its accidents.[34] Since predicamental participation is the foundation of generic and specific perfections, Fabro explains that it concerns univocal formalities.[35]

In contrast to predicamental participation, transcendental participation does not involve the participants sharing in the same way in a formality; rather, they participate in a given perfection according to a deficiency of likeness. Such a perfection, unlike those of predicamental participation, exists outside of the participant either as a property of a higher entity or in itself as a pure and subsistent formality in its full possession, for example, as beings *(entia)* participate in *esse*. Since the participated perfections here are shared in by the participants according to differing degrees and cannot be predicated of them univocally, this is an analogical mode of participation, and Fabro regards it as the strongest meaning of "participation."[36]

He thus considers a creature to be a being by participation in a twofold manner: first, according to the transcendental order inasmuch as it is a composite of essence and *esse;* and second, according to the predicamental order inasmuch as it is a composite

33. Fabro, *La nozione*, 317–18.
34. Fabro, *La nozione*, 145–46.
35. Fabro, *Participation et causalité*, 626; id., "Intensive Hermeneutics," 471.
36. Fabro, *La nozione*, 318.

of matter and form, or of substance and accidents.[37] Although he emphasizes the distinction between these two modes of participation, Fabro is careful to note that Thomas considers them to be in close relationship to one another.[38] Still, regarding this structure of participation, Fabro stresses the importance of the real composition between essence and *esse* within a creature. As he explains, "since the essence of a creature has also its own participated act of being *(actus essendi)*, its actualization is not merely a relation of extrinsic dependence; rather, it is based on the act of *esse* in which it participates and which it preserves within itself and is the proper terminus of divine causality."[39]

Like Fabro, Louis Geiger discerns in Thomas's writings two modes of participation: what he terms "participation by composition" and "participation by similitude" or "formal hierarchy." Historically, Geiger argues, these have been two distinct systems, but Thomas comes to adopt them both. As Geiger explains in *La participation dans la philosophie de s. Thomas d'Aquin,* the fundamental element of the first type of participation is composition itself, namely, of a receiver and that which it receives. To participate in this sense, then, is to possess something that one has received. If the receiving subject is less perfect than its received perfection, the subject will limit that perfection. Thus, Geiger explains, limitation occurs in nearly all instances of composition. Those philosophical systems that adopt this type of participation (such as Platonism) account for limitation by reason of the composition itself. In light of these observations, Geiger offers the following definition of participation by composition: "the *reception* and consequently the *possession* of an element playing the role of form by a subject playing the role of matter."[40]

37. Fabro, "Intensive Hermeneutics," 480–81.

38. Ibid., 471–72.

39. Ibid., 481.

40. Geiger, *La participation,* 27–28: "On peut donc la définir de la manière suivante: la participation est la *réception* et conséquemment la *possession* d'un élément, jouant le rôle de forme, par un sujet jouant le rôle de matière."

The second system of participation that he describes, participation by similitude or formal hierarchy, involves states of greater and lesser perfection and is founded precisely on this unequal perfection. As Geiger explains regarding this system, "participation expresses the diminished, particularized, and, in this sense, participated state of an essence each time that it is not realized in the absolute fullness of its formal content." Thus, if two things both imitate the same source for their perfection, each does so to its own degree. This system of participation may also involve composition, but even then the principle of limitation is not presented as resulting from the composition itself; rather, philosophical systems that adopt this type of participation (such as Neoplatonism) account for limitation by reason of the formal inequality that we have described.[41]

Hence, as Geiger explains, these two systems of participation are not distinguished from each other because of the presence or absence of composition in the participant but rather because of their explanation of limitation. If composition explains the limitation of the received perfection, then we have an instance of participation by composition. If, however, the limitation is prior by nature to any composition, then we have an instance of participation by similitude, or formal hierarchy. Again, Geiger considers these two types of participation to be distinct systems. Still, he is careful to note that they need not be exclusive. Participation by composition could be seen as offering an account of the complex structures of the beings of our experience: an account intended simply to make participation by formal hierarchy more intelligible to us. In fact, Geiger argues, this is precisely what we find in Thomas's metaphysics of participation.[42]

According to Geiger, Thomas recognized that neither of these

41. Geiger, La participation, 28–29. "La participation exprime l'état diminué, particularisé, et, en ce sens, participé, d'une essence, chaque fois qu'elle n'est pas réalisée dans la plénitude absolue de son contenu formel." Emphasis is in the original.

42. Ibid., 29–30.

systems is sufficient without the other: participation by composition is incapable of explaining the origin of either formal multiplicity or the subject that limits forms, whereas participation by formal hierarchy seems incapable of explaining the composition between matter and form, essence and *esse*, or subject and accident.[43] Hence, Thomas adopts both systems. Geiger, however, argues that Aquinas nonetheless assigns primacy to the latter.[44]

Looking at the commentary on the *De Hebdomadibus*, Geiger focuses only on the second and third modes of participation described there, since the first is according to the order of reason and not of reality. Geiger notes that the second mode of participation (that of matter in form and of a subject in its accidents) involves composition. This composition accounts for limitation in its own order, but he argues that there must be a prior limitation to account for the very subject of the composition. Looking to the third mode of participation described by Thomas (that of an effect in its cause), Geiger maintains that if an effect is produced by its cause, the effect cannot receive before it even exists the very thing that makes it to be—in short, its limitation must precede its composition.[45]

Regarding the relation of created essence to *esse*, Geiger acknowledges that there is a composition of the two principles in any created being: the two are really distinct, and essence is the proper principle of the limitation of *esse* within the being. If we wish to avoid an infinite regress of limiting compositions, however, this limitation of *esse* cannot be due simply to essence as such since the essence does not exist prior to its act of being *(esse)*, he argues. Geiger concludes, therefore, that we must appeal here to a prior participation: the participation of formal hierarchy by which participants share in a greater or lesser likeness to the First Perfection. As he explains, "the essence that participates *in (à)* existence is itself a

43. Ibid., 301.
44. Ibid., 392–98.
45. Ibid., 48–52.

participation *of (de)* the First Perfection, of which it conveys only a limited and fragmentary aspect."[46]

Geiger's division regarding the two systems of participation bears some similarity to Fabro's own division; nevertheless, there are fundamental differences between their two interpretations of Thomas. Whereas Geiger assigns primacy to participation by similitude to account for the limitation of *esse* in finite beings, Fabro assigns primacy to composition. Fabro, moreover, considers Geiger to have made too strict a division between composition and formal hierarchy. Fabro argues that to accept Geiger's division is to compromise the real distinction between essence and *esse* in finite beings.[47] Still, despite these differences between Geiger and Fabro, John Wippel has suggested more recently that their interpretations can in some sense be reconciled into a single approach, as long as each is considered within the context of its proper perspective.

In *The Metaphysical Thought of Thomas Aquinas,* Wippel examines participation and the problem of the one and the many.[48] Like his predecessors, Wippel looks principally to Thomas's commentary on the *De Hebdomadibus* for answers, focusing his attention in particular on the participation of finite beings in (substantial) *esse.* As regards the first mode of participation described by Thomas, Wippel explains that participation in *esse* cannot be reduced to

46. Ibid., 60–61n3: "L'être, au sens plein, c'est le sujet concret: ens. Il est tel par son essence, il est réel par son existence. Et parce que l'essence, réellement distincte de l'existence, est le principe propre de la diversité et de l'inégalité dans l'être, le problème se pose de l'origine de cette inégalité, voire de sa possibilité. On ne peut évidemment expliquer cette limitation par une composition, antérieure. Ce serait confondre les principes de l'être et l'être subsistant. Ce serait aller à l'infini dans la série des compositions sans rien expliquer. Il faut faire appel à la participation par hiérarchie formelle: l'essence qui participe à l'existence est elle-même une participation de la Perfection Première, dont elle ne dit qu'un aspect limité et fragmentaire." ·

47. Fabro, "Intensive Hermeneutics," 469.

48. Wippel, *Metaphysical Thought,* chap. 4, 94–131. An earlier version of this chapter originally appeared as "Thomas Aquinas and Participation," in *Studies in Medieval Philosophy,* ed. John F. Wippel, Studies in Philosophy and the History of Philosophy, vol. 17 (Washington, D.C.: The Catholic University of America Press, 1987), 117–58.

that mode for several reasons: (1) because participation in *esse* is not a logical participation but a real one; (2) because it involves a real distinction between the participant and that in which it participates; (3) because *esse* is not predicated essentially of the participant;[49] and (4) because participation in *esse* does not allow for univocal predication, whereas logical participation does.[50]

As regards the second mode of participation, Wippel acknowledges that, unlike the first, it is a real participation that does involve a distinction between the participant and that which is participated. Nevertheless, he offers several reasons why participation in *esse* cannot be reduced to this mode either. (1) First, for a subject to participate in its accidents, the subject must already exist for this participation to be possible—an existence that it has only because it participates in *esse*. Hence, Wippel concludes, participation in *esse* is more fundamental than that of a subject in its accidents. And, he adds, it is more fundamental than the participation of matter in its form since a matter-form composite must participate in *esse* for it to exist. (2) In the two examples that Thomas gives to illustrate this second mode of participation, a third thing or *tertium quid* is the result, since the participation of form in matter results in the essence of a material thing, and (we might add) the participation of a subject in its accidents results in a new accidental unity. By contrast, however, the composition of essence and *esse* does not result in a third thing; *esse* is rather the act whereby a "thing" (*viz.*, essence) exists.[51] (3) The third difference that Wippel brings to light is that in matter-form composition, the specification of the kind of being that results from the participation (e.g., a

49. For this reason, Thomas at times describes *esse* as an accident in relation to essence. As Wippel notes, however, "He does not mean by this that *esse* (the act of being) is a predicamental accident, but only that it is not part of the essence of any creature" (Wippel, *Metaphysical Thought,* 106). For Thomas's clarification of this point, see *In IV Meta.,* lect. 2, n. 558 (Marietti ed., 187); *Quod.* 12, q. 4, a. 1 (Leonine ed., vol. 25.2.404:27–37).

50. Wippel, *Metaphysical Thought,* 103, 105–6.

51. See, e.g., *Quod.* 2, q. 2, a. 1 (Leonine ed., vol. 25.2.214–15).

human being as opposed to a dog) is determined by the act principle, namely, the form. In the composition of essence and *esse*, however, the specification of the kind of being is determined by the potency principle, namely, the essence. (4) Finally, this second mode of participation, like the first, allows for univocal predication. As we have already noted, however, *esse* can only be predicated analogically of whatever participates in it.[52]

Having eliminated these first two modes of participation, Wippel concludes that participation of beings in *esse* corresponds to the third mode that Thomas describes: that of an effect in its cause, especially when the effect is not equal in power to that cause. But what does it mean to participate in *esse*? Here, Wippel brings some clarity to a point that, as he notes, has received too little attention.[53] When Thomas speaks of beings participating in *esse*, he is not always using the term *esse* in the same respect: sometimes he uses it to refer to *esse commune*, sometimes to *esse subsistens* (i.e., God), and other times he uses it to refer to the *actus essendi* of finite beings. Still, Wippel argues that in each of these three senses, participation in *esse* corresponds to the third mode of participation outlined in the commentary on the *De Hebdomadibus*.

As he explains, to speak of participation in *esse commune* is to say that each finite being merely shares in *esse* without possessing the fullness of the perfection that is signified by the term. To speak of participation in *esse commune* is not to posit a sort of Platonic subsisting universal, however; rather, it is to say that individual beings are said to *have esse* but are not identical with it. Apart from these individual beings, *esse commune* exists only according to reason.[54] Here, we might add as an analogy that just as Socrates really participates in the common form of whiteness even though whiteness does not really exist apart from him, so too individual beings participate in *esse commune* even though it too does not really exist apart from

52. Wippel, *Metaphysical Thought*, 103–6.
53. Ibid., 95.
54. Ibid., 115–16, 120–21.

them.[55] Nonetheless, Wippel concludes that participation in *esse commune* belongs to the third mode of participation for two reasons: because it does not belong to the first two and because it is closely associated with participation in *esse subsistens,* as we shall see next.[56]

As Wippel explains, sometimes when Thomas speaks of participation in *esse* he refers to participation in the First Act, or the First *Esse,* or the First Being. When he does so, Thomas commonly adds that such participation is by similitude or imitation. Thomas adds this qualification to emphasize that this participation does not involve created beings sharing or taking a part of God's *esse.* Rather, as Wippel explains, it means that every finite being has a participated likeness to or similitude of that divine *esse,* that is, each has its own intrinsic *actus essendi,* which is efficiently caused in it by God. By positing such participation in the divine *esse* as a participation of the divine similitude, Thomas avoids the problem of pantheism. Thus, the divine essence remains uncommunicated and unparticipated although its likeness is nevertheless communicated to every created being.[57] God is the exemplar, efficient, and final cause of every finite being, and inasmuch as the *actus essendi* of each being depends upon God, so too does *esse commune.*[58]

The third sense of *esse* to which Thomas refers when he speaks of participation in *esse* is the created being's own *actus essendi.* Wippel notes that this usage may at first strike the reader as unusual. However, as he explains, it is helpful to recall that when Thomas does speak of participation in this context, he employs the term *participare* as a transitive verb with *esse* as its direct object.[59] Fur-

55. Here we must keep in mind, of course, that the participation of a subject in its accident falls under the second mode of participation, whereas participation of an individual being in *esse commune* does not.

56. Wippel, *Metaphysical Thought,* 116–17.

57. Ibid., 120–21.

58. Ibid., 116.

59. In support of this reading, Wippel cites *In I Sent.,* d. 19, q. 5, a. 2 (Mandonnet ed., vol. 1.491): "quaelibet res participat suum esse creatum, quo formaliter est, et unusquisque intellectus participat lumen per quod recte de re judicat."

thermore, when Thomas speaks of participation in *esse* in this third way, he is implicitly indicating that finite beings participate in *esse commune*, for their own *actus essendi* does not exhaust its fullness. Moreover, participation in *esse commune*, Wippel goes on to note, does not exclude participation in *esse subsistens* since this is its ultimate metaphysical foundation. Indeed, it is because finite beings participate in the likeness of *esse subsistens* that they participate in *esse commune*.[60]

In light of this analysis of participation, Wippel concludes that the differing approaches of Fabro and Geiger can, in a sense, be reconciled. To begin with, he reminds us that neither Fabro's division between transcendental and predicamental participation nor Geiger's division between participation by composition and participation by similitude appears as such in Thomas's writings. Nevertheless, although these terms might not be Thomas's own, elements of what they denote are undoubtedly present in the commentary on the *De Hebdomadibus*, as well as in other texts.[61]

Wippel himself chooses to adopt Geiger's terminology, although he alters it to some extent. He explains that composition is involved in Thomas's account of participation in *esse*, namely, the composition of essence and *actus essendi*. As we have seen, Wippel argues that this is not the sort of composition that Thomas describes in his second division in his commentary on the *De Hebdomadibus*, but Wippel insists that it is a composition nonetheless. In cases of real participation, the participant is united with its participated perfection as potency to act. This is no less true regarding the relation between the essence principle in a finite being and its own *actus essendi*. Furthermore, Wippel argues, Thomas holds that act as such is not self-limiting. If limited instances of *esse* are found in finite beings, this must be because in such beings act is received and limited by a really distinct potency principle. For this reason, Wippel concludes that we must posit a composition between essence and *esse* to account for

60. Ibid., 120–21.
61. Ibid., 127–28.

this limitation. Hence, against Geiger and Rudi A. te Velde, he concludes that, on this point, Fabro's interpretation is correct.[62]

Since the essence principle in a finite being is created simultaneously with its *actus essendi*, Wippel concludes that there is little justification for Geiger's concern that such an appeal to participation by composition might imply some sort of preexistence of the essence principle. Wippel posits that this concern might be due to Geiger's assumption regarding the nature of composition. It is true that what *he* understands participation by composition to entail (*viz.*, as it pertains to the participation of matter in form or of a subject in its accidents) does not pertain to the participation of beings in *esse;* nevertheless, Wippel suggests, Geiger's limited application of the term "composition" does not detract from the fact that Thomas does describe a composition within beings of essence and *esse:* one that results in the limitation of *esse.*[63]

Wippel reminds us here of two points: (1) that causes can simultaneously be causes of one another according to different lines of causality, and hence that principles can be mutually dependent upon one another; and (2) that what is prior in the order of nature is not necessarily so in the order of time. Hence, on the one hand we can say that the act of being *(esse)* causes a finite being *(ens)* to exist by actualizing its essence principle; on the other hand we can say that the essence principle simultaneously receives and limits that act of being. In this way, we see that neither exists apart from the other and that each is prior in the order of nature as regards its ontological function.[64]

Having acknowledged the truth in Fabro's position regarding the role of composition in Thomas's theory of participation, Wip-

62. Ibid., 128. For textual justification regarding the position that act as such is not self-limiting, see John F. Wippel, "Thomas Aquinas and the Axiom that Unreceived Act Is Unlimited," *Review of Metaphysics* 51 (1998): 533–64.

63. Wippel, *Metaphysical Thought,*128–29. Wippel notes on these pages that te Velde seems to share Geiger's same concern (see te Velde, *Participation and Substantiality,* 82–83).

64. Wippel, *Metaphysical Thought,* 129–30.

pel then addresses what he considers to be the truth of Geiger's position. As he notes, an appeal to composition does account for the fact that a finite being is of this kind rather than of any other, and hence that it participates in *esse* to its limited degree, but it does not fully account for the essence principle itself. Participation by composition must ultimately entail causal dependence in the orders of both efficient and exemplar causality inasmuch as God wills a created being to imitate his divine essence according to its proper respect. Here, then, Wippel agrees with Geiger that participation by similitude or formal hierarchy is needed to account fully for the origin of created essence.[65]

Wippel thus concludes that Thomas's theory of participation in *esse* entails both composition and assimilation. He contends, however, that participation by composition is first in the order of discovery for the philosopher. Looking at finite beings, the philosopher is able to discern that they must participate in *esse commune* and that this participation entails a real distinction within them between the essence principle and the *actus essendi*. Only after God's existence has been demonstrated, Wippel argues, can participation in *esse subsistens* be discerned inasmuch as God is seen to be both the efficient and exemplar cause of all finite beings. Hence, he concludes that participation by similitude or formal hierarchy comes later in the order of discovery. Nevertheless, it does enjoy priority according to the order of nature (although not according to the order of time) since explanation in terms of exemplar causality is concerned. As Wippel explains, "Creatures actually exist because God wills them to exist and efficiently causes them. But God can will a creature of a certain kind to exist only if it can exist. And it can exist only if it is viewed by God as a possible way of imitating the divine essence."[66]

---

65. Ibid., 130.
66. Ibid., 131. Clarifying this statement, Wippel notes, "To this I would add, in order to forestall any possible misunderstanding, that this is not to imply that the creaturely essence enjoys any actual reality in itself apart from the divine essence prior to its

CONCLUSIONS REGARDING THOMAS'S DOCTRINE OF PARTICIPATION

As we have seen, Thomas describes participation as occurring when something receives in a particular way that which another has in a universal way. The participant thus does not possess the participated perfection according to its fullness but rather does so in a limited way. Hence, the doctrine of participation accounts for the fact that a single perfection can be possessed by many different subjects. In short, it offers an answer to the ancient Parmenidean problem of the one and the many.[67]

The structure of participation, therefore, involves a receiver and a received characteristic or perfection. Moreover, it involves a third element. As Thomas explains, "Everything that participates [in] something receives it from that *from which* it participates, and in this respect that from which it participates is its cause."[68] Regarding real or ontological participation, furthermore, the receiver stands as potency to the received principle, which stands as act.[69] Concerning the relation of essence to *esse,* Thomas explains that

Everything that is after the First Being, since it is not its *esse,* has an *esse* that is received in something through which that *esse* is contracted. Thus in every creature the nature of the thing that participates *esse* is other than that participated *esse.* And since every thing participates in the First Act through

actual creation in an existing entity together with its corresponding act of being. The actual creation of any such an entity, including both its essence and its act of being, also requires the simultaneous exercise of divine efficient causality."

67. Wippel, *Metaphysical Thought,* 96–97.

68. *De sub. sep.,* c. 3 (Leonine ed., vol. 40.46:11–15): "Omne autem participans aliquid accipit id quod participat ab eo a quo participat, et quantum ad hoc id a quo participat est causa ipsius: sicut aer habet lumen participatum a sole, quae est causa illuminationis ipsius."

Commenting on this passage, Wippel observes that "This text is interesting because it makes three points: (1) something may participate (in) some perfection (accusative case); (2) it then participates in that *from* something else (ablative case); (3) the source is identified as the cause which accounts for the presence of the participated perfection in the participant" (Wippel, *Metaphysical Thought,* 117).

69. *ST* I, q. 75, a. 5, ad 1 (Leonine ed., vol. 5.202).

assimilation inasmuch as it has *esse,* the participated *esse* in each thing must be compared to the nature that participates in it as act to potency.[70]

It is because essence participates in *esse,* then, that it receives the perfection of *esse* and limits it as potency limits act. This received act is its own individual *actus essendi.* But we see that the essence also participates in the First Act by way of assimilation, thus receiving a likeness to the divine essence.[71]

What is key here, as we have seen, is that the divine essence remains in itself unparticipated: it does not enter into composition with the creature. Rather, it is the *likeness* of the divine essence that is participated.[72] And this likeness is itself the principle of all the principles that enter into the composition of things.[73] Hence, participation by composition must ultimately depend upon participation by similitude. We can thus conclude with Wippel that Thomas's structure of participation includes both composition and assimilation.[74]

70. *De spir. creat.,* a. 1 (Leonine ed., vol. 24.2.13–14:375–85): "Omne igitur quod est post primum ens, cum non sit suum esse, habet esse in aliquo receptum, per quod ipsum esse contrahitur: et sic in quolibet creato aliud est natura rei quae participat esse et aliud ipsum esse participatum. Et cum quaelibet res participet per assimilationem primum actum in quantum habet esse, necesse est quod esse participatum in unoquoque comparetur ad naturam participantem ipsum, sicut actus ad potentiam."

71. See, e.g., *In I Sent.,* d. 36, q. 2, a. 2 (Mandonnet ed., vol. 1.842); *ST* I, q. 15, a. 2 (Leonine ed., vol. 14.202). *ST* I, q. 44, a. 3 (Leonine ed., vol. 14.460).

72. *In II De div. nom.,* lect. 3, n. 158 (Marietti ed., 51): "Nam in processione divinarum Personarum ipsa eadem divina Essentia communicatur Personae procedenti et sic sunt plures Personae habentes divinam Essentiam, sed in processione creaturarum, ipsa divina Essentia non communicatur creaturis procedentibus, sed remanet incommunicata seu imparticipata; sed similitudo eius, per ea quae dat creaturis, in creaturis propagatur et multiplicatur et sic quodammodo Divinitas per sui similitudinem non per essentiam, in creaturas procedit et in eis quodammodo multiplicatur, ut sic ipsa creaturarum processio possit dici divina discretio, si respectus ad divinam similitudinem habeatur, non autem si respiciatur divina Essentia."

73. Thus, speaking of God's knowledge of singulars, Thomas observes that "species intelligibilis divini intellectus, quae est Dei essentia, non est immaterialis per abstractionem, sed per seipsam, principium existens omnium principiorum quae intrant rei compositionem, sive sint principia speciei, sive principia individui. Unde per eam Deus cognoscit non solum universalia, sed etiam singularia" (*ST* I, q. 14, a. 11, ad 1 [Leonine ed., vol. 4.183–84]).

74. Wippel, *Metaphysical Thought,* 118, 131.

᷾

If we consider the three modes of participation Thomas presents in his commentary on the *De Hebdomadibus,* we can quickly discern that the exemplarism of the divine ideas does not entail either of the first two modes. Unlike the first mode, this exemplarism involves a real relation of a finite being *(ens)* to its divine idea since a finite being is really dependent upon its exemplar idea in order for it to exist as that being. Furthermore, in contrast to the participated perfections of the first mode of participation which are only logically distinct from the participant, a divine idea is ontologically or really distinct from what it exemplifies. Unlike the second mode of participation, the exemplarism of the divine ideas does not involve a composition between the idea and what it exemplifies. If it did, God's essence would enter into the composition of a creature since the divine ideas are ontologically the same as the divine essence. As we have seen, however, Thomas rejects such a pantheistic model as impossible.

By a process of elimination, then, we can conclude that if the exemplarism of the divine ideas does involve a mode of participation, it is the third mode: that of an effect in its cause. To put the matter into Geiger's terminology, such exemplarism would involve participation by similitude rather than by composition. In fact, as we have seen, Thomas identifies the notion of similitude or likeness as a fundamental characteristic of exemplarism, for he commonly describes an exemplar as "that in the likeness of which something is made."[75]

But what is it that stands in likeness to a divine idea? Is it a finite being's essence alone? Or is it that being's entire entity, essence and *esse* together? Thomas does not offer much detail on this point. As

---

75. See the section "What is an Exemplar" in chap. 1. In Thomas, see, e.g., *In Lib. de caus.,* prop. 14. ". . . exemplar est id ad cuius similitudinem fit aliud" (Saffrey ed., 85.12–13). Cf. *De ver.,* q. 3, a. 1 (Leonine ed., vol. 22.1.99.177–82); *Quod.* 8, q. 1, a. 2 (Leonine ed., vol. 25.1.54.42–43); *In V Div. nom.,* lect. 3, n. 665 (Marietti ed., 249); *ST* I, q. 35, a. 1, ad 1 (Leonine ed., vol. 4.372).

we have seen, in q. 3, a. 8 of the *De veritate* he notes that an idea tak-en in its proper sense (i.e., as an exemplar) corresponds to the spe-cies, genus, and individual characteristics of a created being—all seemingly essential notes.[76] Earlier in q. 2, a. 4 of the same work, he observes that "God knows a thing in an idea, that is, through an idea that is the likeness of all that is in the thing, both acciden-tal and essential, although [the idea] itself is neither an accident of a thing nor its essence."[77] Here, again, we find that a divine idea is not presented as the likeness of a thing's act of being *(esse)*. If we were to take this list as exhaustive, then, we could conclude that the divine ideas only exemplify created essences and their accidents.

Other passages, however, seem to depict a finite being's *esse* as also sharing in a similitude of that being's exemplar idea. In *In I Sent,*. Thomas notes that "an idea that is in the divine mind is the cause of all that is in a thing; hence, through an idea God knows not only the nature of a thing, but also that this thing *is* at such a time *(sed etiam hanc rem esse in tali tempore),* and all the conditions that accompany a thing either on the side of matter or on the side of form."[78] Here, when Thomas refers to God's knowledge of the thing's *esse,* he is re-ferring to the thing's factual existence rather than to its existential act. Nonetheless, the former presupposes the latter.

We find a stronger intimation of a correspondence of created *esse* to the divine ideas in q. 2, a. 3 of the *De veritate.* There, in an

76. *De ver.,* q. 3, a. 8, ad 2 (Leonine ed., vol. 22.1.116:74–84).

77. *De ver.,* q. 2, a. 4, ad 6 (Leonine ed., vol. 22.1.58:261–71): "Deus cognoscit res in propria natura si ista determinatio referatur ad cognitionem ex parte cogniti; si autem loquamur de cognitione ex parte cognoscentis sic cognoscit res in idea, id est per ide-am quae est similitudo omnium quae sunt in re, et accidentalium et essentialium, qua-mvis ipsa non sit accidens rei neque essentia eius."

78. *In I Sent.,* d. 38, q. 1, a. 3, ad 1 (Mandonnet ed., vol. 1.904): "Aliud est de forma existente in mente artificis et de idea rei quae est in mente divina: quia forma quae est in mente artificis, non est causa totius quod est in artificiato, sed tantum formae; et ideo esse hanc domum, et caetera quae consequuntur naturam per formam artis, ne-scit artifex nisi sensibiliter accipiat: sed idea quae est in mente divina, est causa omnis ejus quod in re est; unde per ideam non tantum cognoscit naturam rei, sed etiam hanc rem esse in tali tempore, et omnes conditiones quae consequuntur rem vel ex parte materiae vel ex parte formae." Emphasis added in translation.

objection, it is argued that a thing is known principally through its causes and, above all, through the causes of its being *(esse)*. Now of the four causes, the efficient and final causes cause the coming-to-be *(fieri)* of a thing, whereas form and matter cause its being *(esse)* since they enter into its constitution. Because God is only the cause of things as an efficient and final cause, the objection concludes that he knows the least about creatures.[79] Thomas responds to this objection as follows,

Although, as Avicenna says, a natural agent is only the cause of coming-to-be *(fiendi)*—a sign of which is that upon its destruction the being *(esse)* of the thing [effect] does not cease but only [its] coming-to-be *(fieri)*—the divine agent that is imparting *(influens)* being *(esse)* to things is still the cause of the act of being *(esse)* for all things, even though he does not enter into the constitution of things; and he is still the likeness of the essential principles that enter into the constitution of a thing. Therefore he knows not only the coming-to-be of a thing but its act of being and its essential principles.[80]

In analyzing this passage, we should first note that Thomas does not refer to the divine ideas by name here. Nevertheless, it is clear that he is describing exemplar causality and that he is doing so, moreover, within the context of discussing the divine knowledge. Regarding God's knowledge of a created being *(ens)*, Thomas tells us that this knowledge is not simply of that being's essential principles but of its act of being *(esse)* as well. Since God knows things other than himself through the divine ideas, this passage might be read to suggest that a divine idea is the exemplar of both the essence and *esse* principles of a finite being.

79. *De ver.,* q. 2, a. 3, obj. 20 (Leonine ed., vol. 22.1.49–50).

80. *De ver.,* q. 2, a. 3, ad 20 (Leonine ed., vol. 22.1.55:537–47): "Quamvis agens naturale, ut Avicenna dicit [*Metaph.,* VI, c. 2], non sit causa nisi fiendi,—cuius signum est quod eo destructo non cessat esse rei sed fieri solum—, agens tamen divinum quod est influens esse rebus est omnibus rebus causa essendi quamvis rerum constitutionem non intret, et tamen est similitudo principiorum essentialium quae intrant rei constitutionem: et ideo non solum cognoscit fieri rei sed esse eius et principia essentialia ipsius."

In interpreting this passage, however, it is important for us to keep in mind the nature of the argument to which Thomas is responding. In the objection, it is argued that God could not know the being *(esse)* of created things because he does not enter into their constitution. Thomas begins his reply to this argument by drawing a distinction between the efficiency of a natural agent and that of God. Unlike the natural agent, he reminds us, God is the cause of the *esse* of things.[81] It is in light of *this* observation regarding efficient causality that Thomas proceeds to discuss the nature of God's knowledge. This context is not insignificant. Here we must recall that exemplarism always entails efficient causality: knowledge is only productive through the mediation of the will. Hence, it is through an act of the divine will that a created essence with the potential to exist actually does exist.

What is described in this passage, then, corresponds to the character of exemplarism inasmuch as it addresses both formal and efficient causality. As we see, Thomas discusses God's efficiency in causing created *esse* as well as God's formal likeness to the essential principles in things. Then, in the final sentence, he offers a conclusion that parallels these two modes of causality: God knows the coming-to-be and the being *(esse)* of a thing (effects that correspond to his role as efficient cause) and also its essential principles (effects that correspond to his role as exemplar cause). I read this passage, then, as suggesting that it is because God *as efficient cause* imparts the act of being to a created thing (or can impart the act of being to a possible thing) that he knows that act of being, whereas it is because he is the exemplar likeness of the essential principles that enter into a thing that he knows its essence.[82] Read in this way,

81. Regarding the distinction between *causa fiendi* and *causa essendi* as well as the role that natural agents play in causing the act of being, see the section "The Double Causality of God and Nature" in chap. 5.

82. Here we are simply considering the role of the divine ideas as exemplar causes. I will discuss below the role of the divine nature as exemplar cause. I will also examine the distinction between the two modes of divine exemplarism and their respective rela-

this passage is consistent with the position that what properly corresponds to a divine exemplar idea is a created thing's essence rather than its entire entity, essence and *esse* together.

Thus, following Thomas's observation that we considered earlier, we can conclude that a divine exemplar idea is the likeness of what is both essential and accidental in a thing. We have been addressing the essential thus far, but we should briefly note that Thomas also includes the accidental as being exemplified by the divine ideas, and for two reasons. The first is that, as we found in chapter 4, he holds that inseparable accidents are exemplified by the same divine idea that exemplifies the individual in which they inhere. This position follows from the fact that inseparable accidents belong *per se* to the thing's essence although they are not contained within it. Hence, when a divine idea exemplifies a thing's essence, it exemplifies these accidents as well. The second reason that Thomas includes the accidental as sharing a likeness to the divine ideas is that, as we also found in chapter 4, he holds that separable accidents are exemplified by ideas that are distinct from ideas that exemplify the things in which they inhere. This position follows because such accidents do not belong *per se* to the thing's essence; hence, they require a separate account for their exemplar cause. In summary, then, we see that there are two types of divine exemplars: one that primarily exemplifies the essence of a finite being and secondarily its inseparable accidents, and another that exemplifies its separable accidents.[83] It is for this reason, therefore, that Thomas describes the divine ideas as the likenesses of what is both essential *and* accidental in a thing. But while both the essences and accidents of finite beings share a likeness to the divine exemplars, it is with the similitude of essence that we are more concerned.

---

tionships to both the essence and *esse* principles in created beings. See the section "Participation and the Twofold Divine Exemplarism."

83. Thus, there would be as many exemplar ideas corresponding to a thing's separable accidents as there are separable accidents inhering in that thing.

Returning to our consideration of participation, we find that the relation of created essences to their divine exemplars appears to involve some manner of what Geiger terms participation by similitude. Here, even Fabro is in agreement: "To the extent that participation allows one to conceive the created universe in the complexity of its natures as a reflection of divine ideas or exemplars, one may speak of participation by similitude *(per similitudinem)* in the transcendental order according to a relation of dependence of the finite on the Infinite."[84] As he explains, the divine ideas act as intermediaries through which created essences are derived from the divine essence.[85] Wippel, too, holds that Thomas's ultimate explanation for the essence principle in a finite being is its imitation of its appropriate idea in the divine mind. On this point, he follows Geiger's position that the finite nature of created essences must depend upon a prior participation by similitude.[86]

But what of the *actus essendi* of a finite being? Certainly we do not want to say that it does not share in any likeness to the divine essence. If the essence principle of a finite being shares in such a likeness, *a fortiori* must its *esse* as well since what is being imitated, namely, the divine essence, is *Esse* itself. Here, it is helpful to recall that Thomas discerns two modes of divine exemplarism. As we have seen, not only does he identify an exemplarism of the divine ideas, but he also identifies an exemplarism of the divine nature. The latter type of exemplarism involves the divine attributes, such as God's goodness and his wisdom. Thomas is careful to note, however, that unlike the divine ideas, the divine attributes do not signify anything other than the divine essence: God can be compared to creatures in different ways according to these attributes, but the attributes themselves are not plural except conceptually. Hence, according to this mode of exemplarism, the divine nature or essence is the exemplar of all things, not as it is under-

84. Fabro, "Intensive Hermeneutics," 476.
85. Fabro, *Participation et causalité*, 630.
86. Wippel, *Metaphysical Thought*, 130.

stood, but simply as it *is* that essence.[87] Thus, Thomas describes a twofold likeness between creatures and God: in one way, creatures are like the divine ideas, but in another way, they are like the divine nature. In light of this fact, we must consider how this twofold similitude that creatures share to these exemplars fits into the structure of participation.

PARTICIPATION AND THE TWOFOLD DIVINE EXEMPLARISM

In considering divine exemplarism, we have thus far focused principally on the causality of the divine ideas. As Geiger observes, however, the metaphor that we have drawn from art is insufficient if we wish to address accurately the relationship between creatures and God. As we have just seen, the similitude that is involved in divine exemplarism is not limited to the relationship between the creature and the divine intellect. Looking at the two modes of divine exemplarism, he thus discerns two acts of participation: one by which finite beings participate in the divine ideas and another by which they participate in the divine nature. Geiger describes these two modes of exemplarism as "radically diverse," but he does not consider in detail what he terms "this difficult problem," reserving what little he does have to say on this point for a footnote.[88]

Geiger explains that both types of participation are real; moreover, he emphasizes that they are not the same. The distinction between the two types of participation is founded upon the distinction between what he terms the "perfections" and "modes" of things. A finite being participates in the divine nature according to its perfections inasmuch as it has being, life, goodness, and so

---

87. *Quod.* 4, q. 1, a. 1 (Leonine ed., vol. 25–2.319:31–38): "Nominat enim idea formam exemplarem, est autem una res quae est omnium exemplar, scilicet divina essentia, quam omnia imitantur in quantum sunt et bona sunt. Alia vero pluralitas est secundum intelligentiae rationem, et secundum hoc sunt plures ideae."

88. Geiger, *La participation*, 232–33 and 233n1.

forth. By contrast, it participates in only one divine idea since it has *this* mode of being and no other, that is, since it has a determinate nature. This difference in participation derives from the different ways that forms are in God. As Thomas explains, "the form of a horse and life are not in God in the same way since the form of a horse is not in God except as a *ratio* that is understood, but the *ratio* of life is in God not only as understood but also as fixed in the nature of a thing."[89]

Thomas's examples may be clear enough, but Geiger notes that the distinction itself is nonetheless full of obscurities. As he explains,

[I]f life is really found in God whereas the essence of a horse has only one corresponding idea in God, how is the distinction made between the life proper to the horse and its nature? If the mode is intrinsic to the *reason* that it modifies, should we not say that the essence of the horse is a mode of life, that is to say, life modified in a certain manner? And if we consider the transcendentals and their immanence in all that is, how do we separate in a being that by which it participates in the nature, the being, or the goodness of God and that by which it is only the resemblance of the idea?[90]

Geiger himself does not offer a positive solution to this problem. Instead, he simply counsels the students of Thomas to avoid two errors. On the one hand, he notes that we must not view the distinction between the proper and metaphorical names of God as if

89. *In I Sent.*, d. 36, q. 2, a. 2, ad 2 (Mandonnet ed., vol. 1.842): "Non enim eodem modo est in Deo forma equi et vita; quia forma equi non est in Deo nisi sicut ratio intellecta, sed ratio vitae in Deo est non tantum sicut intellecta, sed etiam sicut in natura rei firmata."

90. Geiger, *La participation*, 233n1: "Il reste que la distinction entre les perfections et les modes demeure pleine d'obscurités. Pour reprendre l'exemple cité plus haut, si la vie se trouve réellement en Dieu alors que l'essence du cheval n'a en Dieu comme répondant qu'une idée, comment se fait le partage entre la vie propre au cheval et sa nature? Si le mode est intrinsèque à la *raison* qu'il modifie ne faut-il pas dire que l'essence du cheval est un mode de la vie, c'est-à-dire la vie modifiée d'une certaine manière? Et si on envisage les transcendentaux et leur immanence en tout ce qui est, comment séparer dans un être ce par quoi il participe la nature, l'être ou la bonté de Dieu et ce par quoi il n'est que la ressemblance de l'idée?"

it were founded upon some multiplicity within him, what Geiger terms "zones of increasing depth"; although the richness of the divine essence is infinite, it is still one. On the other hand, he notes that we must not view the distinction in created beings between absolute perfection and mode as an adequate real distinction. To do so, he contends, would be to introduce errors into Thomas's system, such as creation by intermediaries (although Geiger does not explain why this last point would necessarily follow).[91]

Although Geiger does not offer a solution as to how the two modes of divine exemplarism may be reconciled, it should be noted that neither does Thomas himself explicitly do so. Writing more recently on the subject of participation, Rudi te Velde concludes from this fact that Thomas does not consider the distinction to have a "principal character." As evidence for his position, te Velde cites the fact that Thomas often mentions the two aspects together.[92] I would contend, however, that far from diminishing the significance of the distinction, this fact emphasizes it. Thomas discusses the two types of divine exemplarism together precisely to show the difference between them, but he also does so to show how these two modes of causality are *interrelated*. Unless we understand both the differences and the interrelationship between them, we will not have a full picture of the character of the divine ideas.

To grasp the distinction between the two modes of divine exemplarism, we must first consider the limited nature of finite beings. Unlike God, a finite being is not its *esse* but rather participates in *esse*. For this reason, even though a finite being is good, goodness does not belong to it essentially but only by participation. Offering an example to illustrate this point, Thomas notes that humanity does not have the formality *(ratio)* of goodness except to the extent that it has *esse*.[93] In short, perfections such as goodness are

---

91. Ibid.

92. te Velde, *Participation and Substantiality*, 111.

93. *De ver.,* q. 21, a. 5 (Leonine ed., vol. 22.1.606:133–41): "Essentialis enim bonitas non attenditur secundum considerationem naturae absolutam sed secundum esse ip-

transcendental ones that only follow from the act of being. Now, Aquinas explains, a creature is a being and is good because it imitates the exemplar that is the divine nature, an exemplar that is the First Being and the First Good.[94] Through the exemplarism of the divine nature, then, the finite being receives its total entity *as* a being, both its essence and its *esse;* for in imitating that exemplar, the finite being imitates the absolute perfection that is being itself *(ipsum esse).* By contrast, through the exemplarism of the divine ideas, the finite being receives only its essence; for in imitating *that* exemplar, the finite being imitates but one limited mode of being *(esse).* Contrary to Geiger's position, then, the distinction between absolute perfection and mode of being *is* an adequate real distinction in creatures. Indeed, this distinction forms the foundation of the very distinction between essence and *esse* in any finite being.

The two modes of divine exemplarism thus entail two moments within the structure of participation. As Fabro explains, the first moment is constituted by the "diremption," or division, of the divine essence in the formal order such that it comprises the multiplicity of divine ideas that are the exemplars of created things.[95] Because of this diremption, every real created formality is referred to its respective exemplar according to its mode of being. This constitutes the derivation of the created essence. Then there is the derivation of all the transcendental perfections that follow from the divine nature which embraces *esse* in all of its intensity.[96] And this

---

sius; humanitas enim non habet rationem boni vel bonitatis nisi in quantum esse habet. Ipsa autem natura vel essentia divina est eius esse; natura autem vel essentia cuiuslibet rei creatae non est suum esse sed est esse participans ab alio." Cf. *De ver.,* q. 21, a. 5, ad 5 and ad 6 (Leonine ed., vol. 22.1.607:192–209).

94. *De pot.,* q. 3, a. 4, ad 9 (Marietti ed., vol. 2.48): "Quamvis inter Deum et creaturam non possit esse similitudo generis vel speciei; potest tamen esse similitudo quaedam analogiae, sicut inter potentiam et actum, et substantiam et accidens. Et hoc dicitur uno modo in quantum res creatae imitantur suo modo ideam divinae mentis, sicut artificiata formam quae est in mente artificis. Alio modo secundum quod res creatae ipsi naturae divinae quodammodo similantur, prout a primo ente alia sunt entia, et a bono bona, et sic de aliis."

95. Fabro, *Participation et causalité,* 435.

96. Ibid., 518–19.

double exemplarism, Fabro explains, is founded before all on that very act of intensive *esse* that is the divine essence.[97]

Thus, if we consider the foundation of exemplarism and real participation, I suggest that we find the following logical "moments": in the first moment, there is the divine essence, or nature, which is imitable in itself; in the second moment, God knows his nature as imitable and thus "discovers" ideas;[98] in the third moment, he looks to these ideas and, by an act of his will, creates essences in their likeness, simultaneously creating the corresponding acts of being that these essences receive inasmuch as created beings *(entia)* participate in a likeness of the divine nature.[99] Thus, created beings simultaneously share a likeness to both their respective exemplar ideas and to the divine nature. Developing Thomas's analogy from art, we could compare these moments to those of an artist's painting a self portrait. In the first moment, the artist's likeness is imitable in itself; in the second moment, he has an idea of its imitability; in the third, he paints his likeness, a likeness that is simultaneously similar to both his idea and, in a certain respect, himself as a whole.

As with any analogy, this one has its limitations.[100] With the ex-

97. Ibid., 435.

98. *De ver.,* q. 3, a. 2, ad 6 (Leonine ed., vol. 22.1.105:277–82): "Una prima forma ad quam omnia reducuntur est ipsa divina essentia secundum se considerata, ex cuius consideratione intellectus divinus adinvenit, ut ita dicam, diversos modos imitationis ipsius in quibus pluralitas idearum consistit." See also *SCG* I, c. 50 (Leonine ed., vol. 13.144–45): "Quicumque scit naturam aliquam, scit an illa natura sit communicabilis: non enim animalis naturam sciret perfecte qui nesciret eam pluribus communicabilem esse. Divina autem natura communicabilis est per similitudinem. Scit ergo Deus quot modis eius essentiae aliquid simile esse potest. Sed ex hoc sunt diversitates formarum quod divinam essentiam res diversimode imitantur: unde Philosophus formam naturalem *divinum quoddam* nominat. Deus igitur de rebus habet cognitionem secundum proprias formas." As I have discussed above, the reference to God's discovering *(adinvenit)* ideas should not be read as suggesting that Thomas is a voluntarist (see chap. 4, n. 43).

99. It is important to remember here that, as we have seen, God does not create (indeed cannot create) an essence prior to its act of being, for the former cannot actually exist without the latter.

100. For a detailed consideration of both the similarities and the differences between divine and human art, see Francis J. Kovach, "Divine Art in Saint Thomas Aquinas," in

emplarism of human art, the moments we have described are temporally successive. By contrast, the moments belonging to divine
exemplarism are purely logical. God does not literally excogitate
or discursively think out his ideas because he is eternal and unchanging and because they are based on his knowledge of himself as imitable; furthermore, since there is no real distinction in
God between his intellect and will, neither is there a real distinction between his knowing and his willing. Thus, there is no process
in God whereby he moves from first considering speculative ideas
of things that he could possibly create, then to choosing to create those things, and finally to considering practical ideas of those
things as actually created. Rather, in one simple act, God knows
created things and wills them to be.[101]

Another significant difference between human art and divine
exemplarism concerns the dependence had by the effect on its exemplar. As Thomas explains,

An exemplar form is twofold. In one [way it is *that*] *in representation of
which* something is made, and for this the form is not required except as
a likeness alone—just as we say that real things are the exemplar forms
of pictures. In another way an exemplar form is called [*that*] *in likeness of
which* something is made and by participation in which it has an act of being *(esse)*, as the divine goodness is the exemplar form of every goodness,
and the divine wisdom of every wisdom.[102]

*Arts libéraux et philosophie au môyen age. Actes du Quatrième congrès international de philoso-
phie médiévale* (Montreal: Institut d'études médiévales, 1969), 663–71.

101. As Brian Shanley explains, "The distinctions between various kinds of divine
knowledge, imposed by us according to different intelligible perspectives and different
objects, do not imply any real distinction in God. There is no mental process whereby
God first speculatively considers the various possibilities *(scientia simplicis intelligentiae)*, then practically decides to execute one plan *(scientia approbationis)*, and finally contemplates the finished product *(scientia visionis)*; Molinists typically misread Aquinas
in this way. This and other errors stem from an anthropomorphic failure to make the
requisite distinctions between the human artist and the divine artist. God's practical
knowledge of contingent singulars does not involve the kind of logical, temporal, and
operational stages involved in human production" (Shanley, "Eternal Knowledge,"
217–18). Regarding the debate between Ross, Dewan, and Maurer concerning whether
Aquinas is a voluntarist, see chap. 4 above, n. 43.

102. *In III Sent.*, d. 27, q. 2, a. 4, ad 1 (Moos ed., vol. 3.889–90): "*Forma exemplaris est*

In our analogy from art, then, the artist's likeness is only *that in representation of which* the portrait is made—what we termed earlier an "external exemplar." Hence, the portrait is not dependent upon that exemplar likeness for its very existence. By contrast, the divine essence is *that in likeness of which* everything is made; hence everything is dependent upon this exemplar likeness for its very existence. Again, the mode of divine exemplarism that Thomas presents here is the exemplarism of the divine nature and not that of the divine ideas; for the latter is the exemplar cause of a finite being's essence, but the former is the exemplar cause of its total being *(ens)*.

One final difference that we can point out between human art and divine exemplarism rests in a distinction that Thomas makes in the *De potentia* between art and nature. In q. 7, a. 2, an objector argues that if a multitude of forms is found in God, there must be composition within him. Thomas responds by noting that an effect is found in one way in an agent that acts through its nature and in another in an agent that acts through art. In the former agent, the form of an effect is found because the agent likens *(assimilat)* the effect to itself in its nature—for as Thomas reminds us, *omne agens agit sibi simile.* Such assimilation occurs when an effect is perfectly assimilated to the agent, that is, when it is equal to the agent in power. Thus, the form of the effect is in the agent according to the same formality *(ratio)*, as is the case with univocal agency. But assimilation can also occur when an effect is *not* perfectly assimilated to the agent, that is, when it is not equal to the agent's power. Thus, the form of the effect is in the agent according to a higher

---

duplex. *Una ad cujus repraesentationem aliquid fit,* et ad hanc non exigitur nisi similitudo tantum; sicut dicimus res veras picturarum esse formas exemplares. *Alio modo* dicitur forma exemplaris *ad cujus similitudinem aliquid fit et per cujus participationem esse habet;* sicut divina bonitas est forma exemplaris omnis bonitatis, et divina sapientia omnis sapientiae." Emphasis added in translation. Regarding the distinction between the two modes of divine exemplarism in Thomas's commentary on the *Sentences,* see Bernard Montagnes, *La doctrine de l'analogie de l'être d'après saint Thomas d'Aquin* (Louvain: Publications Universitaires, 1963), 45–53.

mode of formality, as is the case with equivocal agency. Now, regarding agents that act through art, Thomas notes that forms do indeed preexist in them according to the same formality but *not* according to the same mode of being *(esse)*, for in the effects these forms have a material being *(esse materiale)*, but in the mind of the artisan, they have an intelligible being *(esse intelligibile)*.

Having drawn these distinctions, Thomas explains that the forms of things preexist in God in both his nature and his mind, for when God makes a thing through his intellect, it is not without the action of his nature. In this respect, he differs significantly from the human artisan:

In lower artisans, art acts by the power of an extraneous nature that it employs as an instrument—just as a potter employs fire for baking a brick. The divine art, however, does not employ a nature exterior to [its] acting but makes its effect by a power proper to its nature. Thus, the forms of things are in the divine nature as in an operative power, [but] not according to the same formality *(ratio)* since no effect is equal to that power. Hence, all forms that are multiplied in effects are there as one; and so no composition arises from that. Similarly, in his intellect there are many things that are understood through one and the same thing, which is his essence.[103]

This passage is significant, not only because of the distinction that it draws between human and divine art, but because of what it tells us about the nature of divine exemplarism. If we consider the exemplarism of the divine nature, the forms of created things preexist in God according to a higher formality. Thus, creatures are beings, but God is being itself; creatures are good, but God is good-

---

103. *De pot.,* q. 7, a. 1, ad 8 (Marietti ed., vol. 2.190): "Utroque autem modo formae rerum sunt in Deo: Cum enim ipse agit res per intellectum, non est sine actione naturae. In inferioribus autem artificibus ars agit virtute extraneae naturae, qua utitur ut instrumento, sicut figulus igne ad coquendum laterem. Sed ars divina non utitur exteriori natura ad agendum, sed virtute propriae naturae facit suum effectum. Formae ergo rerum sunt in natura divina ut in virtute operativa, non secundum eamdem rationem, cum nullus effectus virtutem illam adaequet. Unde sunt ibi ut unum omnes formae quae in effectibus multiplicantur; et sic nulla provenit inde compositio. Similiter in intellectu eius sunt multa intellecta per unum et idem, quod est sua essentia."

ness itself; and so forth. If we consider the exemplarism of the divine ideas, the forms of created things preexist in God according to the *same* formality but not according to the same being *(esse)*. Thus, the created essences of singular things are material in themselves but exist immaterially in the mind of God.

We see in this passage, furthermore, that while these two modes of divine exemplarism differ in formality, each is dependent in a certain respect upon the other for its causality. As Thomas notes, when God acts through his intellect he does so through the action of his nature as well. As we saw in chapter 5, knowledge as such only signifies that something is in the knower, not that an effect proceeds from the knower. It is only by acting through his will that God makes something. And unlike the human artisan, he needs no external instrument to make his effects; rather, he makes them through the operative power of his own nature. Thus, there is no exemplarism on the part of the divine ideas without the exemplarism of the divine nature, and there is no exemplarism on the part of that nature without the exemplarism of the divine ideas.

In summary, regarding their *formal content,* the two modes of divine exemplarism are distinguished from each other because one concerns the divine nature and the other concerns the ideas in the divine mind. But regarding *what is exemplified,* they are distinguished from each other because the former mode of exemplarism concerns the transcendental perfections that a creature receives through its act of being (perfections that it receives by participating in the likeness of the divine nature), whereas the latter mode concerns the very essence that a creature receives in the likeness of its corresponding divine idea. Furthermore, while these two modes of divine exemplarism can be distinguished in this way, neither is the cause of its effect apart from the causality of the other. This is because created essence cannot be created without an act of being and because an act of being that is created must be limited by a created essence. Or to put it in terms of participation, there must be a finite essence that participates in the likeness of the divine nature in order for an act of being to be received. But what of the essence itself? Does a finite being *(ens)* receive its essence because that essence participates in its exemplar idea? If so, the question arises what the subject is that receives the participated perfection. If not, then the question arises what the relationship is between the essence of the finite being and its corresponding divine idea.

DO FINITE BEINGS INDEED PARTICIPATE IN THE DIVINE IDEAS?

As noted at the beginning of this chapter, the history of the philosophical doctrine of participation is closely linked with the Platonic and Neoplatonic doctrines of exemplarism—involving a participation by things either in ideas that are separately subsisting or in ones that exist within some divine mind. The reader may have noticed, however, that as regards Thomas's doctrine, I have only referred in the conditional to creatures participating in their exemplar ideas, except when I have discussed the observations of other scholars on this topic. This is because I would contend that if we follow Thomas's thought, creatures do *not* participate in the divine ideas.

Looking at Thomas's writings on both the divine ideas and participation, I find three principal reasons to support the position that things do not participate in their exemplar ideas. First, the divine ideas that are exemplars (i.e., actually practical ideas) are ideas of individuals. Indeed, as discussed in this chapter, the essence of each finite being is exemplified by its own divine idea: thus, for example, the idea of Socrates is the exemplar of his essence. Now, as has also been mentioned, Thomas holds that for something to be essentially *(substantialiter)* and for it to be by participation are opposites. Following this position, therefore, if we were to say that Socrates is Socrates by participating in his divine idea, then we would be saying that Socrates is not Socrates in his essence. Given Thomas's Aristotelianism, however, such a conclusion is clearly absurd.[104] For the same reason, we must conclude that creatures do not participate in the divine ideas of species or genera. Just as Socrates is Socrates essentially, so too is he essentially a man and an animal.[105]

The second reason that I would offer in support of my position that things do not participate in the divine ideas concerns the nature of real participation. If finite beings were to participate in their exemplar ideas, such participation would either be by composition or by similitude. From what we have seen, it is clear that creatures do not enter into composition with their ideas, for to do so would be to enter into composition with the divine essence. But neither could they participate by similitude. It is true that the essence principle of a finite being is made in the likeness of its respective exemplar idea, but the similitude here is not of the same kind as that involved in participation *by* similitude. As we have seen, such participation involves a formal hierarchy whereby participants are similar to a perfection according to a greater or lesser degree, with no participant being identical to that perfection. Thus, the participant does not realize the fullness of the likeness in which it participates.

In contrast to this manner of similitude, however, the similitude of a created essence to its divine idea does not involve a formal hierarchy. For as we have seen, although the divine nature does not have the same formality *(ratio)* as the creatures that it exemplifies,

104. Little notes that "Individuals also participate in the idea of their essence abstracted from them and considered as representing the whole perfection that the essence is capable of realising. If however the essence is considered as included wholly in each individual it is not participated, for no *part* of its virtue is considered to be confined in the individual but the whole of it" (Little, *Platonic Heritage,* 39–40).

105. It must be recalled that when Thomas describes an individual as participating in its species and a species as participating in its genus, he is referring to a logical participation, not a real one. Furthermore, since the divine ideas of species and genera are speculative and not practical, they are only cognitive principles of God's knowledge, not ontological ones by which he creates—a fact that would rule out any real participation of creatures in such ideas. Thus, if we follow the distinction above, the likeness of a creature to the divine idea of either its species or its genus is due to the fact that such an idea is *that in representation of which* something is made rather than *that in likeness of which* something is made.

the exemplar forms in the divine *mind* do have the same formality as found in creatures—although not according to the same mode of being *(esse)*. Hence, Socrates cannot be more or less similar to the divine idea of Socrates: either he is like it or he is not; either he is Socrates or he is not. In short, he enjoys a perfect likeness to his divine idea.

Just as created essences do not participate by similitude in their divine ideas, neither do separable accidents. It is true that Socrates' whiteness, for example, can admit of degrees of intensity regarding the fullness of whiteness itself. It might seem, therefore, that his whiteness participates by formal hierarchy in the divine idea of whiteness itself, that is, in the idea of the species "whiteness." Here we must recall, however, that for Thomas only God's ideas of particulars can function as exemplars. The exemplar of Socrates' whiteness, therefore, is just that: the exemplar of his *own* whiteness. It is not the divine idea of whiteness itself. And this idea of his whiteness exemplifies the intensity of that accidental form as it is in Socrates at any given point in time. Thus, at any point in time that accident perfectly imitates its divine idea. Indeed, as we have seen, Thomas holds that all created beings perfectly imitate their exemplar ideas because they have the same formality *(ratio)* as those ideas. The likeness, therefore, between a separable accident and its idea is not one according to formal hierarchy. Thus, whether we consider substances or their accidents, the exemplarism of the divine ideas does not involve participation by similitude.[106]

---

106. Thomas discusses accidents that admit of intensity in *Summa theologiae* I-II, q. 52, a. 1. There, he notes that some accidents, such as whiteness or heat, do not increase or decrease in themselves because such a change would result in a change in species; rather, they are participated in more or less intensively by the subject, i.e., through participation by composition. In contrast to such accidents, another type receives its specific determination from something to which it is related. These accidents admit of increase and decrease both by means of the subject's participation *and* (what is more important for our consideration) in themselves. Thomas gives the examples of accidents such as motion and science (*ST* I-II, q. 52, a. 1 [Leonine ed., vol. 6.330–31]). This second type of accident presents more of a challenge to my position that nothing participates in the divine ideas. Since this type of accident admits of increase and decrease

The third and final reason that I would offer in support of the position that things do not participate in the divine ideas is that Thomas himself does not speak in such terms. If we look at his *ex professo* considerations of the divine ideas, any mention of participation is in reference to the creature's participating, not in its divine idea, but in a likeness of the divine essence. Thus, in the *Summa theologiae,* Thomas notes that "every single creature has a proper species as it participates in some way [in] a likeness of the divine essence. Hence, inasmuch as God knows his essence as imitable thusly by such a creature, he knows it as the proper notion *(ratio)* and idea of that creature. And similarly regarding others."[107] In short, the language that speaks of a participation in the divine ideas is not Thomas's own.[108]

---

in itself, it seems at first glance to involve a formal hierarchy of the sort that is the mark of participation by similitude. Still, even the degrees of intensity that belong to this type of accident are not due to participation by similitude.

We have seen that participation by similitude involves not only states of greater and lesser perfection in the subject but also a source that possesses that perfection according to the absolute fullness of its formal content. The limitation of the perfection in the subject is due to a formal inequality and is prior by nature to any composition. This is not, however, the account that Thomas offers for the greater and lesser states found in accidents that admit of increase in themselves. In a. 2 of q. 52, he explains that such accidents increase by way of *addition.* Motion, for example, increases according to the time that it occurs or according to the course that it follows, and the habit of science increases when someone learns several geometric conclusions. In both cases, Thomas tells us, the form maintains the same species according to the unity of the term. Furthermore, in both cases, the form is not limited *by* itself but rather is limited in its relation to something else. Thus, he notes, we speak of the habit of science as being greater or lesser as it extends to more or fewer things (*ST* I-II, q. 52, a. 2 [Leonine ed., vol. 6.334]). We see, therefore, that even though these sorts of accidents admit of degrees of intensity in themselves, it is not due to a participation by similitude or formal hierarchy. Regarding accidents that admit of degrees of intensity, see John F. Wippel, "Godfrey of Fontaines on Intension and Remission of Accidental Forms," *Franciscan Studies* 39 (1979): esp. 319–20.

107. *ST* I, q. 15, a. 2 (Leonine ed., vol. 14.202): "Unaquaeque autem creatura habet propriam speciem, *secundum quod aliquo modo participat divinae essentiae similitudinem.* Sic igitur inquantum Deus cognoscit suam essentiam ut sic imitabilem a tali creatura, cognoscit eam ut propriam rationem et ideam huius creaturae. Et similiter de aliis" (emphasis added). Cf. *In I Sent.,* d. 36, q. 2, a. 2 (Mandonnet ed., vol. 1.842); *ST* I, q. 44, a. 3 (Leonine ed., vol. 14.460).

108. The sole mention that I have found in Thomas's writings of participation in

Indeed, it is only because things participate in a likeness of the divine nature that God has ideas—or, more precisely, it is only because the likeness of that nature is *able* to be so participated. As Thomas explains in *In I Sent.*, all creatures imitate God's nature as regards being *(esse)*, some as regards life, and so forth. Because things participate in the likeness of his nature either more or less nobly, they have different relations to it. It is on account of these relations (or possible relations) to God's nature that he is able to understand it as imitable in different ways. This imitability of the divine nature is the ground for the diversity of ideas.[109] As Thomas explains in the *Summa theologiae*, "He [God] knows his essence perfectly; hence, he knows it according to every mode by which it is knowable. But it can be known not only as it is in itself, but as it is "participable" *(participabilis)* according to some mode of likeness by creatures."[110] Rather than themselves being participated, then, the divine ideas are what we might term the "participabilities" of the divine nature, that is, known ways in which the likeness of God's essence can be participated.[111]

Still, to deny that there is a participation by similitude of creatures in their ideas is not to deny any similitude between the two:

---

the divine ideas occurs in the words of an objector. See *De ver.*, q. 3, a. 7, obj. 3 (Leonine ed., vol. 22.1.113:18–22): "Omne quod habet ideam est participativum ipsius; sed accidentia nihil participant cum participare sit tantum substantiarum, quae aliquid recipere possunt; ergo non habent ideam." In his reply to this objection, Thomas does not respond to the objector's position that everything having an idea participates in that idea. He does, however, reject the position that there are no ideas of accidents. See below, n. 132.

109. *In I Sent.*, d. 36, q. 2, a. 2 (Mandonnet ed., vol. 1.842).

110. *ST* I, q. 15, a. 2 (Leonine ed., vol. 14.202): "Ipse enim essentiam suam perfecte cognoscit: unde cognoscit eam secundum omnem modum quo cognoscibilis est. Potest autem cognosci non solum secundum quod in se est, sed secundum quod est participabilis secundum aliquem modum similitudinis a creaturis."

111. Geiger thus refers to the ideas themselves as being, in a sense, "participations": "Les idées sont les participations de l'essence divine, connues, en tant qu'elles sont exprimées par Dieu, non pas l'essence divine en tant qu'elle est quasi forme actualisante de l'intellect de Dieu" ("Les idées divines," 179). But Geiger also thinks that created things do participate in their divine ideas.

instead of a similitude of formal hierarchy, it is a similitude according to the *same* formality for, as we have seen, a creature enjoys a perfect likeness to its idea. If, however, we consider that the divine ideas derive from the participability of the divine nature, then we must conclude that the likeness of a creature to its exemplar idea must, in a sense, be a secondary likeness. Through his ideas, God intends to create beings that are like his divine nature; but it is only as creatures are like that nature that they are in turn like their ideas.

Regarding a creature's similitude to the divine nature, we have seen that this likeness involves the divine attributes. Creatures are like God's nature inasmuch as they are good, wise, and so forth, and they share this likeness because they have an act of being. Thus, it is precisely because a creature receives an act of being that it participates in the divine nature by assimilation.[112] But what of the creature's likeness to the divine intellect? Here, too, Thomas explains that the creature possesses this likeness because it participates in an act of being.[113] If this is so, then it is like its divine idea because it participates in *esse*. Such a conclusion seems to pose a problem for us, for as we have seen, what stands in likeness to an exemplar idea is a creature's essence, not its *esse*. Why, then, would Thomas hold that a creature is likened to its divine idea by participating in an act of being? To begin to answer this question, we need to take a closer look at the nature of the essence principle in finite beings.

---

112. See, e.g., *De spir. creat.,* a. 1 (Leon ed., vol. 24.2.13–14:375–85). For the Latin, see n. 70 above.

113. *De ver.,* q. 2, a. 5 (Leonine ed., vol. 22.1.63:297–301): "Sed similitudo rerum quae est in intellectu divino est factiva rei; res autem sive forte sive debile esse participet hoc non habet nisi a Deo, et secundum hoc similitudo omnis rei in Deo existit quod res illa a Deo esse participat."

CREATED ESSENCE AND
THE DIVINE IDEAS

As we have seen, within the structure of participation the essence principle of a finite being is really distinct from its act of being. Through participation in *esse commune,* the essence principle
receives and limits the act of being, standing in relation to it as potency to act. Thus, while a finite being has *esse,* it is not *Ipsum Esse.*
It is for this reason that a finite being's likeness to the divine nature is deficient, for every created being *(ens)* in some respect falls
short of imitating the divine nature. Given this fact, Thomas notes
in response to an objection in *De veritate,* q. 2, a. 3 that since a creature approaches God only as it participates in a finite act of being,
it is infinitely distant from God and is thus said to have more non-
being *(non esse)* than being.[114] He expresses this notion again in a
subsequent response in the same article. There, Thomas explains
that if we can compare a creature to God according to commensu-
ration (i.e., as one being to another), we find that the creature is, as
it were, nothing *(quasi nihil).* In short, there is no true comparison.
We can, however, also compare a creature to God as it receives its
act of being from him. Only in this way, Thomas concludes, can
the creature be compared to God because only in this way does it
have an act of being by which it can be so compared.[115]

Passages like these, and others, suggest that although creatures

114. *De ver.,* q. 2, a. 3, ad 16 (Leonine ed., vol. 22.1.54:504–15): "Esse simpliciter et
absolute dictum de solo divino esse intelligitur sicut et bonum, ratione cuius dicitur
Matth. cap. XIX, vers. 17 «Nemo bonus nisi solus Deus»; unde quantum creatura accedit ad Deum tantum habet de esse, quantum vero ab eo recedit tantum habet de non
esse; et quia non accedit ad Deum nisi secundum quod esse finitum participat, distat
autem in infinitum, ideo dicitur quod plus habet de non esse quam de esse: et tamen
illud esse quod habet cum a Deo sit, a Deo cognoscitur."

115. *De ver.,* q. 2, a. 3, ad 18 (Leonine ed., vol. 22.1.54:521–28): "Aliquid comparatur
Deo dupliciter: vel secundum commensurationem, et sic creatura Deo comparata invenitur quasi nihil; vel secundum conversionem ad Deum a quo esse recipit, et sic hoc
solum modo esse habet quo comparatur ad Deum, et sic etiam a Deo cognoscibilis
est."

are beings in one respect, in another respect they are non-beings. This point has been discussed on more than one occasion by Wippel.[116] As he explains, since the essence principle of a finite being is other than its act of being, we can describe its essence as *non esse* or non-being—not absolute non-being, but rather in a relative sense as the negation of the act of being.[117] As Wippel explains, this principle of relative non-being is also a real principle of diversity, for it is only because the essence of a finite being limits its act of being that it is different both from Being Itself (*viz., Ipsum Esse* or God) and from any other finite being. Understood in this way, the notion of created essence as relative non-being complements Thomas's theory of participation in *esse:* a particular being can participate in *esse* precisely because its received act of being is not identical with the subject in which it is received, namely, the being's essence.[118]

Since the exemplar ideas in the mind of God correspond to created essences, they too must in some way include non-being. As I discussed in chapter 3, just as creatures fall short of the infinite perfection of the divine essence, so do their respective divine ideas. Thus, non-being must in some way enter as a negating principle into the mind of God; for in knowing things other than himself, God knows how they are *not* himself.[119] In short, God can only consider himself as imitable by creatures through combining being (*esse*) and non-being (*non esse*) in his very act of understanding.[120] But again, this non-being is not absolute nothingness, for noth-

---

116. See Wippel, "The Many from the One," esp. 585–89; and *Metaphysical Thought,* chap. 6, 177–94.

117. Wippel, *Metaphysical Thought,* 187–88. Wippel explains that in itself, essence must have formal or positive content for three reasons: (1) because essence determines or specifies a thing; (2) because act is not self-limiting, hence something other than *esse* must account for its limitation; and (3) because the structure of participation requires a receiver to participate in *esse* (*Metaphysical Thought,* 190–92).

118. Wippel, *Metaphysical Thought,* 188–90.

119. Branick, "Unity of the Divine Ideas," 199.

120. Wippel, "The Many from the One," 583–84. Wippel grants, however, that "It is at this point that my interpretation may go beyond Thomas's *ipsissima verba*" (ibid., 583n42).

ingness cannot enter into the divine essence, which is being itself. Rather, such non-being is a relative non-being.[121]

It is because the divine ideas include this relative (yet nonetheless real) non-being that they share a similitude with all that is entailed in created essences: both being and non-being. By contrast, the divine nature as exemplar does not do this. The divine nature is imitable in itself, but in itself it is simply being *(esse)* and, hence, is the exemplar of finite beings because *they* are beings. Only through God's knowledge of how his nature can be imitated *and fallen short of* does non-being enter in to allow for diversification, for non-being can only be present in God intentionally since it does not actually exist. Thus, it is through the exemplarism of the divine ideas that finite beings are able to participate in a likeness of the divine nature. Fabro nicely sums up this order for us:

Essence is a positive-negative because it expresses the mode and degree of the participation of being and expresses it in a positive way, thanks to derivation through "imitation" of the divine Ideas. This allows that which exists to move away from nothingness and to surpass it effectively, so that nothingness does not enter directly, as for Hegel, into the dialectical constitution of the finite, but indirectly because of its limitation: this is not a pure negation, as for Spinoza and idealist metaphysics, but a limit which has a double intentionality so to speak, towards nothing, through relation to which the finite ex-ists, and towards Being in which it per-sists.[122]

---

121. As Wippel notes, however, the relative non-being of the divine ideas is not the same as that of created essences: "The frame of reference is different in the two cases, since this time what is negated—the absolute fullness of divine perfection—is not and cannot be an intrinsic constituent of the existing entity, if and when this particular essence should be brought into being by God's causal activity" ("The Many from the One," 589).

122. Fabro, *Participation et causalité,* 635: "Mais saint Thomas, tout différent de Hegel, conçoit l'essence sur la base de la création de l'être à partir du néant: l'essence est un positif-négatif, car elle exprime le mode et le degré de la participation de l'être et l'exprime d'une manière positive, grâce à la dérivation par «imitation» des Idées divines. Ceci permet à ce qui existe de s'éloigner du néant et de le dépasser effectivement, de sorte que le néant n'entre pas directement, comme pour Hegel, dans la constitution dialectique du fini, mais indirectement, à cause de sa limitation: celle-ci n'est pas une pure négation, comme pour Spinoza et la métaphysique idéaliste, mais une

The relative non-being of finite essence, then, presupposes the relative non-being of the divine ideas. It is this prior limitation in the divine mind regarding the degree to which it is imitated that accounts for the limitation found in a created essence. Through imitating the divine ideas, a created essence can participate in and receive *esse*, simultaneously limiting it. But, again, if a created essence imitates the divine ideas, what are we to make of Thomas's observation that a creature is likened to the divine intellect by participating in an act of being *(esse)*? Is this a circular account? Here, the notion of essence as relative non-being provides an answer.

Because a finite essence is not its own act of being, it exists only by participating in being *(esse)*. In itself, such an essence is non-being, or *non esse*. When Thomas tells us, therefore, that a creature is likened to the divine intellect by participating in an act of being, I take him to mean that through such participation a finite essence is made actually like its respective divine idea. For considered simply in itself, the essence is only *potentially* like that idea. Thus, regarding the difference between the exemplarism of the divine ideas and that of the divine nature, Fabro notes that with the former, the resemblance of the exemplate to the exemplar is but of a formal nature, leaving intact the divine isolation; but with the latter, the relationship becomes real in the creature.[123] As he explains,

Thomism does not seem to admit of doubts regarding this order: created essences derive from the divine essence by the intermediary of the divine Ideas, and this derivation formally follows the relationship of exemplarity. Next, every essence, although it is act in the formal order, is created as potency that becomes actualized by the participated *esse* that it receives: its actuality is thus given by the "mediation" of *esse*.[124]

limite qui présente pour ainsi dire une double intentionalité, vers le néant, par rapport auquel le fini ex-iste, et vers l'Etre dans lequel il in-siste."

123. Ibid., 519.

124. Ibid., 630: "Le thomisme ne semble pas admettre de doutes quant à cet ordre: les essences créées dérivent de l'essence divine par l'intermédiaire des Idées divines, et cette dérivation suit ainsi formellement le rapport d'exemplarité. Ensuite, toute essence, bien qu'elle soit acte dans l'ordre formel, est créée comme puissance qui devient

According to the formal order, then, a created essence is assimilated to its divine idea through itself. But according to the order of *reality*, it is assimilated to its idea through the mediation of its act of being; for in itself the essence is only potentially like that exemplar. It is for this reason, therefore, that Thomas holds a thing to be like the divine intellect through participating in *esse*.[125]

This distinction between these two orders derives in part from the fact that the divine ideas, in themselves, are not productive. As we have seen, knowledge as such signifies simply that something is in the knower, not that an effect proceeds from him. It is only through the mediation of the will that intelligible forms receive an inclination to their effects. Thus, even though the essence of a finite being is determined by its exemplar idea, it is by means of a command of the divine will that that essence is determined actually to exist. This has been termed by te Velde the traditional interpretation of Thomas's metaphysics of creation, but it is an interpretation that te Velde himself contends "breaks the unity of the act of creation."[126]

According to te Velde, if we hold that God knows essences through the divine ideas and produces them into existence by an act of his will, then prior to an act of God's will there is a phase involving the constitution of the possibility of existence. This interpretation, he contends, necessarily leads to the assumption of a double participation—a position that te Velde finds absurd: "A double participation makes an empty metaphor of the concept of participation. For why should one speak of participation if creation consists in attributing factual existence to a possible essence? God's freedom in creation does not correspond to the contingency of existence."[127]

---

actualisée par l'*esse* participé qu'elle reçoit: son actualité est ainsi donnée par la «médiation» de l'*esse*."

125. *De ver.*, q. 2, a. 5 (Leonine ed., vol. 22.1.63:297–301). For the Latin, see n. 113 above.

126. te Velde, *Participation and Substantiality*, 282.

127. Ibid. Te Velde thus also rejects the notion that there are divine ideas of pure

We might ask, however, what this double participation is that concerns te Velde. Is it a participation in both the divine ideas and the divine will? Or is it a participation in the divine ideas and the divine nature? Unfortunately, he does not elaborate upon this point but notes simply that "There is no place for a double participation in Aquinas."[128] Either way, however, one can respond immediately by observing, as I have already done, that for Thomas there is no participation in the divine ideas. This is not to deny the model of creation whereby God wills into existence the essences that he conceives; rather, it is simply to note that the similitude between created essence and idea does not involve the essence's participating in the idea.

Furthermore, te Velde's concern about a double participation is unfounded because even though created essence participates in *esse,* there is no participation that results in created essence. Here we must recall that real or ontological participation involves both a receiver and a received principle. Created essence receives an act of being, but there is nothing ontologically prior to receive that essence itself.[129] This is why Geiger notes that "the essence that participates *in (à)* existence is itself a participation *of (de)* the First Perfection, of which it conveys only a limited and fragmentary aspect."[130]

It must be granted that Thomas himself does not appear to have referred to created essence as being a "participation"; instead,

---

possibles: "Creation cannot be seen, as frequently happens in Thomistic literature, as the act by which God actualizes the many pre-conceived possibilities by attributing them *esse* or actual existence. In this way the act of creation already presupposes the formal differences of things and results therefore in a kind of common existence the same for all regardless of their formal differences. But the doctrine of ideas does not serve to explain the possibility of something prior to its actual existence; as the formal differences of things are differences in being, they must be reduced to the common cause of being" (te Velde, *Participation and Substantiality*, 114n46). Thomas's writings on the *possibilia* would seem to contradict te Velde's position.

128. Ibid., 114n46.
129. Geiger, *La participation*, 52.
130. Ibid., 60–61n3. For the French, see n. 46, above.

he employs this term to refer to a perfection that a participant receives from that which it participates.[131] Still, essence is nonetheless a perfection in its own right even though it is not itself received
by anything. Geiger's terminology is useful, therefore, because it
conveys the difference between essence and *esse* as perfections. A
structure analogous to that described by Geiger can be found in
Thomas's account of the relationship between accidental form and
the divine ideas. In the *De veritate,* Thomas defends the position
that there are divine ideas of accidents by noting that "Although an
accident is not *that which participates,* it nevertheless is itself a *participation.* Thus, it is clear that an idea or likeness in God corresponds
to it as well."[132] Following Geiger's language, I would suggest that
created essence, like an accident and like other created formal perfections, could be termed a participation—namely, a participation
of the likeness of the divine essence. Unlike other created perfections, however, essence is not received into anything—that is, it is
not participated *by* anything. Nor does it need to be since essence,
according to the ontological order, is not an act that needs to be
limited by potency; rather, it is itself a principle of potency that
limits the act of being. From where, then, does its own limitation
come? As we have noted before, from its corresponding idea in the
divine mind which is itself limited.

Furthermore, the fact that Thomas does not think essence is received into anything does not pose a problem for our terming it a
"participation." As he reminds us, "'Creation' does not mean the
constitution of a composite thing out of preexisting principles, but
it means that the composite is created such that it is produced into
being *(in esse)* simultaneously with all of its principles."[133] Hence,

131. As we have seen, however, Thomas does refer to essence as participating in *esse.*
On this point, see *De spir. creat.,* a. 1 (Leonine ed., vol. 22.4.13–14:363–408). See also
Wippel, *Metaphysical Thought,* 108n39.

132. *De ver.,* q. 3, a. 7, ad 3 (Leonine ed., vol. 22.1.115:118–21): "Quamvis accidens non
sit participans, est tamen ipsa participatio, et sic patet quod ei etiam respondet idea in
Deo vel similitudo." Emphasis added in translation.

133. *ST* I, q. 45, a. 4, ad 2 (Leonine ed., vol. 14.468): "Creatio non dicit constitutio-

he also explains that "God, at the same time giving *esse*, produces that which receives *esse*, and thus it is not necessary that he act from something preexisting."[134] Despite the fact, then, that created essence is not received into anything, we could still term it a "participation," for it does not *need* to be received into anything in order to exist. Rather, it exists through the act of being that God bestows on it through creation: "From the very fact that *esse* is attributed to a quiddity, the quiddity is not only said to be but to be created, since before it has *esse* it is nothing—except perhaps in the creator's intellect, where it is not a creature but the creative essence."[135] Here, then, Thomas affirms precisely what te Velde claims that he does not, namely, that the ideas in the divine intellect are ontologically (but not temporally) prior to created essence. It is because God bestows *esse* upon a possible essence that it is created, and the finite being that results from this composition is what participates in a likeness of the divine nature.

Hence, te Velde's concern that the traditional interpretation of Thomas's metaphysics of creation requires a double participation is unfounded. His criticism of the traditional interpretation stems from a concern that created essence not be understood to preexist its act of being. As Wippel observes, however, because of this concern he appears to have fallen prey to Geiger's error, missing two key notions. As we saw above, the first is that the principles of essence and *esse* can be mutually dependent upon each other according to different orders of dependency. The second is that the priority in the order of nature does not necessarily imply a priority in the order of time. Thus the act of being actualizes a created

---

nem rei compositae ex principiis praeexistentibus: sed compositum sic dicitur creari, quod simul cum omnibus suis principiis in esse producitur."

134. *De pot.,* q. 3, a. 1, ad 17 (Marietti ed., vol. 2.41): "Deus simul dans esse, producit id quod esse recipit: et sic non oportet quod agat ex aliquo praeexistenti."

135. *De pot.,* q. 3, a. 5, ad 2 (Marietti ed., vol. 2.49): "Ex hoc ipso quod quidditati esse attribuitur, non solum esse, sed ipsa quidditas creari dicitur: quia antequam esse habeat, nihil est, nisi forte in intellectu creantis, ubi non est creatura, sed creatrix essentia."

essence, while that very essence principle simultaneously receives and limits the same act of being. In this way, Wippel concludes, "Neither preexists as such apart from the other, and each enjoys its appropriate priority in the order of nature (not in the order of time) with respect to its particular ontological function within a given entity."[136]

SUMMARY

Inasmuch as the divine ideas are the causes of things that God creates, they are exemplars; inasmuch as they are exemplars, they are the similitudes of both the essences and accidents of finite beings. But even though both essences and accidents share a likeness to their respective exemplar ideas, neither actually participates in those ideas: Socrates is indeed exemplified by the divine idea of Socrates, but he is who he is through his very essence, not through participation. Despite this fact, divine exemplarism plays an integral role in the structure of participation for Thomas. Although created essence does not participate in its exemplar idea, the finite being (ens) of which it is a principle does participate in a likeness of the exemplar that is the divine nature. Through such participation, the created essence receives and limits esse. This limitation, however, is dependent upon the ontologically prior formation of the divine idea that determines the created essence's limited mode of being. Thus, while the divine nature is imitable in itself, a finite being actually imitates it only because God knows his nature as imitable and wills it actually to be imitated.

Esse is thus limited from the bottom up, as it were, inasmuch as a created essence is a real principle that receives and limits the act of being. But it is also limited from the top down inasmuch as God "excogitates" the divine ideas, thinking *this* essence instead of *that* one as potentially receiving esse in a given being. As regards a cre-

136. Wippel, *Metaphysical Thought*, 129–30.

ated essence itself, therefore, its mode of being is determined by its divine idea, but its actuality is determined by the participation of the finite being *(ens)* in a likeness of the divine nature. The principles of essence and *esse* in any finite being are thus mutually dependent upon each other, and ultimately they are so because the two modes of *divine exemplarism* are mutually dependent upon each other. As the exemplar causes of created essence, the divine ideas are the causes of a principle of potency that requires a principle of act; as the exemplar cause of the act of being, the divine nature is the cause of an act that requires a principle of limitation.

Neither mode of exemplarism, therefore, can be exercised without the other, and both are dependent upon the mediation of the divine will, for an exemplar is effective only because an agent determines the end of that which is exemplified. We might add, furthermore, that each mode of divine exemplarism is prior in its own order. According to the intentional order, the causality of the divine ideas is prior to that of the divine nature because it determines the mode of being *(esse)* of created essence; but according to the order of reality, the exemplarism of the divine nature is prior to that of the divine ideas because it makes that essence actually to exist.

Although created essence does not participate *in* its exemplar idea, we can in a sense say that it is a participation *of* a likeness of the divine nature: a participation that does not need to be received into anything because of its relation to *esse.* Nevertheless, even if we choose to refer to essence in this way, we must recall that Thomas himself never does. For him, participation involves a finite being's sharing in a likeness of the divine nature. The divine ideas, therefore, are not themselves participated but are rather the *participabilities* of that likeness as known by God, that is, his knowledge of the ways in which his essence can be participated by creatures.

CONCLUSION

~

Thomas's doctrine of the divine ideas touches upon some of the most fundamental elements of his metaphysical thought. In the course of exploring his doctrine, we examined such issues as the nature of causality, the real distinction between essence and existence, and the theory of participation, to name a few. As a result, we have a fuller picture of Thomas's doctrine of divine ideas and can understand why exemplarism is indeed an essential element of his philosophy. Central to Thomas's notion of exemplarism is the characteristic of similitude or likeness *(similitudo)*. As we saw in chapter 1, Thomas commonly describes an exemplar as "that in the likeness of which something is made." Following this general notion of exemplarism, he identifies different types of exemplars. In one sense, the form of a natural agent is an exemplar since it causes an effect that shares the same species as itself. We identified this as a "natural exemplar" because what is made in its likeness is made according to nature, not to art. For Thomas, however, the form of a natural agent is an exemplar only in an improper sense because the natural agent does not itself determine its intended end, but rather nature does.

Another sort of exemplar that Thomas identifies is the object or model toward which an artisan looks in making his work. Aquinas refers to this model as an "external exemplar" since it exists externally to both the agent's mind and his nature. Since the sort of exemplarism that it exercises does involve the agent himself determining the end of his work, the artisan's external model more truly deserves the name "exemplar" than does a natural agent's form. Nevertheless, it still is not an exemplar according to the primary sense of the term because this external object is dependent for its exemplarism on the causality of a prior exemplar, namely, the artisan's idea. It is *this* form in the mind of the artisan that Thomas considers to be an exemplar according to the primary sense of the term.

Since an idea is an exemplar only inasmuch as something is made in its likeness, Thomas identifies exemplar ideas as belonging to the practical and not the speculative intellect. In its role as a productive principle, an exemplar idea acts as the measure of the thing made. Thus, the idea is a formal cause of the thing that it exemplifies even though it is not intrinsic to that thing. As we saw, Thomas considers the fundamental characteristic of form to be that it is a pattern by which something is the kind of thing that it is. For this reason, he concludes that form is not limited to an intrinsic mode of causality: it can be extrinsic as well. And this is what he considers an exemplar to be, namely, an extrinsic formal cause. Hence, he does not postulate a fifth type of cause but adheres to the fourfold Aristotelian division. In the course of considering ideas as exemplar causes, Thomas comes to define an idea as "a form that something imitates because of the intention of an agent who predetermines the end for himself."[1]

Still, even though an exemplar idea is properly a formal cause of the thing it exemplifies, its causality involves more than just formality. Following Thomas's mature use of the term "exemplar," we found that he only considers actually practical ideas to be exemplars, for only they in fact exemplify something. Inasmuch as these ideas do exemplify something, their causality necessarily also entails efficient and final causality: it entails efficient causality be-

---

1. *De ver.,* q. 3, a. 1 (Leonine ed., vol. 22.1.100:220–23): "Haec ergo videtur esse ratio ideae, quod idea sit forma quam aliquid imitatur ex intentione agentis qui praedeterminat sibi finem."

cause the exemplar's causality is caused by the efficient cause, and it entails final causality because the exemplar, acting as an end, must first motivate the intention of the agent for him to produce his work. Nevertheless, we found that in its capacity as an exemplar cause, an idea's causality is properly reduced to the order of formal causality since the characteristic that is proper to it as an exemplar is its imitability.

Having discerned these general characteristics of exemplarism, we proceeded in chapter 2 to examine Thomas's arguments for the existence of *divine* exemplars. We found that he offers three different types of arguments: from natural teleology, from divine similitude, and from divine self-knowledge. Following these three arguments, Thomas comes to the conclusion that just as there are exemplar ideas in the mind of the human artisan, so too there must be exemplar ideas in the mind of God. In the course of examining these arguments, moreover, we found that these divine ideas can only exist within the mind of God. On this point, Thomas is emphatically clear: divine ideas are not the *per se* subsistent universals posited by Plato. Since God is pure act, Thomas insists that it is impossible for God's ideas to come from anywhere other than himself.

Nevertheless, the divine ideas are not simply God's essence, nor are they even that essence as it is known by God. Rather, as we saw in chapter 3, Thomas concludes that the ideas are the divine essence inasmuch as that essence is known by God *as imitable.* In this way, the one divine essence is the medium by which God understands the many ways that he can be imitated. His knowledge of these diverse ways is what constitutes the multiplicity of ideas. By positing these distinctions, Thomas is able to affirm the plurality of the divine ideas without compromising the simplicity of the divine essence. For even though there can be no real multiplicity of ideas within the divine essence, there can still be a logical multiplicity of them as objects that are understood by God. In chapter 4, we found that this multiplicity includes ideas of genera, species, individuals, and even pure possibles. Thomas does not consider all of these divine ideas, however, to be exemplars. As we have seen, only actually practical ideas in fact exemplify something. Thus, when discussing the divine ideas, Thomas comes to restrict the term "exemplar" to refer to an idea of an individual thing that God makes at some point in time—whether that idea is of a substance or of a separable accident.

We also saw in this chapter that Thomas in fact identifies two different types of divine exemplarism: one type is the exemplarism of the divine ideas, which is a kind of intellectual exemplarism; the other type is the exemplarism of the divine nature, which is a kind of natural exemplarism. Although both types are ultimately reduced to the one divine essence, they differ in significant ways. The exemplarism of the ideas involves a perfect likeness between a finite being and its respective divine idea. By contrast, the exemplarism of the divine nature involves degrees of imitation with a more and a less, for no creature is the perfect likeness of God's essence. Thus, a created being such as Socrates falls short of imitating the infinite perfection of God's nature, but he does not fall short of imitating the divine idea of "Socrates," for he truly and fully is Socrates in his very essence.

In chapter 5, we considered precisely how the divine ideas act as exemplar causes. As with other types of exemplarism, the exemplarism of the divine ideas entails efficient causality. In this case, the efficient cause is the divine will. Since God's will is perfectly free, Thomas concludes that the exemplarism of the divine ideas does not result from the necessity of God's nature, as some Neoplatonists maintain, but rather from the freedom of his will. Even though the divine ideas do require an act of God's will to exercise their causality, their primary mode of causality is not efficiency but formality: as with other exemplars, they are extrinsic formal causes. As such, these ideas are the cause of form in the things that they exemplify. But the divine ideas are not the cause of form alone. Since God knows all the principles that enter into created beings, he knows even the *matter* of physical substances. Thus, his ideas of such substances exemplify not only their forms but their matter as well. In short, God's exemplar ideas are formal causes of the entire essence of a created being. Having attained clarity on this point, we saw that Thomas is careful to avoid the problem of occasionalism. The divine exemplars are the cause of form in physical substances, but their causality does not compromise the operations of nature: the proximate causes of generation are natural agents, not the divine ideas. Properly speaking, he explains, the ideas are not generative principles but creative ones, concreating form in the potency of matter.

Nevertheless, even though Thomas does not consider the divine ideas to be the proximate causes of generation, he does see a role for them in the operations of nature. Natural agents are properly the cause of *this* form coming to be in *this* matter, but in themselves they are not able to cause form as such. They can only do so, Thomas argues, as the instruments of universal causes. Following Aristotle, therefore, he looks to the motion of the heavens to account for this universal causality. But this motion itself must be reduced to the intelligible species in the angelic intellect and, ultimately, to the ideas in the mind of God. Thus, Thomas's doctrine of divine exemplarism does not exclude natural agency but, rather, facilitates it, for the whole natural effect is caused by the combined agencies of God and the natural agent, although each causes the same effect in a different respect.

This study culminated in chapter 6 with a consideration of the causal role of the divine ideas within the structure of Thomas's theory of participation. As we have seen, God's exemplar ideas are the similitudes of both the essences and the accidents of finite beings. But even though both essences and accidents share a likeness to their respective exemplar ideas, we found that neither actually participates in those ideas: Socrates is indeed exemplified by the divine idea of Socrates, but he is who he is through his very essence, not through participation. Despite this fact, divine exemplarism plays an integral role in the structure of participation for Thomas. Here we again saw the importance of the distinction that he draws between the exemplarism of the divine ideas and that of the divine nature. Although the essences of finite beings do not participate in their exemplar ideas, they do participate in the exemplar that is God's nature. And it is through such participation that created essences receive and limit *esse*. This limitation, however, is dependent upon the ontologically prior formation of the divine ideas, which determine the limited modes of being *(esse)* received by created essences. Thus, even though the divine nature is imitable in itself, it is only imitated by a finite being because God both knows his nature as imitable and wills it actually to be so imitated. As regards created essence, its mode of being is determined by its divine idea, but its actuality is determined by the finite being's participating in a likeness of the divine nature. Thus, we found that for Thomas, the divine ideas are not themselves participated but are rather the "participabilities" of the likeness of the divine nature as it is known by God, that is, they are his knowledge of the ways in which the likeness of his essence can be participated.

I would like to conclude this work by returning to Gilson's observation that exemplarism is an essential element of Thomistic philosophy (even though Gilson did not say the same of the divine *ideas*). Why, we might ask, is this the case? What would Thomistic philosophy be lacking without this doctrine? In light of the themes that we have considered, we are now in a position to answer this question. Here, I believe, it is helpful to turn to Thomas's own words. Let us review what he has to say about divine exemplarism in q. 44, a. 3 of *Summa theologiae* I:

[I]n the production of any thing, an exemplar is necessary so that an effect may receive a determinate form; for an artisan produces a determinate form in matter according to the exemplar to which he looks, whether that be an exemplar that he looks to without or whether it be an exemplar conceived by the mind within. Now it is clear that things that are naturally made receive determinate forms. But this determination of forms must be reduced, as to a first principle, to the divine wisdom that has discerned (excogitavit) the order of the universe, which [order] consists in the distinction of things. Therefore we must say that in the divine wisdom there are notions (rationes) of all things, which we have previously called "ideas" (ideas)—that is, exemplar forms existing in the divine mind. And these [ideas], although they are multiplied according to a relation to things, are nevertheless in reality nothing other than the divine essence inasmuch as its likeness can be participated by different things in different ways. Thus, God himself is the first exemplar of all things.[2]

Here, in this short passage, we see Thomas touch upon each of the major themes that we have considered in this work: he proves to us why the divine ideas must exist; he shows us how they can exist as a multiplicity; he illustrates their causal role; and he acknowledges their relationship to the exemplarism of the divine nature, addressing the metaphysical role of participation.

Why, then, is the doctrine of divine exemplarism essential to Thomistic philosophy? Because it provides a necessary epistemological and ontological account of the order of reality. As regards their epistemological role, the divine ideas account for God's having a proper knowledge of a multiplicity of created things. Without a doctrine of exemplarism, Thomas's metaphysics would reduce God to an Aristotelian "thought thinking itself" that thinks only itself: a first principle that is blissfully unaware of the world that it

---

2. *ST*, I, q. 44, a. 3 (Leonine ed., vol. 4.460): "Deus est prima causa exemplaris omnium rerum. Ad cuius evidentiam, considerandum est quod ad productionem alicuius rei ideo necessarium est exemplar, ut effectus determinatam formam consequatur: artifex enim producit determinatam formam in materia, propter exemplar ad quod inspicit, sive illud sit exemplar ad quod extra intuetur, sive sit exemplar interius mente conceptum. Manifestum est autem quod ea quae naturaliter fiunt, determinatas formas consequuntur. Haec autem formarum determinatio oportet quod reducatur, sicut in primum principium, in divinam sapientiam, quae ordinem universi excogitavit, qui in rerum distinctione consistit. Et ideo oportet dicere quod in divina sapientia sunt rationes omnium rerum: quas supra diximus *ideas*, id est formas exemplares in mente divina existentes. Quae quidem licet multiplicentur secundum respectum ad res, tamen non sunt realiter aliud a divina essentia, prout eius similitudo a diversis participari potest diversimode. Sic igitur ipse Deus est primum exemplar omnium."

moves.³ As regards their ontological role, the divine ideas account for the determination of form and the directedness of nature. Without a doctrine of exemplarism, Thomas's metaphysics would either imply that the natural world acts according to chance rather than teleologically, or it would imply that God's creative act results from the necessity of his own nature rather than freely through his intellect and will.⁴ Neither of these possibilities, however, is consonant with Thomas's metaphysical thought as a whole. Hence, for these reasons, exemplarism is an essential element of his philosophy.

3. *Metaphysics*, 12.9.1074b15–35 (Barnes ed., vol. 2.1698) and 1075a5–10 (Barnes ed., vol. 2.1699). For an argument that Aristotle's God does know the world, see Thomas De Koninck, "Aristotle on God as Thought Thinking Itself," *Review of Metaphysics* 47 (1994): 471–515. On at least one occasion, Thomas himself is of the opinion that Aristotle in fact has a doctrine of divine ideas. In his *Commentary on the Gospel of John,* Thomas considers the significance of the phrase: *and the Word was with God.* He observes that the Evangelist writes these words in part to avoid the error of Plato, who held that the ideas exist separately from God. Other Platonists held that the ideas exist in a mind, but one that is beneath God. In order to avoid this error, Thomas explains, the Evangelist adds the words: *and the Word was God.* Finally, Thomas notes that in contrast to these philosophers, "Aristoteles vero posuit in deo rationes omnium rerum, et quod idem est in deo intellectus et intelligens et intellectum"; Thomas continues, however, by noting that "tamen posuit mundum coaeternum sibi fuisse. Et contra hoc est quod evangelista dicit hoc, scilicet verbum solum, erat in principio apud deum; ita quod ly hoc non excludit aliam personam, sed aliam naturam coaeternam" (*Lect. super Ioann.,* c. 1, lect. 2 [Busa ed., vol. 6.231:125–75]). Boland describes Thomas's interpretation of Aristotle on this matter as being early in his career (Boland, *Ideas in God,* 284). Torrell, however, places this commentary between 1270 and 1272, although he grants that there is debate concerning the precise dating of this work. If Torrell is correct, then Thomas's observation here would indicate that he held this interpretation even toward the end of his career. It should be noted, however, that in his commentary on Aristotle's *Metaphysics* (1270–71), Thomas does not attribute such an opinion to Aristotle (*In XII Meta.,* lect. 11, nn. 2614–16 [Marietti ed., 736]).

4. *De ver.,* q. 3, a. 1 (Leonine ed., vol. 22.1.100:224–40): "Secundum hoc ergo patet quod illi <qui> ponebant omnia casu accidere non poterant ideam ponere: sed haec opinio a philosophis reprobatur quia quae sunt a casu non se habent eodem modo nisi ut in paucioribus, naturae autem cursum videmus semper eodem modo progredi aut ut in pluribus. Similiter etiam secundum eos qui posuerunt quod a Deo procedunt omnia per necessitatem naturae et non per arbitrium voluntatis, non possunt ponere ideas quia ea quae ex necessitate naturae agunt non praedeterminant sibi finem: sed hoc esse non potest quia omne quod agit propter finem si non determinat sibi finem determinatur ei finis ab alio superiore et sic erit aliqua causa eo superior, quod non potest esse quia omnes loquentes de Deo intelligunt eum esse causam primam entium."

Although it may not be *the* key to understanding Thomas's metaphysical thought, the doctrine of divine exemplarism is certainly *a* key to understanding that thought, and an important one at that. It helps to account for the intelligibility and order of the created world; for as Josef Pieper has observed, it is of the very essence of finite beings to be creatively thought: "It was, as it seems, St. Thomas's view that the notion that things have an essence cannot be separated from the other notion: that this essential character is the fruit of a form-giving thought that plans, devises, and creates."[5] It is the role of this form-giving thought that we have been considering throughout these pages: for Thomas Aquinas, this is the role of the divine ideas as exemplar causes.

5. Pieper, *The Silence of St. Thomas,* 51.

BIBLIOGRAPHY

Aertsen, Jan. *Nature and Creature.* Translated by Herbert Donald Mor-
ton. New York: E.J. Brill, 1987.
———. *Medieval Philosophy and The Transcendentals.* New York: E.J.
Brill, 1996.
Algazel. *Algazel's Metaphysics: A Medieval Translation.* Edited by J. T.
Muckle. Toronto: The Institute of Medieval Studies, 1933.
Anderson, James. *The Cause of Being.* St. Louis: Herder, 1952.
Albinus. *Didaskaliko.* In *Alcinoos,* edited by John Whittaker. Paris: Les
Belles Lettres, 1990.
Aristotle. *Metaphysics.* Edited by W. D. Ross. 2 vols. New York: Oxford
University Press, 1924.
———. *Metaphysics.* Translated by W. D. Ross. In *The Complete Works
of Aristotle,* edited by Jonathan Barnes. Vol. 2. Princeton: Princeton
University Press, 1991.
———. *Nicomachean Ethics.* Edited by I. Bywater. London: Oxford
University Press, 1890.
———. *Nicomachean Ethics.* Translated by W. D. Ross revised by
J. O. Urmson. In *The Complete Works of Aristotle,* edited by Jonathan
Barnes. Vol. 2. Princeton: Princeton University Press, 1991.
———. *On Generation and Corruption.* In *Aristotelis Opera,* edited by
Immanuel Bekker. Vol. 2. Oxford: Oxford University Press, 1837.
———. *On Generation and Corruption.* Translated by H. H. Joachim.
In *The Complete Works of Aristotle,* edited by Jonathan Barnes. Vol. 1.
Princeton: Princeton University Press, 1991.
———. *Posterior Analytics.* In *Analytica Priora et Posteriora,* edited by
W. D. Ross. New York: Oxford University Press, 1964. Reprint 1989.
———. *Posterior Analytics.* Translated by Jonathan Barnes. In *The
Complete Works of Aristotle,* edited by Jonathan Barnes. Vol. 1. Princ-
eton: Princeton University Press, 1991.
———. *Physics.* Edited by W. D. Ross. New York: Oxford University
Press, 1936.
———. *Physics.* Translated by R. P. Hardie and R. K. Gaye. In *The*

Complete Works of Aristotle, edited by Jonathan Barnes. Vol. 1. Princeton: Princeton University Press, 1991.

Armstrong, Arthur H. *The Architecture of the Intelligible Universe in the Philosophy of Plotinus.* New York: Cambridge University Press, 1940.

———. ed. *The Cambridge History of Later Greek and Early Medieval Philosophy.* London: Cambridge University Press, 1967.

Augustine, Saint. *Sancti Aurelii Augustini episcopi opera.* Corpus Scriptorum Ecclesiasticorum Latinorum. Vol. 33, *Confessiones.* Edited by Pius Knöll. Vindobon, 1896.

———. *Contra Academicos.* Edited by William McAllen and Klaus Detlef Daur. In *Aurelii Augustini opera.* Corpus Christianorum. Series Latina, vol. 29. Turnhout, 1970.

———. *Sancti Aurelii Augustini episcopi opera.* Corpus Scriptorum Ecclesiasticorum Latinorum. Vol. 40, *De civitate Dei.* Edited by Emanuel Hoffmann. Vindobon, 1899.

———. *De diversis quaestionibus LXXXIII.* Edited by Almut Mutzenbecher. In *Aurelii Augustini opera.* Corpus Christianorum. Series Latina, vol. 44A. Turnhout, 1975.

———. *De Genesi ad litteram.* Edited by Joseph Zycha. In *Sancti Aurelii Augustini episcopi opera.* Corpus Scriptorum Ecclesiasticorum Latinorum, vol. 28.1. Vindobon, 1894.

———. *De libero arbitrio.* Edited by William McAllen and Klaus Detlef Daur. In *Aurelii Augustini opera.* Corpus Christianorum. Series Latina, vol. 29. Turnhout, 1970.

———. *De natura et origine animae.* Edited by Carl F. Urba and Joseph Zycha. In *Sancti Aurelii Augustini episcopi opera.* Corpus Scriptorum Ecclesiasticorum Latinorum, vol. 60. Vindobon, 1913.

———. *Aurelii Augustini opera.* Corpus Christianorum. Series Latina. Vols. 50 and 50A, *De Trinitate.* Edited by William John Mountain. Turnhout, 1968.

———. *De vera religione.* Edited by William McAllen Green. In *Sancti Aurelii Augustini episcopi opera.* Corpus Scriptorum Ecclesiasticorum Latinorum, vol. 77. Vindobon, 1961.

———. *Sancti Aurelii Augustini episcopi opera.* Corpus Scriptorum Ecclesiasticorum Latinorum. Vol. 34, *Epistula.* Edited by Alois Goldbacher. Vindobon, 1895.

———. *Aurelii Augustini opera.* Corpus Christianorum. Series Latina. Vol. 36, *In Iohannis Evangelium tractatus.* Edited by Radbodus Willems. Turnhout, 1954.

———. *Aurelii Augustini opera.* Corpus Christianorum. Series Latina. Vol. 57, *Retractationes II.* Edited by Almut Mutzenbecher.Turnhout, 1984.

Averroes. *Destructio destructionum philosophiae Algazelis.* Edited by Beatrice H. Zedler. Milwaukee: The Marquette University Press, 1961.

Avicebron. *Fons vitae.* Translated into Latin by John of Spain and Dominic Gundissalinus. In *Die dem Boethius fälschlich zugeschriebene abhandlung des Do-*

minicus Gundisalvi De unitate, edited by Paul Correns. Beiträge zur Geschich-te der Philosophie und Theologie des Mittelalters, vol. 1, bks. 2–4.. Münster: Aschendorff Buchhandlung, 1891.

Avicenna. *Liber de philosophia prima sive scientia divina: I–IV.* Edited by Simone Van Riet. Louvain: Peeters and Leiden: E.J. Brill, 1977.

———. *Liber de philosophia prima sive scientia divina: V–X.* Edited by Simone Van Riet. Louvain: Peeters and Leiden: E.J. Brill, 1980.

Avicenna. *Liber primus naturalium.* Edited by Simone Van Riet. Louvain-La-Neuve: Peeters and Leiden: E.J. Brill, 1992.

Balmaceda, Federico. "Ejemplaridad y Causalidad: Estudio de Las Ideas Divinas en Tomás de Aquino." Ph.D. diss., University of Navarra, 1980.

———. "La Doble Causalidad Ejemplar Divina en Santo Tomás de Aquino." *Philosophica* 9–10 (1986–87): 155–66.

Berchman, Robert M. *From Philo to Origen.* Chico, Calif.: Scholars Press, 1984.

Blumenthal, Henry J. "Did Plotinus Believe in Ideas of Individuals?" *Phronesis* 11 (1966): 61–80.

Bobik, Joseph. "Aquinas' Fourth Way and the Approximating Relation." *The Thomist* 51 (1987): 17–36.

Boethius. *The Consolation of Philosophy.* Translated by Richard Green. New York: Macmillan Publishing Company, 1962.

———. *The Theological Tractates with an English Translation; The Consolation of Philosophy.* Translated by H. F. Stewart, E. K. Rand, and S. J. Tester. Loeb Classical Library. Cambridge: Harvard University Press, 1973.

Boland, Vivian. *Ideas in God According to Saint Thomas Aquinas.* New York: E.J. Brill, 1996.

Bonaventure, Saint. *Collationes in hexaemeron.* In *Doctoris seraphici S. Bonaventurae, opera omnia.* Vol. 5. Quaracchi: 1891.

Bonino, Serge-Thomas. *Thomas d'Aquin: De la Vérité ou La science en Dieu.* Fri-bourg: Éditions Universitaires de Fribourg, 1996.

Brady, Jules M. "Note on the Fourth Way." *The New Scholasticism* 48 (1974): 219–32.

Branick, Vincent P. "The Unity of the Divine Ideas." *The New Scholasticism* 42 (1968): 171–201.

Burrell, David B. "Distinguishing God from the World." In *Language, Meaning and God,* edited by Brian Davies, 75–91. London: Geoffrey Chapman, 1987.

———. *Freedom and Creation in Three Traditions.* Notre Dame: University of Notre Dame Press, 1993.

Burnet, John. *Platonism.* Berkeley: University of California Press, 1928.

Burt, Donald X. *Augustine's World.* Lanham, Md.: University Press of America, 1996.

Carlo, William. *The Ultimate Reducibility of Essence to Existence in Existential Meta-physics.* The Hague: Martinus Nijhoff, 1966.

Cascante-Fallas, Luis Diego. "La metafisica de la luz, una categoria de la ontologia bonaventuriana." *Revista de Filosofía de la Universidad de Costa Rica* 36 (1998): 341–48.

Chadwick, Henry. *Boethius: The Consolations of Music, Logic, Theology, and Philosophy.* Oxford: Clarendon Press, 1981.

Chambat, Lucien. "La «Quarta Via» de saint Thomas." *Revue Thomiste* 33 (1928): 412–22.

Charlier, Louis. "Les cinq voies de saint Thomas: Leur structure métaphysique." In *L'existence de Dieu.* Cahiers de l'actualité religieuse 16 (Tournai and Paris, 1961), 181–227.

Chenu, Marie-Dominique. *Introduction à l'étude de saint Thomas d'Aquin.* Montreal: Université de Montréal, 1954.

Clark, Mary T. *Augustine.* Washington, D.C.: Georgetown University Press, 1994.

Clarke, Norris. "The Limitation of Act by Potency in St. Thomas: Aristotelianism or Neoplatonism?" *The New Scholasticism* 26 (1952): 167–94.

———. "The Meaning of Participation in St. Thomas." In *Proceedings of the American Catholic Philosophical Association* 26 (1952): 147–57.

———. "The Platonic Heritage of Thomism." *Review of Metaphysics* 8 (1954): 105–24.

———. "What Is Really Real?" In *Progress in Philosophy,* edited by J. A. McWilliams, 61–90. Milwaukee: Bruce, 1955.

———. "The Problem of the Reality and Multiplicity of Divine Ideas in Christian Neoplatonism." In *Neoplatonism and Christian Thought,* edited by Dominic J. O'Meara, 109–27. Albany: State University of New York Press, 1982.

Collins, James. *The Thomistic Philosophy of the Angels.* Washington, D.C.: The Catholic University of America Press, 1947.

Conway, James I. "The Reality of the Possibles." *The New Scholasticism* 33 (1959): 139–61, 331–53.

Cortest, Luis. "Was St. Thomas Aquinas a Platonist?" *The Thomist* 52 (1988): 209–19.

Corvez, Maurice. "La quatrième voie vers l'existence de Dieu selon saint Thomas." In *Quinque sunt viae,* edited by Leo Elders, 75–83. Vatican City, 1980.

Couesnongle, Vincent de. "La causalité du maximum. L'utilisation par S. Thomas d'un passage d'Aristote." *Revue des sciences philosophiques et théologiques* 38 (1954): 433–44.

———. "La causalité du maximum. Pourquoi Saint Thomas a-t-il mal cité Aristote?" *Revue des sciences philosophiques et théologiques* 38 (1954): 658–80.

Cousins, Ewert. "Truth in St. Bonaventure." *Proceedings and Addresses of the American Philosophical Association* 43 (1969): 204–10.

Crabbe, Anna. "Literary Design in *De Consolatione.*" In *Boethius: His Life, Thought and Influence,* edited by Margaret Gibson, 237–77. Oxford: Basil Blackwell, 1981.

Cullen, Christopher M. *Bonaventure.* New York: Oxford University Press, 2006.

Cunningham, Francis A. "A Theory on Abstraction in St. Thomas." *Modern Schoolman* 35 (1958): 249–70.

Davies, Brian. "Classical Theism and the Doctrine of Divine Simplicity." In *Language, Meaning and God,* edited by Brian Davies, 51–74. London: Geoffrey Chapman, 1987.

————, ed. *Language, Meaning and God.* London: Geoffrey Chapman, 1987.

De Koninck, Thomas. "Aristotle on God as Thought Thinking Itself." *Review of Metaphysics* 47 (1994): 471–515.

Dewan, Lawrence. "St. Thomas and the Possibles." *The New Scholasticism* 53 (1979): 76–85.

————. "St. Thomas, James Ross, and Exemplarism: A Reply." *American Catholic Philosophical Quarterly* 65 (1991): 221–34.

Dionysius. *See Pseudo-Dionysius.*

Durantel, Jean. *Saint Thomas et le Pseudo-Denis.* Paris: Librairie Félix Alcan, 1919.

Ewbank, Michael B. "Diverse Ordering of Dionysius's *Triplex Via* by St. Thomas Aquinas." *Mediaeval Studies* 52 (1990): 82–109.

Fabro, Cornelio. "Sviluppo, significato e valore della 'IV Via.'" *Doctor Communis* 7 (1954): 71–109.

————. *Participation et causalité selon s. Thomas d'Aquin.* Louvain: Publications Universitaires, 1961.

————. *La nozione metafisica di partecipazione.* 2nd ed. Turin: Società Editrice Internazionale, 1963.

————. "Platonism, Neoplatonism and Thomism: Convergencies and Divergencies." *The New Scholasticism* 44 (1970): 69–100.

————. "The Intensive Hermeneutics of Thomistic Philosophy: The Notion of Participation." *Review of Metaphysics* 27.3 (Commemorative Issue Thomas Aquinas 1224–1274): 449–91 (1974).

Farthing, John Lee. "The Problem of Divine Exemplarity in St. Thomas." *The Thomist* 49 (1985): 183–222.

Fay, Thomas. "Participation: The Transformation of Platonic and Neoplatonic Thought in the Metaphysics of Thomas Aquinas." *Divus Thomas* 76 (1973): 50–64.

Garrigou-Lagrange, Réginald. *God: His Existence and His Nature.* Translated by Bede Rose. 2 vols. St. Louis and London: B. Herder, 1949.

Gauthier, René-Antoine. Introduction to *Somme contre les gentils,* by Saint Augustine. Paris: Éditions Universitaires, 1993.

Geiger, Louis B. "Abstraction et séparation d'après s. Thomas *In de Trinitate,* q. 5, a. 3." *Revue des sciences philosophiques et théologiques* 31 (1947): 3–40.

————. *La participation dans la philosophie de s. Thomas d'Aquin.* 2nd ed. Paris: Librairie Philosophique J. Vrin, 1953.

————. "Les rédactions successives de *Contra Gentiles,* I, 53 d'après l'autographe." In *Saint Thomas d'Aquin aujourd'hui,* 221–40. Paris: Desclée de Brouwer, 1963.

————. "Les idées divines dans l'oeuvre de S. Thomas." In *St. Thomas Aquinas, 1274–1974: Commemorative Studies,* edited by Armand Maurer et al. Vol. 1, 175–209. Toronto: Pontifical Institute of Mediaeval Studies, 1974.

Gersh, Stephen. *From Iamblichus to Eriugena: An Investigation of the Prehistory and Evolution of the Pseudo-Dionysian Tradition.* Leiden: E.J. Brill, 1978.

———. *Middle Platonism and Neoplatonism: The Latin Tradition.* Publications in Medieval Studies, ed. Ralph McInerney, no. 2. Notre Dame: University of Notre Dame Press, 1986.

Gilson, Étienne. *The Spirit of Mediaeval Philosophy.* Translated by A. H. C. Downes. New York: Charles Scribner's Sons, 1939.

———. *History of Philosophy and Philosophical Education.* Aquinas Lecture 1947. Milwaukee: Marquette University Press, 1948.

———. *The Christian Philosophy of St. Thomas Aquinas.* Translated by L. K. Shook. New York: Random House, 1956. Reprint, Notre Dame, Ind.: University of Notre Dame Press, 1994.

———. *The Christian Philosophy of Saint Augustine.* Translated by L. E. M. Lynch. New York: Random House, 1960.

———. *Introduction à la philosophie Chriétienne.* Paris: Librairie Philosophique J. Vrin, 1960.

———. *The Philosophy of St. Bonaventure.* Translated by Dom Illtyd Trethowan. Paterson, N.J.: St. Anthony Guild Press, 1965.

———. *Le Thomisme.* 6th ed. Revised. Paris: Librairie Philosophique J. Vrin, 1965.

———. *Christian Philosophy: An Introduction.* Translated by Armand Maurer. Toronto: Pontifical Institute of Mediaeval Studies, 1993.

Girardi, Giulio. *Metafisica della causa esemplare in san Tommaso d'Aquino.* Turin: Scuola Grafica Salesiana, 1954.

Goodenough, Erwin R. *An Introduction to Philo Judaeus.* 2nd ed. Revised. Oxford: Basil Blackwell, 1962.

Greenstock, David L. "Exemplar Causality and the Supernatural Order." *The Thomist* 16 (1953): 1–31.

Guthrie, William K. C. "The Development of Aristotle's Theology." *Classical Quarterly* 28 (1934): 90–98.

Haldane, John. "Aquinas on the Active Intellect." *Philosophy* 67 (1992): 199–210.

Hankey, Wayne J. *God in Himself: Aquinas' Doctrine of God as Expounded in Summa theologiae.* Oxford: Oxford University Press, 1987.

Hart, Charles A. "Participation and the Thomistic Five Ways." *The New Scholasticism* 26 (1952): 267–82.

———. *Thomistic Metaphysics.* Englewood Cliffs, N.J.: Prentice Hall Inc., 1959.

Henle, Robert J. *Saint Thomas and Platonism.* The Hague: Martinus Nijhoff, 1956.

Hessen, Johannes. *Augustins Metaphysik der Erkenntnis.* 2nd ed. Leiden: E.J. Brill, 1960.

Hughes, Christopher. *On a Complex Theory of a Simple God.* Ithaca, N.Y.: Cornell University Press, 1989.

Isaye, Gaston. *La Théorie de la mesure et l'existence d'un maximum selon saint Thomas.* Archives de Philosophie, vol. 16, bk. 1. Paris: Beauchesne et Ses Fils, 1940.

Jaeger, Werner. *Aristotle: Fundamentals of the History of His Development.* Translated by Richard Robinson. Oxford: Clarendon Press, 1948.

Jansen, Lawrence F. "The Divine Ideas in the Writings of St. Augustine." *The Modern Schoolman* 22 (1945): 117–31.

Johnson, Mark F. "Did St. Thomas Attribute a Doctrine of Creation to Aristotle?" *The New Scholasticism* 63 (1989): 129–55.

Jones, Roger Miller. "The Ideas as the Thoughts of God." *Classical Philology* 21 (1926): 317–26.

Jordan, Mark D. "The Intelligibility of the World and the Divine Ideas in Aquinas." *Review of Metaphysics* 38 (1984): 17–32.

Kenny, Anthony. *The Five Ways.* Notre Dame: The University of Notre Dame Press, 1980.

Klibansky, Raymond. *The Continuity of the Platonic Tradition During the Middle Ages.* London: The Warburg Institute, 1939. Reprint with new prefaces and supplement, Millwood, N.Y.: Kraus International Publications, 1982.

Klubertanz, George P. "St. Thomas' Treatment of the Axiom, 'Omne Agens Agit Propter Finem'." In *An Etienne Gilson Tribute,* edited by Charles J. O'Neil. Milwaukee: The Marquette University Press, 1959. 101–17.

Kondoleon, Theodore J. "Divine Exemplarism in Augustine." *Augustinian Studies* 1 (1970): 181–95.

———. *Exemplary Causality in the Philosophy of St. Thomas Aquinas.* Ann Arbor, Mich.: UMI. Microfilm. ProQuest document ID: 758691971.

Kovach, Francis J. "Divine Art in Saint Thomas Aquinas." In *Arts libéraux et philosophie au môyen age. Actes du Quatrième congrès international de philosophie médiévale,* 663–71.. Montreal: Institut d'études médiévales, 1969.

Kretzmann, Norman. *The Metaphysics of Theism.* Oxford: Clarendon Press, 1997.

Lavatori, R. "La quarta via di san Tommaso d'Aquino secundo il principio dell'ordine." *Divinitas* 18 (1974): 62–87.

Lee, Patrick. "Saint Thomas and Avicenna on the Agent Intellect." *The Thomist* 45 (1981): 41–61.

Leclercq, Jean. "Influence and Noninfluence of Dionysius in the Western Middle Ages." In *Pseudo-Dionysius: The Complete Works,* translated by Colm Luibheid, with notes by Paul Rorem, 25–32. New York: Paulist Press, 1987.

Litt, Thomas. *Les corps célestes dans l'univers de saint Thomas d'Aquin.* Louvain: Publications Universitaires and Paris: Béatrice-Nauwelaerts, 1963.

Little, Arthur. *The Platonic Heritage of Thomism.* Dublin: Golden Eagle Books, 1949.

Lonergan, Bernard B. *Verbum: Word and Idea in Aquinas.* Edited by David B. Burrell. Notre Dame: University of Notre Dame Press, 1967.

Macrobius. *Summa de homine.* Borgnet, 1891.

Maimonides, Moses. *The Guide of the Perplexed.* Translated by Shlomo Pines. Chicago: University of Chicago Press, 1963.

Maquart, François-Xavier. *Elementa philosophiae.* Paris: Andreas Blot, 1938.

Maurer, Armand A. "Form and Essence in the Philosophy of St. Thomas." *Mediaeval Studies* 13 (1951): 165–76.

———. "St. Thomas and Eternal Truths." *Mediaeval Studies* 32 (1970): 91–107

———. "James Ross on the Divine Ideas: A Reply." *American Catholic Philosophical Quarterly* 65 (1991): 213–20.

———, trans. *The Division and Methods of the Sciences* by Thomas Aquinas. 4th ed. Toronto: Pontifical Institute of Mediaeval Studies, 1986.

McCall, Raymond J. "St. Thomas on Ontological Truth." *The New Scholasticism* 12 (1938): 9–29.

McEvoy, James. "The Divine as the Measure of Being in Platonic and Scholastic Philosophy." In *Studies in Medieval Philosophy,* ed. John F. Wippel, 85–116. Studies in Philosophy and the History of Philosophy, vol. 17. Washington, D.C.: The Catholic University of America Press, 1987.

McInerney, Ralph. *Boethius and Aquinas.* Washington, D.C.: The Catholic University of America Press, 1990.

Meehan, Francis X. *Efficient Causality in Aristotle and St. Thomas.* Washington, D.C.: The Catholic University of America Press, 1940.

Meyerhoff, Hans. "On the Platonism of St. Augustine's *Quaestio De Ideis.*" *The New Scholasticism* 16 (1942): 16–45.

Montagnes, Bernard. *La doctrine de l'analogie de l'être d'après saint Thomas d'Aquin.* Louvain: Publications Universitaires, 1963.

Obertello, Luca. *Severino Boezio.* 2 vols. Genoa: Accademia ligure di scienze e lettere, 1974.

O'Connell, Robert J. *St. Augustine's Theory of Man, A.D. 386–391.* Cambridge: Harvard University Press, 1968.

———. "Faith, Reason, and Ascent to Vision in St. Augustine." *Augustinian Studies* 21 (1990): 83–126.

———. "Where the Difference Still Lies." *Augustinian Studies* 21 (1990): 139–52.

O'Meara, Dominic J. *Plotinus: An Introduction to the Enneads.* New York: Oxford University Press, 1993.

O'Meara, John J. *Porphyry's Philosophy from Oracles in Augustine.* Paris: Études Augustiniennes, 1959.

———. "The Neoplatonism of Saint Augustine." In *Neoplatonism and Christian Thought,* edited by Dominic J. O'Meara, 34–41. Albany: State University of New York Press, 1982.

———. O'Rourke, Fran. *Pseudo-Dionysius and the Metaphysics of Aquinas.* New York: E.J. Brill, 1992.

Owens, Joseph. "Thomistic Common Nature and Platonic Idea." *Mediaeval Studies* 21 (1959): 211–23.

———. "Aquinas and the Proof from the 'Physics.'" *Mediaeval Studies* 28 (1966): 119–50.

———. *The Doctrine of Being in the Aristotelian Metaphysics.* 3rd ed. Revised. Toronto: Pontifical Institute of Mediaeval Studies, 1978.

————. *An Elementary Christian Metaphysics.* Houston: Center for Thomistic Studies, 1985.

————. "Deo Intus Pandente." *Modern Schoolman* 69 (1992): 369–78.

Paulus, Jean. "La théorie du premier moteur chez Aristote." *Revue de philosophie* 33 (1933): 259–94, 394–424.

Péghaire, Julien. "L'axiome *bonum est diffusivum sui* dans le néoplatonisme et le thomisme." *Revue de l'Université d'Ottawa* 1 (1932): 5*–30*.

Pegis, Anton C. *Saint Thomas and the Greeks.* Aquinas Lecture 1939. Milwaukee: Marquette University Press, 1939.

————. "The Dilemma of Being and Unity." In *Essays in Thomism,* edited by Robert E. Brennan, 149–83. New York: Sheed & Ward, 1942.

————. "A Note on St. Thomas, *Summa Theologica,* I, 44, 1–2." *Mediaeval Studies* 8 (1946): 159–68.

————. "St. Thomas and the Coherence of the Aristotelian Theology." *Mediaeval Studies* 35 (1973): 67–117.

————. Pelikan, Jaroslav. "The Odyssey of Dionysian Spirituality." In *Pseudo-Dionysius: The Complete Works*, translated by Colm Luibheid, with notes by Paul Rorem. New York: Paulist Press, 1987. 11–24.

Perret, Marie-Charles. "La notion d'exemplarité." *Revue Thomiste* 41 (1936): 446–69.

Philo. *De Opificio Mundi.* Translated by G. H. Whitaker. In *Philo.* Vol. 1. Loeb Classical Library. New York: G. P. Putnam Sons, 1929.

————. *De Specialibus Legibus.* Translated by F. H. Colson. In *Philo.* Vol. 7. Loeb Classical Library. Cambridge: Harvard University Press, 1968.

————. *De Virtutibus.* Translated by F. H. Colson. In *Philo.* Vol. 8. Loeb Classical Library. Cambridge: Harvard University Press, 1968.

————. *Legum Allegoria.* Translated by F. H. Colson and G. H. Whitaker. In *Philo.* Vol. 1. Loeb Classical Library. New York: G. P. Putnam Sons, 1929.

Pieper, Josef. *The Silence of St. Thomas.* Translated by John Murray and Daniel O'Connor. New York: Pantheon Books, Inc., 1957.

Plotinus. *Enneads.* Translated by A. H. Armstrong. Loeb Classical Library. Cambridge: Harvard University Press, 1989.

Proclus. *The Elements of Theology.* Transated by E. R. Dodds. 2nd. ed. Revised. New York: Oxford University Press, 1992.

Pseudo-Dionysius. *De divinis nominibus.* In *In librum beati Dionysii De divinis nominibus expositio,* edited by C. Pera. Turin and Rome, 1952.

————. *Dionysiaca.* Edited by Philippe Chevallier. 2 vols. Paris: Desclée, de Brouwer & Cie., 1937.

————. *Pseudo-Dionysius: The Complete Works.* Translated by Colm Luibheid with notes by Paul Rorem. New York: Paulist Press, 1987.

Ramos, Alice. "Ockham and Aquinas on Exemplary Causality." In *Proceedings of the PMR Conference,* vols. 19–20, 199–213. Villanova: The Augustinian Historical Institute, 1994–96.

Reale, Giovanni. *Aristotele.* 6th ed. Milan: Vita e Pensiero, 1994.

Renard, Henri. *Philosophy of God.* Milwaukee: Bruce, 1949.

Rist, John M. "The One of Plotinus and the God of Aristotle." *Review of Metaphysics* 27 (1973): 75–87.

Rocca, Gregory P. *Plotinus: The Road to Reality.* London: Cambridge University Press, 1967.

———. *Speaking the Incomprehensible God.* Washington, D.C.: The Catholic University of America Press, 2004.

Ross, David. *Plato's Theory of Ideas.* Oxford: Clarenden Press, 1951.

Ross, James F. "Aquinas' Exemplarism; Aquinas' Voluntarism." *American Catholic Philosophical Quarterly* 64 (1990): 171–98.

———. "Response to Maurer and Dewan." *American Catholic Philosophical Quarterly* 65 (1991): 213–20.

Saffrey, Henri-Dominique. "New Objective Links Between the Pseudo-Dionysius and Proclus." In *Neoplatonism and Christian Thought,* ed. Dominic J. O'Meara, 64–74. Albany: State University of New York Press, 1982.

Shanley, Brian. "Eternal Knowledge of the Temporal in Aquinas." *American Catholic Philosophical Quarterly* 71 (1997): 197–224.

———. "Aquinas on God's Causal Knowledge: A Reply to Stump and Kretzmann." *American Catholic Philosophical Quarterly* 72 (1998): 447–57.

———. "Divine Causation and Human Freedom in Aquinas." *American Catholic Philosophical Quarterly* 72 (1998): 99–122.

Simonin, H.-D. "Immatérialité et Intellection." *Angelicum* 7 (1930): 460–86.

Sparks, Timotheus. *De divisione causae exemplaris apud S. Thomam.* River Forest, Ill.: Dominican House of Studies, 1936.

Stump, Eleonore, and Norman Kretzmann. "Eternity and God's Knowledge: A Reply to Shanley." *American Catholic Philosophical Quarterly* 72 (1998): 439–45.

TeSelle, Eugene. *Augustine the Theologian.* New York: Herder and Herder, 1970.

Thomas Aquinas, Saint. *De potentia.* Edited by R. P. Pauli and M. Pession. In *Quaestiones disputatae.* Vol. 2. Turin and Rome: Marietti, 1949.

———. *De virtutibus in communi.* Edited by P. A. Odetto. In *Quaestiones disputatae.* Vol. 2. Turin and Rome: Marietti, 1949.

———. *The Division and Methods of the Sciences.* Translated by Armand Maurer. 4th ed. Toronto: Pontifical Institute of Mediaeval Studies, 1986.

———. *In librum beati Dionysii De divinis nominibus expositio.* Edited by C. Pera. Turin and Rome: Marietti, 1950.

———. *In Metaphysicam Aristotelis commentaria.* Edited by M.-R. Cathala. Turin: Marietti, 1935.

———. *Lectura super evangelium Johannis.* In *S. Thomae Aquinatis opera omnia,* edited by R. Busa. Vol. 1. Stuttgart-Bad Cannstatt, 1980.

———. *Sancti Thomae de Aquino Opera omnia.* Leonine edition. Rome, 1882–. Vol. 1*.1, *Expositio Libri Peryermenias.* Vol. 1*.2, *Expositio Libri Posteriorum.* Vol. 2, *In octo libros Phyiscorum Aristotelis.* Vol. 3, *In libros Aristotelis De caelo, In libros*

BIBLIOGRAPHY

Aristotelis De mundo, De principiis naturae. Vols. 4–12, *Summa theologiae.* Vols. 13–15, *Summa Contra Gentiles.* Vols. 22.1, 22.2, 22.3, *Quaestiones disputatae de veritate.* Vol. 23, *Quaestiones disputatae de malo.* Vol. 24.1, *Quaestiones disputatae de anima.* Vol. 24.2, *Quaestio disputata de spiritualibus creaturis.* Vol. 25.1, 25.2, *Quaestiones de quolibet.* Vol. 40, *De substantiis separatis.* Vol. 42, *Compendium theologiae.* Vol. 43, *De ente et essentia, De operationibus occultis naturae.* Vol. 45.1, *Sentencia libri De anima.* Vol. 47, *Sententia libri Ethicorum.* Vol. 50, *Expositio libri Boetii De ebdomadibus, Super Boetium De Trinitate.*

―――. *Sancti Thomae de Aquino Super librum de causis.* Edited by H. D. Saffrey. Fribourg: Société philosophique de Fribourg, 1954.

―――. *Scriptum super libros Sententiarum.* Vols. 1 and 2, edited by P. Mandonnet. Paris: Lethielleux, 1929.

―――. *Scriptum super Sententiis.* Vols. 3 and 4, edited by M. F. Moos. Paris: Lethielleux, 1933 and 1947.

―――. *Super Epistolam S. Pauli Apostoli ad Hebraeos.* Turin: Marietti, 1929.

―――. *Thomae Aquinatis Opera omnia: cum hypertextibus in CD-ROM.* 2nd ed. Edited by Robert Busa. Milan: Editoria Elettronica Editel, 1996.

Torrell, Jean-Pierre. *Saint Thomas Aquinas.* Vol. 1, *The Person and His Work.* Translated by Robert Royal. Washington, D.C.: The Catholic University of America Press, 1996.

Urban, Linwood. "Understanding St. Thomas's Fourth Way." *History of Philosophy Quarterly* 1 (1984): 281–95.

Van Fleteren, Frederick. "A Reply to Robert O'Connell." *Augustinian Studies* 21 (1990): 127–37.

Van Steenberghen, Fernand. *Ontology.* Translated by Martin J. Flynn. New York: Joseph F. Wagner, Inc., 1952.

―――. *Le problème de l'existence de Dieu dans les écrits de s. Thomas d'Aquin.* Philosophes Médiévaux, vol 23. Louvain-La-Neuve: Éditions de l'Institut Supérieur de Philosophie, 1980.

―――. "Prolégomènes à la «quarta via»." *Rivista di Filosofia Neo-Scolastica* 70 (1978): 99–112.

Velde, Rudi A. te. *Participation and Substantiality in Thomas Aquinas.* New York: E.J. Brill, 1995.

Wagner, Marion. *Die Philosophischen Implikate der "Quarta Via." Eine Untersuchung zum Vierten Gottesbeweis bei Thomas von Aquin (S. Th. I, 2, 3c).* Leiden: E.J. Brill, 1989.

Weisheipl, James A. "Thomas' Evaluation of Plato and Aristotle." *The New Scholasticism* 48 (1974): 100–124.

―――. *Thomas d'Aquino and Albert His Teacher.* Etienne Gilson Series, no. 2. Toronto: Pontifical Institute of Mediaeval Studies, 1980.

White, Kevin. "Creation, Numbers, and Natures: On Aquinas's *Quodlibet* 8.1.1." In *Medieval Masters,* edited by R. E. Houser, 179–90. Houston: Center for Thomistic Studies, 1999.

Wiele, Joseph Vande. "Le problème de la vérité ontologique dans la philosophie de saint Thomas." *Revue philosophique de Louvain* 52 (1954): 521–71.

William of Auvergne. *De Universo.* Vol. 1. Paris, 1674.

Winston, David. *Logos and Mystical Theology in Philo of Alexandria.* Cincinnati: Hebrew Union College Press, 1985.

Wippel, John F. "Godfrey of Fontaines on Intension and Remission of Accidental Forms." *Franciscan Studies* 39 (1979): 316–35.

———. *The Metaphysical Thought of Godfrey of Fontaines.* Washington, D.C.: The Catholic University of America Press, 1981.

———. "The Reality of Nonexisting Possibles According to Thomas Aquinas, Henry of Ghent, and Godfrey of Fontaines." *Review of Metaphysics* 34 (1981): 729–58.

———. *Metapysical Themes in Thomas Aquinas.* Washington, D.C.: The Catholic University of America Press, 1984.

———. "Thomas Aquinas on the Distinction and Derivation of the Many from the One: A Dialectic between Being and Nonbeing." *Review of Metaphysics* 38 (1985): 563–90.

———. "Thomas Aquinas and Participation." In *Studies in Medieval Philosophy,* ed. John F. Wippel. Studies in Philosophy and the History of Philosophy, vol. 17. Washington, D.C.: The Catholic University of America Press, 1987. 117–58.

———. "Truth in Thomas Aquinas." *Review of Metaphysics* 43 (1989–90): 295–326, 543–67.

———. *Thomas Aquinas on the Divine Ideas.* The Etienne Gilson Series, no. 16. Toronto: Pontifical Institute of Mediaeval Studies, 1993.

———. "Thomas Aquinas and the Axiom that Unreceived Act Is Unlimited." *Review of Metaphysics* 51 (1998): 533–64.

———. *The Metaphysical Thought of Thomas Aquinas.* Washington, D.C.: The Catholic University of America Press, 2000.

———. "Thomas Aquinas on Creatures as Causes of *Esse.*" *International Philosophical Quarterly* 40 (2000): 197–213.

———. "Thomas Aquinas on Our Knowledge of God and the Axiom that Every Agent Produces Something Like Itself." Proceedings of the *American Catholic Philosophical Association* 74 (2000): 81–101.

Witt, Reginald E. *Albinus and the History of Middle Platonism.* London: Cambridge University Press, 1937. Reprint, Amsterdam: Adolf M. Hakkert, 1971.

Wolfson, Harry A. *Philo: Foundations of Religious Philosophy in Judaism, Christianity and Islam.* 2 vols. Cambridge: Harvard University Press, 1948.

———. "Extradeical and Intradeical Interpretations of Platonic Ideas." *Journal of the History of Ideas* 22 (1961): 3–32.

Zedler, Beatrice Hope. "Why Are the Possibles Possible?" *The New Scholasticism* 55 (1981): 113–30.

INDEX OF SUBJECTS

~~~

INDEX OF NAMES

Aquinas on the Divine Ideas as Exemplar Causes was designed and typeset in Maiola Pro by Kachergis Book Design of Pittsboro, North Carolina. It was printed on 60-pound Natures Natural and bound by Thomson-Shore of Dexter, Michigan.